Basics of Entrepreneurship

FOURTH EDITION

Editor:

Cecile Nieuwenhuizen

Basics of Entrepreneurship

First published 2004

Second edition 2011

Reprinted 2012

Reprinted 2013 (twice)

Reprinted 2014 (thrice)

Third edition 2014

Fourth edition 2020

Juta and Company (Pty) Ltd
First Floor, Sunclare Building, 21 Dreyer Street, Claremont, 7708

PO Box 14373, Lansdowne, 7779, Cape Town, South Africa

ISBN 978 1 48513 051 2

Project Manager: Deidre Dupreez and Valencia Wyngaard-Arenz

Proofreader: Martin Rollo

Cover designer: Drag and Drop

Indexer: Lexinfo

Typesetter: Lebone Publishing Services

Typeset in Palatino LT Std 9.5/13.5

Contents

Preface

This book is written by a team of entrepreneurship and business management experts to guide you, the entrepreneur to plan and start your own business. You probably have a good business idea or have identified a business opportunity. Now you would like to evaluate the viability of this idea or opportunity. But perhaps not, you might need guidance on how to identify an opportunity or determine the viability of a business idea. To assist you, the start-up entrepreneur, we have combined relevant work of entrepreneurs and specialists in the different phases as well as related fields of entrepreneurship to better understand the business environment and relevant business concepts.

We guide you through process of identifying feasible business ideas, testing the viability of these ideas, plan, start and grow your own business. We are well aware that many successful entrepreneurs go through this process informally and never put anything down in writing. In this book we guide you through the process, as it is especially necessary for the younger, less experienced and nascent entrepreneur to work through it in the process of establishing and growing a business.

The benefit of this book is that successful entrepreneurs contributed by providing valuable information about what had been needed in the different phases of start-up and establishing their businesses. In addition, all the authors of this book have personal experience as entrepreneurs, as business advisors and as subject specialists.

Some of the most important and essential functions that have to be addressed by the entrepreneur, such as product, pricing, distribution and marketing communication decisions as well as managing operations, human resources as well as finances are also dealt with.

We aim to guide you on:

- being positive about even your seemingly most insignificant talents, skills and knowledge, and using them, while acknowledging your weak points and doing something about them;
- being creative yet practical in your search for business ideas, and believing in whatever you attempt;
- researching your business idea and ensuring that it will be profitable;

- planning the way you will be doing business; and
- establishing and managing important functions like financing, marketing, operations and human resources.

Willingness to learn is the first step in understanding entrepreneurship and business. By learning, looking and doing, you can achieve success.

Have fun in planning and starting your own business, and good luck!

Cecile Nieuwenhuizen

About the authors

Dr Alex Antonites is a senior lecturer in the Department of Business Management and Chair for Entrepreneurship, at the University of Pretoria. He specialises in the field of entrepreneurship and small business development with a specific focus on the pre-entrepreneurial phase concerning creativity, innovation and opportunity finding.

Andreas de Beer is a senior lecturer in the Department of Business Management at the University of South Africa (Unisa).

Prof Michael Cant is a professor in marketing and retail at the University of south Africa. He specialised in Retailing, small business management and entrepreneurship.

Prof Willie Conradie is a retired professor of the Department of Business Management, at the University of Johannesburg, formerly a marketing executive at Absa Bank and currently a successful entrepreneur. He holds the degrees BA, MBA (University of Pretoria) and DBA (NWU).

Dr Edmund Ferreira is a self-employed, retired professor, previously from the Department of Business Management at UNISA. He holds the degrees BMil (Commercial Sciences) (US); BCom Hons (HR Management) (UNISA); MCom (Business Management) (UJ) and DCom (UNISA). He has co-authored several books on business management, small business management and office administration. He has also published various articles in accredited national and international academic journals.

Ms Welma Fourie (CA) SA has formerly been a senior lecturer in Accounting and Financial management at Stellenbosch University, KwaZulu Natal University and Technikon SA. She has also gain extensive corporate experience since 2008 as financial manager and currently is a director of her own accounting and taxation services practise, Balance ur Act (Pty) Ltd.

Dr Hannelize Jacobs is an innovative academic, a strategist and a leader-manager who habitually strives for excellence. In her career of 25 years she has gained extensive experience of the South African, as well as the international higher education environment. She holds a DCom Strategic Management degree and has authored and co-authored numerous textbooks and accredited articles.

Richard Marchado is a Senior Lecturer in the Department of Marketing and Retail Management at UNISA. He is co-author of a number of books.

Prof Cecile Nieuwenhuizen is a Professor and the Chair of the SARChI Entrepreneurship Education, a National Research Foundation Chair funded by the Department of Higher Education and the University of Johannesburg. She is involved in extensive family businesses since 1980 and in academia from 1994. She is the author and co-author of various books, articles and conference proceedings focused on entrepreneurship, innovation and management. She is editor of Basics of Entrepreneurship and author of Chapter 2.

Prof Rigard Steenkamp is a lecturer in operations management in Unisa's Department of Business Management. He is author of several books and articles on operations management. Rigard has received several research awards and entrepreneurship is one of his interests. He and his partners were actively involved in a small business that was awarded the AHI Business of the Year.

Chapter 1

Basic business concepts and the business environment

1.1 LEARNING OUTCOMES

After you have studied this chapter, you should be able to:

- explain the motivation for setting up a business
- analyse the relationship between the business and its establishment
- distinguish between the terms 'branch of industry' and 'production branch', using examples to illustrate them and their use in classifying a business
- arrange the three sectors in which businesses are grouped and provide suitable examples
- draw an industrial column for a product to illustrate the route it follows – from the raw material stage, to delivery, to the customer
- describe the micro environment of the business
- explain the market environment and the variables that influence the business's growth and existence
- identify the macro environment and all the forces and influences that affect the business.

1.2 INTRODUCTION

We are going to look at two important concepts in this chapter – basic business concepts and principles, and the reason why the environment is so important in the business world.

The first part of this chapter will look at the enterprise as a need-satisfying organisation in the free-market system and show the relationship between the enterprise and the establishment. This section will clarify how entities are categorised into branches of industry and production. After the categorisation we will explain the different sectors of the economy in which these entities operate and describe how raw materials and products move through these sectors to reach the end-consumer. These are all 'basic business concepts'.

Every society consists of people who have basic needs and wants that must be satisfied in order for them to survive. The satisfying of needs and wants occurs through the process of economic activity. Economic activity includes the factors of production. The combination of the production factors in the enterprise lead to the production of service in the establishment to deliver goods and services. Section 1.3 will explain the relationship between an enterprise (business) and an establishment in more detail. In South Africa enterprises are part of a business system which allows people to own their own business and receive profits from it. Consider whether it is possible for a business to exist in total isolation. Ask yourself if it is possible for a business to grow and exist if factors such as the customer and his or her needs, competitor activity and prevailing economic and political conditions are not taken into consideration. The answer to these questions should be 'No': of course it is not possible for any business, large or small, to function in isolation.

To be successful, a business must stay in constant contact with the market environment so that it remains up to date with changing customer needs, changing technology and competitor activities. The business and the community in which it functions are therefore mutually dependent and influence each other. The entrepreneur takes the initiative, continually looking for new ideas, new products and improved methods of doing business. The entrepreneur's motivation is to make a profit and also to stimulate the environment to innovate and change.

A business manufactures long-playing records (LPs). Because of technological changes, most people today prefer compact discs (CDs and DVDs).

What do you think will happen to this business? Do you think there is still a demand for long-playing records? How many of you know what a long-playing record is? Or listen to long-playing records? The need (demand) and environment for this type of business has changed.

Every business functions within an environment (the business environment) where events and variables influence its activities. These events may pose opportunities or threats to the business. Technological development is a good illustration (think about the example above) of fluctuations in the market. On the one hand technology offers opportunities because new products and services are created, while on the other hand it can constitute a threat because it may result in products or services becoming obsolete.

NB

As an entrepreneur, you must be aware of environmental variables and changes. With knowledge of these changes, you can develop a plan of action to deal with potential opportunities or threats. Without this knowledge, your business will not grow or may even cease to exist.

It is also important that you understand some basic business concepts, such as the role your business (or proposed business) plays in a free-market system, how different entities are categorised into branches of industry and production, the different sectors of the economy and how raw materials and products move through these sectors to reach the customer.

1.3 THE BUSINESS

D

A business or enterprise can be described as an independent institution, established by an entrepreneur to make a profit by producing goods or providing services that satisfy customers' needs. Therefore, the entrepreneur identifies a customer need and creates a business to produce goods and/or provide services to satisfy that need. The motive for the entrepreneur's action is to make a profit. In both cases the entrepreneur and the customer benefit from the creation of the business – the customer is able to satisfy his or her needs, while the entrepreneur makes a profit.

1.3.1 The relationship between the business and the establishment

D

The establishment can be described as the place where inputs such as raw materials and other components are processed to produce a product or provide a service. Production activities take place in the establishment.

The best way of explaining the relationship between the business and the establishment is to look at Figure 1.1. The figure illustrates the bakery business started by Tumi Lekoto. Tumi combines the production factors of natural resources, capital, labour and entrepreneurship in his business. Tumi (the entrepreneur) will employ people to work for him (labour). He will also buy (capital) the raw materials (natural resources) he needs to bake bread and cakes.

Once the production process is complete, the end product (bread and cakes) can be sold using the marketing activities to generate income for Tumi's business. He will also use the external relations activities to improve the image of his business. The general management and administrative functions will oversee all the activities.

NB

The establishment is one part of the business. The 'business' or 'enterprise' is the place where all the business functions take place (for example, marketing, management, administration) but the establishment refers only to the place where the product is made or the service is provided.

Figure 1.1: The relationship between the enterprise and its establishment

1.3.2 Classification of a business and its establishment in the economy

The branch of industry and the production branch

Table 1.1 explains the difference between a branch of industry and the production branch.

Table 1.1: Branch of industry versus production branch

Branch of industry	Production branch
A branch of industry refers to all the businesses that produce more or less the same product or provide the same service.	The production branch refers to all the businesses that use more or less the same production processes.
For example:	For example:
Gold mines produce the same product – gold.	All mines, eg gold, diamond and coal, form part of the mining production branch because they all use the same production process – the extraction of natural resources through mining.

The different sectors in which a business can operate

There are three sectors in which a business can operate:

- primary sector
- secondary sector
- tertiary sector.

The activities that take place in the establishment determine the sector in which the business operates.

- The primary sector: This sector is responsible for the exploitation of natural resources in their raw, unprocessed form.
- The secondary sector: In the secondary sector, the exploited natural resources are processed and transformed into products demanded by customers.
- The tertiary sector: This sector is responsible for distributing the final products from the manufacturer to the customer.

The industrial column

The industrial column is the course that a product follows from its unprocessed, natural resource state to the final form in which it is supplied to the customer. This includes all the processes and transactions that take place from the primary sector, through the secondary sector and along to the tertiary sector, from where it is passed on to the customer.

The diagram below illustrates the industrial column, using the manufacture and distribution of paper as an example.

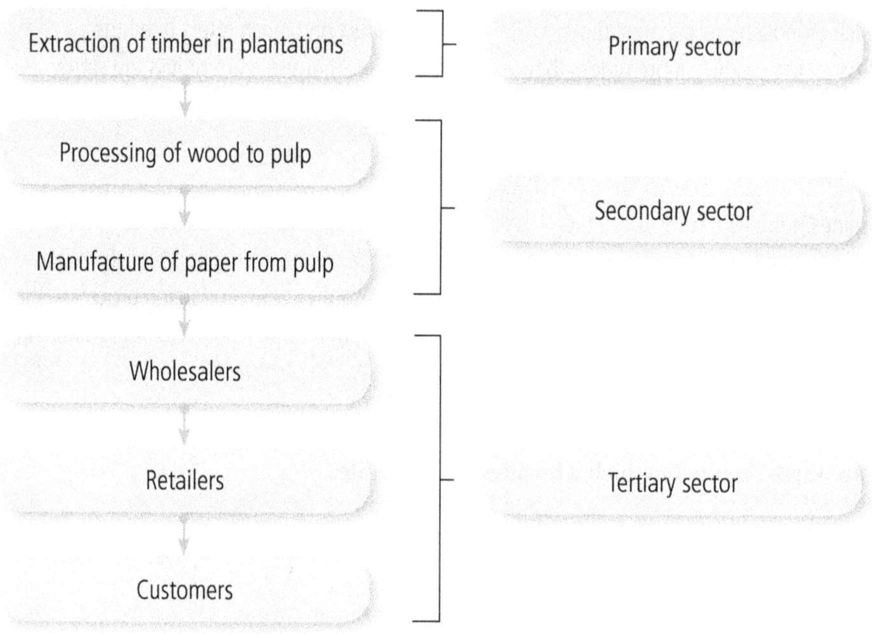

Figure 1.2: The industrial column

1.4 THE BUSINESS ENVIRONMENT

The business environment is the sum total of all the factors and variables that influence the creation, growth and continued existence of a business either positively or negatively, thereby promoting or hindering the achievement of its objectives.

The effect of the business environment on a business will be determined by the place and role of the business in the total economy of a country. The business environment has several characteristics:

- Interrelatedness of environmental factors or variables – a change in one external factor may cause a change in the micro-environment and, similarly, a change in one external factor may influence other external environmental variables. A practical example is the instability and fluctuation of the value of the rand against the dollar, pound and other currencies. A drastic fall in the value of the rand means that imported goods such as cars and fuel become more expensive. This initially results in inflationary pressures, which are followed by high interest rates to contain the inflation. This in turn means that consumer spending declines and that certain industries suffer.

- Increasing instability – the interdependence between environmental factors results in increasing instability and change in the environment. Even if there is a general increase in the rate of change in the environment, environmental fluctuations are greater for some businesses than for others.
- Environmental uncertainty – is a function of the amount of information available on environmental variables. There are both opportunities and threats in the business environment. Opportunities and threats arise as a result of certain occurrences in the environment and they influence the function of the business. An opportunity is a favourable situation for the business. The business must decide how to react to these opportunities and threats.
- Complexity of the environment – this characteristic indicates the number of external variables to which the business must react, as well as fluctuations in the variables themselves. The business management environment changes constantly. Factors that influence the business today will not necessarily have the same influence tomorrow. A good example is the rapid change in technology over the last few years, like cell phones.
- Unpredictability of the environment – the current business environment is revolutionary, which is unpredictable and is characterised by discontinuous change. The business must be in step with the changing environment. During the past few years, environmental emphasis has increasingly been placed on the protection of the ozone layer and this has resulted in businesses having to adapt their products accordingly.

The business environment is usually divided into three components, namely the micro (the internal environment), the market, and the macro environments (both part of the external environment). These three components each have a variety of variables that can influence the business either positively or negatively.

These variables are discussed in the following sections. Figure 1.3 gives an overall picture of the business environment. (The business is identified as the central point in this figure.) Table 1.2 illustrates the three components and their variables.

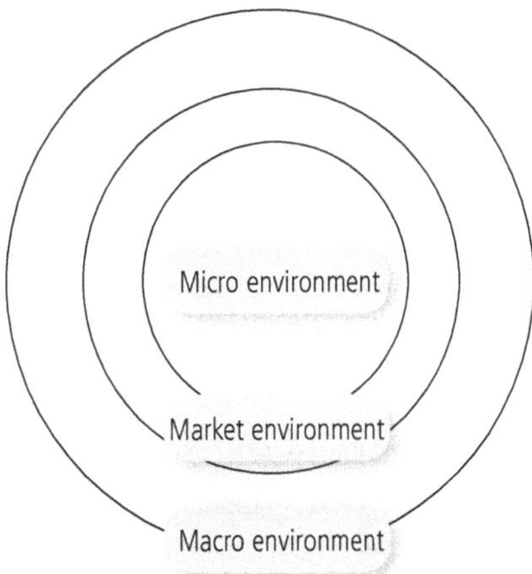

Figure 1.3: The internal and external business environment

Table 1.2: The components and variables of the business environment

The micro environment
This is the business itself. We can distinguish between the following variables: • the mission statement and objectives of the business • the functions of the business • the production factors of the business.
The market environment
This setting surrounds the business and is part of the external environment. The main variables include: • the market • the competition • the suppliers of resources and services (without which the business would not be able to manufacture and market its products and/or provide services).
The macro environment
The macro environment surrounds the market environment and the business. We can distinguish between the following sub-environments: • economic environment (economic conditions) • social environment • technological environment • physical environment • political and statutory environment • international environment.

1.4.1 The micro environment

The micro environment is the heart of the business. It indicates to what extent the business is able to utilise opportunities or oppose threats in the external environment.

The micro environment is the sum total of all the factors and variables which occur internally in the business and are influenced in a direct or indirect way by management decisions. These factors and variables have a fundamental influence on the establishment and on the growth and continued existence of the business.

What follows is a brief discussion of the three variables of the micro environment.

The mission statement and objectives of the business

This is what the business hopes to achieve and the way in which it can be achieved.

The mission statement and objectives must correspond with the demands of the external environment.

The functions of the business

These include the following divisions that will be discussed in more detail overleaf:

- general management
- personnel management
- operations management
- purchasing management
- marketing management
- public relations management
- administrative management
- financial management.

NB

General management: General management differs from the other functions because it cannot be placed in a department on its own. General management concerns all the activities that are necessary on all levels throughout the entire organisation.

Personnel management: Personnel management includes all the activities concerned with the procurement, development, compensation, integration and maintenance of the personnel of the organisation.

Operations management: This refers to the management process used in both manufacturing and service enterprises. Operations management can be described as those management activities that take place so that products and services can be provided to satisfy the needs of the consumer.

Purchasing management: The purchasing function deals with the procurement of all the resources an organisation needs to achieve its objectives. This includes, among other things, the determination of purchasing needs, the establishment of alternative suppliers who can satisfy these needs and the negotiation of agreements with suppliers to the long-term advantage of the organisation.

Marketing management: Marketing is the process of transferring goods and services to customers in order to satisfy their needs, as well as the activities that make the transfer possible. Marketing therefore entails more than just advertising products and services; it includes a variety of activities cutting across all functions of the enterprise.

Public Relations management: Public relations is the management function that evaluates public attitudes, identifies the policies and procedures of an individual or organisation with a public interest, and plans and executes a programme of action to earn public acceptance and understanding.

Administrative management: The administrative function can be defined as being concerned with the service of obtaining, recording and analysing information, and communicating the results to management who then can safeguard the assets, promote the activities and achieve the objectives of the organisation.

Financial management: Financial management refers to the management of the business's financial activities. The financial functions therefore include all the activities involved in obtaining capital and the efficient use thereof. The financial manager is responsible for the effective planning, organising and control of all the financial activities in the organisation.

The production factors of the business

The production factors consist of:

- *Natural resources*

Natural resources refer to all the means provided by nature. A characteristic of natural resources is that they are scarce and limited. Examples include crude oil, water and minerals.

- *Capital*

During its establishment a business needs capital to start to operate. The capital is used to produce other goods for the purchase by consumers. Normally, this capital is funded by the owners and investors who invest their money in the business.

- *Labour*

No business can function without people. Labour refers to all the physical and mental human effort applied in producing goods and services. Humans have the knowledge (technical and academic), physical capabilities and skills to transfer goods into products, provide a service and take leadership.

- *Entrepreneurship*

Entrepreneurship is the process through which the individual takes capital, labour and natural resources and combines them with the risk linked with the provision of goods and services. Therefore the entrepreneur can be described as the person who brings all the factors of production together and organises them into a system that produces goods, and renders a services.

- *Knowledge*

Traditionally, only four factors of production were identified. However, Peter Drucker added a fifth factor of production: knowledge. Knowledge as a fifth factor of production is embedded in the era of knowledge management. Knowledge Management refers to the process of discovering and harnessing a business's intellectual resources, or utilising the intellect of the people who work for the business.

With these resources the business must utilise opportunities to ward off threats in the external environment. For example, if a business has sufficient capital available, new markets and new products can be explored. On the other hand, a lack of capital may constitute a threat to the business because, unlike its competitors, the business is in a weaker position in the market.

The influence of management on the micro environment

As the manager of your own business, you will exert a direct influence on the mission statement and objectives of the business. You will decide where the business is going and what it will do to get there, and establish guidelines for its day-to-day operation.

1.4.2 The market environment

The market can be defined as the link between the business and the environment in which it functions. It surrounds the micro environment.

The market environment is the sum total of all the factors and/or variables which exist externally that cannot be controlled but can sometimes be influenced so that it will have a positive or negative effect on the growth and existence of a business.

The market environment is surrounded by the macro environment (see Figure 1.3 on page 7). The market environment therefore does not exist in isolation but is in fact influenced by both the micro and macro environments. We can explain this interaction by means of the following examples.

A new shampoo is introduced to the market. Customers prefer the new shampoo to existing products (in other words, it is preferred to the competitors' products).

A company changes its credit and collection policy. This step has an influence on its customers because, for example, some people may prefer to buy items on credit, even if they know that the prices are inflated to make provision for credit risks (the possibility of bad debts). Some customers may therefore prefer to buy clothes from a store such as Edgars, Milady's, Queenspark and Truworths, which offers credit facilities, rather than Erica Fashions, which does not.

The market environment is also influenced by the macro environment. During a downward trend in the economy, for example, customers have less money to spend on luxury items, which will lead to a reduction in the sale of luxury products, such as expensive dinner services, clothing and luxury cars.

Three variables are unique to the market environment, namely:

- the market
- the competition
- suppliers of resources and services.

The market

Here we refer in an abstract sense to 'the market', which concerns the customer and his or her needs rather than the physical marketplace.

The business manufactures or buys products and/or provides services with the objective of selling these (to either individual customers or other businesses or institutions). However, before a customer can become active in the market, he or she must have financial means (money). These financial means can be used to acquire the available goods and/or services. The customer has to choose between different goods and services because he or she has limited financial means. It can also happen, however, that although the customer has the necessary financial means, he or she is not prepared to buy the available goods and services.

From the point of view of the business, the market therefore includes all individuals, groups or institutions who have specific needs for goods and services and who are prepared to use their available financial means to acquire the goods or services.

- The market of a clothing shop such as Edgars, Milady's, Queenspark and Truworths, includes all people with a need for clothing who are prepared to spend their money on the available articles. Their activities are therefore directed at satisfying their needs.
- The market of South African Airways, British Airways, Kulula and Safair, includes all people with a need to travel domestically or internationally who have the financial means to pay for the air tickets. These people must therefore be prepared to spend money on an air ticket in order to satisfy a need (to travel).
- Some manufacturing businesses trade only with wholesalers and retailers and not with the general public. Their market therefore comprises other businesses. For example, you cannot buy a writing pad directly from Sappi; you have to obtain it from a retailer who sells stationery, like CNA, PNA and Walton's. The retailer, in turn, has bought the writing pad from a manufacturer such as Croxley, who bought paper from Sappi.

Different segments of the market have been identified from these examples. Here is a further breakdown.

- **The consumer market:** This market consists of the end-customers who carry out transactions in order to buy and consume items such as clothing, food or cars.
- **The industrial market:** In this market, goods and services are purchased and used for the manufacture of products or the provision of services to end-customers. As mentioned before, Croxley buys paper from a paper and pulp business such as Sappi in order to manufacture writing pads, envelopes and cards. A business that manufactures kitchen cupboards also utilises the industrial market when it buys pressed-wood panels from Sappi Novaboard to manufacture its products.
- **The resale market:** In this market, manufactured goods are purchased by businesses with the sole purpose of reselling them to individuals or other businesses at a profit. Pick n Pay, Spar and Checkers, for example, buy canned vegetables and fruit (such as Koo and All Gold) to sell at a profit to its customers.
- **The international market:** International markets exist outside the borders of a country where a product is produced and include all foreign customers, manufacturers, retailers and authorities. For example, European traders buy South African fruit on the international market.
- **The government market:** In order to provide services and carry out their functions, government and municipal authorities purchase a range of goods and services, such as:
  - furniture and equipment for use in government schools
  - system to pay salaries to teachers, the police, government officials
  - firefighting equipment
  - medical supplies and services.

When discussing the market, we should not forget that the customer has certain rights. As an entrepreneur, you should be aware of these rights in order to keep abreast of customers' needs. Institutions such as the Consumer Council focus on informing customers of their rights. These rights are summarised below.

The customer has the right to:

- **Be informed:** The customer should receive objective information about the available products and/or services. The business may not mislead or harm the customer by withholding information about a specific product. For example, the customer has a right to know the ingredients in a tin of canned food and whether it contains colourants or preservatives.
- **Exercise personal choice:** A variety of products and services are available in the market and the customer has the right to decide which product or service he or she is going to buy. For example, the customer has the right to choose between All Gold and Koo products.
- **Be heard:** The business must be geared towards listening to and responding to customer complaints and requests. For example, if a customer complains about poor service, the entrepreneur/manager should respond to these complaints.
- **Protection:** The customer's safety is important and he or she should be protected against unsafe products, for example by health warnings on cigarette packets.

The competition

An example of competition is the variety of cars available today, as well as the number of dealers who sell these cars. The choice between different products indicates that there is competition in the market.

NB

Competition boils down to the fact that each business tries to convince consumers that its products and services are the best and that consumers should therefore buy from them.

As an entrepreneur, you must be aware of competitor activity because the actions of competitors may constitute a threat to your business. You must be aware of new or improved products on the market. Therefore it is vitally important to be informed about the competition in the external business environment. You must know who your competitors are, where they are situated (the geographic distribution), the products they offer the market, the quality of the products, the specific markets they serve, what their share of the market is, their financial resources and their general image in the marketplace.

Over and above the fact that businesses compete with one another's products and services, we can also distinguish between different types of competition.

The suppliers of resources and services

You must decide which products you are going to manufacture and market, the quantities you can produce and the capital necessary for the project. However, you will be dependent on other institutions in the external environment to carry out your activities because you will not necessarily have the raw materials to manufacture your products. You will therefore have to rely on external suppliers for many products or services.

This example deals with a business that manufactures wooden furniture and how it interacts with the external environment.

- To manufacture its furniture, the company must buy wood, tools, glue, nails and various other products. All of these items must be bought from external suppliers.
- The business uses water, electricity, communication channels and other services. All of these must be bought from the external environment, such as Eskom for electricity and Telkom for communication services.
- The business must make use of a bank or other financial institution so that it can pay wages and salaries and pay its suppliers. They may also need a loan at some stage, for instance if they want to expand the business and build new premises.
- The business decides to build a bigger factory. They must use the services of an external property broker to buy the land and external builders and contractors to build the new premises.
- The larger factory needs additional staff. An external recruitment company is used to fill the new vacancies.
- Finally, the business must sell its furniture. To do this, they use an intermediary – in this case a wholesaler – who markets the product and sells it to a retailer (let's say Joshua Doore), who then sells the furniture to the end-customer.

1.4.3 The macro environment

The macro environment surrounds the business and its marketing environment. It is made up of a wide range of variables which can affect the business and its marketing activities, either positively or negatively.

The macro environment consists of all the variables and factors outside the business which have a positive or negative influence on the growth and continued existence of the business and which encourage or hinder the achievement of its objectives.

The individual business has no control over the macro environment or the variables which operate within it. For example, a business has no control over a rise in interest rates or a change in the exchange rate. However, these changes impact every business in some way.

The macro environment consists of a number of sub-environments which are usually described as 'variables' or 'forces'. Here we refer to economic, sociocultural, political, technological, statutory, physical and international influences and forces.

What follows is a brief discussion of each of the sub-environments already identified.

(a) Economic environment (economic conditions)

The economic environment is that part of the macro environment consisting of factors that influence the personal disposable income of the customer as well as his or her purchasing behaviour. (The term 'customer' is used here in its widest sense, it also includes other businesses.) The customer has limited financial means to satisfy all his or her needs and is therefore forced to make choices.

The customer 's disposable income is influenced by many economic factors, for example, interest rates and exchange rates, inflation, trade cycles and the economic growth rate.

Interest rates

An interest rate is an indication of the price at which money can be bought, in other words, the price at which money is available on the money and capital markets. If the interest rate is 20% per annum for a long-term loan of R100 000, this means that the borrower must pay an additional R20 000 per year (20/100 × R100 000) to secure the loan of R100 000. This is therefore the price that the borrower must pay for the money he or she wishes to borrow.

A rise in interest rates usually results in a decrease in spending. If someone wants to buy a car, for example, he or she will have to pay more to borrow the money and ultimately, pay more for the car. Suppose the buyer buys a car through hire purchase financing and interest rates subsequently rise. This means that the buyer's monthly instalments will also increase and that he or she will pay even more for the vehicle in the long run. The bond on a home loan works in the same way; as soon as the interest rates rise, so do the monthly loan instalments. The opposite scenario is also true.

Inflation

Inflation results in a continual rise in the prices of products and services. This has a depressing effect on the economy because the purchasing power of the rand, and therefore also the purchasing power of the customer, decreases as inflation rises. The customer is able to buy fewer products for the same amount of money because the value of the money has decreased as a result of inflation. Since the late seventies, South Africa has had to deal with the negative influence of inflation, in some years this has reached double figures.

The influence of inflation is clear from the following examples:

- In 1980 we paid 30c for a loaf of white bread. In 2010 we paid R5.90 for the same loaf of bread and today we pay R12.00 up to R18.50, depending on brand and the different enterprise, like Pick n Pay, Checkers or Spar.
- In 1980 we paid 76c for a dozen eggs; in 1985 we paid R1.31. In 2010 we paid R5.95 and today we pay R26.00 up to R48.00 depending on the sizes and brand of eggs and the different enterprise, like Pick n Pay, Checkers or Spar.

Trade cycles

All economies are subject to certain cyclical changes. We can distinguish between different phases in the economic cycle, namely a period of prosperity, followed by a period of recession and depression and then a period of recovery. You should be aware of the phase through which the economy is moving as this influences the management, growth and continued existence of the business.

Each phase makes its own demands on the business.

- During a phase of prosperity, the business (the marketing and production divisions) has the opportunity to manufacture and market new products. The business therefore has the opportunity to explore new markets and to expand its share of the market.
- In contrast, during a recession customers' disposable incomes are lower and they therefore buy less. This has a direct influence on the demand for products and/or services and therefore also on the growth of a business.
- During the recovery phase, the business must prepare itself for the economic growth that will take place and should, for example, pay attention to personnel training programmes, the development of new products and ways to increase its sales and therefore its income.

(b) Social environment

The social environment is governed by the demographics of the population and social and cultural variables. We can distinguish between the following demographic variables, all of which have an impact on the market.

Size and composition of the population

- **Population growth:** The size and composition of the market are directly influenced by the population growth of the country. When you consider the size of the population, remember that families have grown smaller over the past few years and consider what effect this will have on future markets.

- **Market composition:** The market is made up of different ethnic groups. Each group has a distinctive culture and lifestyle.
- **Changing role of women:** Women make up a large proportion of the labour force today. This has a direct impact on the market because the working woman has different needs of a woman who is a homemaker. For instance, more working mothers mean a greater demand for crèches and nursery schools; families with two incomes have a higher disposable income; the clothing needs of the working woman differ from the homemaker; and finally, working women usually spend more money on time-saving goods such as ready-made meals.
- **Life expectancy:** Life expectancy has increased as a result of better medical services and healthier lifestyles. This means that there are many more customers over the age of 60, which presents definite marketing opportunities. For example, in the tourist industry there are many opportunities for travel agents to develop tour packages for this older target group.

Geographic location

Markets in metropolitan areas are larger and more concentrated; therefore a wider variety of products and services can be marketed and sold in and around cities. Urbanisation and the depopulation of rural areas have a direct influence on the distribution of the market.

Development level of the market

In South Africa today great emphasis is placed on training and consumer education. Customers are more informed, which means they know precisely what they want and therefore make greater demands on business. The customer is aware of, and stands up for, his or her rights. In order to continue to exist and grow, every business must focus on the needs of its customers.

Other

Social and cultural forces in the macro environment, which must be considered, include the following:

- **Changing awareness:** The customer today is well informed about quality and available options. They are aware of environmental concerns and consider such aspects as whether the manufacturing of products contributes to pollution or uses scarce natural resources.
- **Time:** In today's busy world, the customer does not want to spend too much time shopping and will look for products that are convenient and save time. Some examples include portable laptop computers that can be used while travelling, or prepared foods as mentioned earlier. A further example is the appearance of convenience supermarkets in residential areas. People returning home from work want to be able to buy essentials as quickly as possible. The convenience and longer

opening hours of smaller supermarkets in suburban areas satisfy this need. The same principle applies to one-stop shopping centres: everything the customer wants is available under one roof.

- **Healthier lifestyle:** The current trend towards fitness and a healthier lifestyle is a further phenomenon that a business must be aware of. There is greater demand for natural foods (foods without colouring agents or preservatives) and an increased demand for products linked to fitness, such as bicycles, running shoes and gym equipment.

(c) Technological environment

Today we live in the era of the Fourth Industrial Revolution. The Fourth Industrial Revolution focuses on technologies. The technological environment embraces numerous aspects that give rise to new products and services being made available on the market. The microwave oven, today a common convenience appliance in the average household, only became commercially available 50 years ago. This product is the result of technological development and it has given many businesses the opportunity to add a new product to an existing product line.

In the music industry, compact discs also constitute a new development which did not exist 40 years ago. These days the compact discs are being replaced by the MP3 and MP4 digital formats that can be downloaded and distributed via digital platforms.

New technological developments or improvements create definite opportunities for business, but they may also constitute certain threats. The development of compact discs meant that long-playing records are no longer manufactured. Factories that used to manufacture the latter have been forced to change their strategies because of developments on the technological front. Currently, record labels and producers are faced with new opportunities and threats of selling music through various digital channels. On the one hand, there are many more opportunities to reach consumers, but on the other hand, there is the threat of piracy or illegal downloading. In addition, think of the continual changes in computer technology and the influence this has on banking, for example. New and technologically improved products are constantly being introduced into the market.

If a business does not keep abreast of changes taking place on the technological front, it will soon find that the products it sells are obsolete. The consumer is not interested in obsolete products – organisations that do not keep abreast of technological change will have to relinquish their share of the market in the long term. A further influence of the technological environment on business is that provision should be made for research and development by means of funds allocated for this purpose. Technological changes do not always result in new products – they can also result in improvements to existing products. A good example of this is the cell phone industry.

(d) Physical environment

The physical environment means the natural resources within the country and incorporates the total management of these resources. Natural resources include gold, coal, diamonds, water and natural forests. The natural beauty of the country can be included here as this influences the tourist market. The following variables in the physical environment should be taken into consideration:

Limited and expensive resources

The world's natural resources are limited and must be managed carefully. Customers today demand that manufacturers recognise these limitations. This could also create opportunities in two ways:

- for the business to advertise its own environmentally friendly procedures and thereby attract customers
- for business opportunities.

Consider the following examples:

South Africa currently has problems with the supply of electricity. Many entrepreneurial opportunities arise from this – solar heating for water, power-saving light bulbs and wind generators etc.

South Africa has limited water supplies. This limitation was highlighted during the drought in the Western Cape during 2017. Suggestions for entrepreneurial opportunities include sprinkler systems using recycled water and toilets with the two-flush option.

Environmentalism and pollution

Industry is often guilty of air, water and noise pollution resulting from their manufacturing processes. The effects of this pollution and the role played by industry in combating pollution are receiving worldwide attention. Manufacturing businesses can play a role by considering issues such as packaging. Packaging in plastic or glass is very convenient, but has definite disadvantages for the environment.

From time to time poisonous waste products, like plastics, which are extremely harmful to human, water and plant life, flow into rivers and the sea. The mining of minerals sometimes elicits strong opposition from conservationists – for example the polemic regarding the mining of minerals in the St Lucia area. The construction of roads can mar natural scenery, and conservationists were strongly opposed to the building of a tar road which would pass the Knysna lagoon in the southern Cape.

(e) Political and statutory environment

The government of the day influences businesses through its fiscal and monetary policies. For instance, interest rates have a direct effect on net income, municipal rates affect property tax, and of course the annual budget influences the total economy of the country. The national budget is a useful document to study because it gives details of likely future government spending and of how income will be generated. Some of the government's income is obtained from taxes paid by individuals and businesses.

Variables which influence the individual business include the following:

Statutory provisions

There are various statutory provisions which businesses must comply with. For example:

- The business must have a trading licence before it can do business.
- The business must register as a taxpayer at the local Receiver of Revenue.
- The Companies Act contains detailed prescriptions on how a company should be established and managed.
- The business cannot conclude contracts unless it complies with the provisions of the closed contract. This means that the business is limited during the concluding of contracts by certain statutory provisions under contract law.
- Certain organisations, for example a restaurant, a home industry concern, or butchery, must comply with certain health requirements as laid down by the relevant municipality. Such businesses must first obtain approval from the municipality before they can commence trading. Inspections are carried out on a regular basis to determine whether these organisations are complying with the necessary requirements.

Two important changes were brought about by the amendments to the Companies Act 71 of 2008, which came into effect on 1 May 2011.

- The new Consumer Protection Act 68 of 2008 (CPA), which came into effect on 31 March 2011, is being implemented by the National Consumer Commission (NCC), which took over from the Department of Trade and Industry's Office of Consumer Protection (OCP).
- The Companies and Intellectual Property Commission (CIPC) was established on 1 May 2011. The CIPC registers companies, promotes awareness of company and intellectual property law, and monitors compliance of financial reporting standards.

There are also a variety of statutory provisions aimed at protecting the customer.

- The regulations regarding advertising; advertising may not be misleading or contain false information. The Advertising Standards Association controls this aspect very strictly.

- The customer must be properly informed about the product and its composition. This information is usually contained on the packaging.
- The customer must be shown how to use the product, if applicable. For example, instructions for use must be included with all electrical products.
- The customer must be properly informed about product safety requirements.
- Product approval granted by the South African Bureau of Standards is aimed at protecting the consumer against inferior, poorly made and dangerous products.

Trade unions

Every business has a responsibility towards its employees. There are various laws which help to maintain a smooth relationship between the employer and employee. Although statutory provisions and regulations protect the rights of the employee, the existence of trade unions is an important variable in the macro environment because the voice of individual employees can easily be ignored by management.

Trade unions fight for the rights of workers who work in the same branch of industry. The employee acquires bargaining power through membership of the trade union which enables him or her to negotiate, for example, for higher salaries or better working conditions. In South Africa there are numerous trade unions, for example trade unions for mine workers, the motor industry, the steel industry and bank officials. If disputes are not resolved or are unfairly resolved, the Labour Relations Act of 1995 has made it possible to refer such cases to external mechanisms, such as the Commission for Conciliation, Mediation and Arbitration (CCMA).

Associations and institutes

In the same way as trade unions look after the interests of organised labour, many business associations and institutes campaign for the interests of businesses in their fields. Earlier on in this chapter we emphasised that a business has little, if any, influence over the macro environment. By means of associations and institutes, a business can promote its interests in the branch of industry in which it functions if it works with other businesses in the same branch of industry.

The following institutes and associations are well known and active in the macro environment:

- Afrikaanse Handelsinstituut (AHI)
- The South African Chamber of Business (Sacob)
- The Chamber of Mines
- The Motor Industries Federation
- Black Management Forum.

(f) International environment

We have seen that the variables influencing individual businesses originate from the local sphere (the business itself) and the national sphere (the market and macro environments). Over and above all these forces, the business must also still keep abreast of variables operating in the international sphere. These influences originate in the environment outside the country's borders and include:

International technology

South Africa is technologically developed in certain areas such as in the fields of synthetic fuels, mining and veterinary science. However, South Africa also imports technology from other countries, for example computer technology from America and engineering technology from Germany and Japan. This phenomenon is common to all developing countries.

International politics

South Africa felt the effect of international politics with the trade sanctions imposed in the mid-eighties. The country did not have access to foreign loan capital, for example, and this had a negative effect on the economic growth rate and job creation.

International economy

Economic factors and variables such as interest rates, exchange rates, the gold price, the economic growth rate, inflation, the availability of capital and a scarcity of resources occur worldwide and influence the economic conditions of all countries. For example, think of the effect inflation has had on the economies of Zimbabwe, Russia and Argentina. Among other things, high inflation rates resulted in very high food prices in these countries.

The rand–dollar and dollar–euro exchange rates have a significant influence on South African import and export activities. If the rand–dollar exchange rate is weak, the cost of importing goods becomes higher for a South African business. An example of this is the cost of overseas textbooks, which are currently expensive because the rand–dollar exchange rate is unfavourable for South African booksellers.

1.5 SUMMARY

It is quite impossible for any business to function in total isolation. Without interaction with the business environment, your business will not continue to grow and may cease to exist. The management of a business should frequently analyse the environment and determine its general trends. This valuable information can be used to help the business achieve its objectives. Achieving the business objectives will remain a dream if this interaction does not take place.

A business is an independent body that is established by an entrepreneur to provide products or services that will meet the needs of consumers, and consists of all the business functions. An establishment is the place where inputs are converted into outputs. This is the place where the physical production takes place, in other words the factory or plant. Businesses are classified into three sectors, according to the activities that they perform:

- Primary sector – exploitation of natural resources in their raw unprocessed form
- Secondary sector – natural resources processed into final products
- Tertiary sector – responsible for conveying or distributing final products from the manufacturer to the consumer.

However, if we look at the route that an individual product follows from its original state until it ends up in the hands of the consumer, we combine the sectors in an industrial column.

The business must also use information to analyse trends in the market. From this information, you can analyse potential opportunities and threats. The business environment offers opportunities which help you to achieve predetermined objectives. The opposite could also be true: if you do not heed important signals in the business environment, it could lead to the potential closure of your business.

The three components of the business environment, identified as the micro, market and macro environments, are in constant interaction with each other and not independent of each other. Keep in mind that the various variables we have identified influence these environments and play a significant role in the growth and continued existence of the business. There is constant interaction between the different sub-environments.

The entrepreneur must continually gather information as a basis for analysing market trends. This information must be transformed into knowledge to bridge the gap between the enterprise, the entrepreneur and the market. From this knowledge, the entrepreneur can analyse potential opportunities and threats. The business environment offers opportunities which help the entrepreneur achieve the objectives of the business. Conversely, if the entrepreneur does not attend to important signals in the business environment, this could jeopardise the business.

Self-evaluation questions

1. With the aid of a practical example, illustrate the relationship between the business and the establishment.
2. Discuss the three sectors in which businesses and establishments can be grouped and motivate your discussion with practical examples.
3. Draw your own industrial column for the production of wine.
4. Explain the meaning of the concept 'business environment' and identify the most important characteristics of this environment in your explanation.
5. Give reasons why a business cannot grow and continue to exist in total isolation.
6. Name three components of the business environment and give a description of each.
7. Discuss the micro environment and its variables.
8. Identify the variables in the market environment and discuss each one.
9. With the help of examples, discuss the different markets in which a business manufacturing wooden furniture can conduct business transactions.
10. Identify your rights as a customer and illustrate each right with the aid of a practical example.
11. Explain the meaning of 'competition'. Illustrate your answer with practical examples.
12. Do you think it is necessary for the business to take the macro-environment into account? Give reasons for your answer by discussing the different variables within the sub-environments.
13. Suppose you are the owner of a business that manufactures and markets wooden kitchen cupboards. Evaluate your business environment on the basis of the variables in the micro, macro and market environments.
14. Martha Mabuso is the owner of a business that sells computer equipment. She realises that she must take the variables in the external environment into account. However, she focuses only on the variables in the market environment and does not consider those in the macro environment. Explain to Martha, with the help of suitable examples, which variables can be identified in the macro environment and what influence these may have on her business.

REFERENCES AND FUTHER READING

Bateman, T.S. & Scott, A.S. 2009. *Management Leading & Collaboration in the Competitive World*. (8th edition). New York: McGraw-Hill.

De Beer, A.A. & Rossouw, D. 2018. *Focus on Operational Management: A generic approach*. (2nd edition). Cape Town: Juta Publishers.

Hellriegel, D., Jackson, S.E., Slocum, J. & Staude, G. 2012. *Management, South African Edition*. (4th edition). Cape Town: Oxford University Press.

Le Roux, E.E., Venter, C.H., Jansen van Vuren, J.E., Jacobs, H., Labuschagne, M., Kritzinger, A.A.C., Ferreira, E.J., de Beer, A.A. & Hübner, C.P. 1999. *Business Management: A practical and interactive approach*. Johannesburg: Heinemann Publishers.

Nel, J. & De Beer, A. 2014. *Business Management: A Contemporary Approach*. Cape Town: Juta.

Van Noordwyk, A., Fernandes, N.M.J. & Van Zyl, J.H. (eds). 2015. *Business Functions: An Introduction*. (2nd ed). Cape Town: Juta.

Williams, C. 2013. *Principles of Management*. (7th edition). Canada: South-Western.

Chapter 2 Entrepreneurship and small, medium and micro enterprises (SMMEs) in perspective

2.1 LEARNING OUTCOMES

After you have studied this chapter, you should be able to:

- define the terms 'entrepreneur' and 'entrepreneurship'
- indicate the relationship between entrepreneurship, a small business enterprise and small business management
- explain the various types of entrepreneurial businesses
- explain corporate entrepreneurship/intrapreneurship
- explain the key success factors of entrepreneurs
- explain how entrepreneurs should deal with external factors that affect entrepreneurship

2.2 INTRODUCTION

Employment opportunities abound in private and public sector organisations. Schools, colleges and universities primarily teach and train us to become employees not employers. However, those of us who identify and evaluate the best employers often agree that one's best employer is oneself. This is measured by work satisfaction, experience, income, self-realisation, job creation and a range of other factors.

Unfortunately, we are often incorrectly informed that entrepreneurship cannot be learned, and that entrepreneurship is an innate ability that few of us are born with. Fortunately, this is untrue: it has been proved that entrepreneurship is a discipline, and therefore can be taught and learnt through specialised entrepreneurship education (Kuratko, 2014:???). Although entrepreneurship is a relatively new discipline, research and education in entrepreneurship have increased tremendously in recent decades. We now know what entrepreneurship is and how it should be taught. Entrepreneurship programmes should not be short, superficial courses but should possess depth. In addition, entrepreneurship education is notably different from business or business management education; lecturers have to learn how to teach true entrepreneurship that makes a difference to the lives of entrepreneurs, their communities and the economy.

Furthermore, entrepreneurial activity has a crucial influence on the national economy: more than a source of income, it is a stimulant – a source of innovation.

Economic development can be directly attributed to levels of entrepreneurial activity in a national economy. In high-growth, globally competitive economies, the ability to nurture entrepreneurial activity, grow businesses, create wealth and sustain competitive advantage is imperative. There is a direct correlation between job creation and the level of entrepreneurial activity in an economy, and a statistically significant association between national economic growth and entrepreneurship (Kuratko, 2014:xxxii).

Entrepreneurial businesses ensure economic growth by means of innovation, which creates wealth for the entrepreneur and adds value to society.

Small, medium or micro enterprises (SMMEs), not necessarily entrepreneurial businesses, form about 90% of all registered businesses in South Africa. Their contribution to the country's Gross Domestic Product (GDP) is 36% and they provide employment to 60% of the workforce. In the United States (US), United Kingdom, Germany, France and other developed countries, small businesses contribute more than 50% to the GDP of each country (GEM, 2018).

Gross Domestic Product (GDP) is the total production of a country. The total number of services and products supplied and produced within the borders of a country in one year is measured in financial terms by GDP. The growth rate of GDP is an indication of how successful a country is in providing jobs and income to its citizens.

In 2018 South Africa was ranked 61st out of 138 countries for private sector organisations, including the establishment and growth of businesses on the Global Competitiveness Index (GCI). This is 28 places down since 2010 and primarily due to local issues such as an inadequately educated workforce; restrictive labour regulations; inefficient government bureaucracy and the burden of government regulations; business cost of crime, theft and violence; corruption; and high unemployment. By contrast, the economic environment in the US and the country's ranking according to the Global Competitiveness Index (GCI) are very favourable at 7th out of 138 countries (WEF 2017:34).

How is South Africa doing?

According to a survey by Brand South Africa:

- 42% of respondents started businesses because they identified an opportunity.
- 87% of respondents lived in Gauteng, KwaZulu-Natal or the Western Cape.
- 5% of respondents lived in rural areas.
- 98% of respondents owned for-profit businesses
  - for-profit businesses are motivated by creating value for the business owner
  - 18% of these were social enterprises.
- 2% owned non-profit businesses
  - non-profit organisations are motivated to bring social change to communities.
- 37% of businesses had no employees, while 51% of businesses that had staff, employed from one to four people.
- Type of customer:
  - 38% business to business
  - 47% business to consumers
  - 12% business to government
  - 36% all of the above.
- 78% needed less than R100 000 to start their businesses; only 5% required more than R1 million to start operating.
- 95% of businesses were funded by owners and their friends and family.
- Only 5% acquired funds from formal sources such as angel funding, bank loans and development finance institutions such as the Industrial Development Corporation.
- 78% of entrepreneurs had engaged in entrepreneur training programmes or had been part of an incubator at some point.
- 45% had previously failed in business, which showed their commitment to the entrepreneurial journey.

Source: Brand South Africa (2017).

This chapter explains how the entrepreneur and entrepreneurship relate to a small business and small business management. Subsequently, the different types of entrepreneurial businesses and corporate entrepreneurship are introduced. The key success factors that contribute to successful entrepreneurship are explained, and information on the external factors affecting entrepreneurship are provided.

2.3 DEFINING ENTREPRENEUR AND ENTREPRENEURSHIP

Entrepreneurs have the ability to identify and seize an opportunity, and create and develop a business by adding value to the business. They do this by applying resources that include finance, time, effort, people and skills. They are willing to take risks; and through their businesses they organise, manage and achieve results.

Entrepreneurs can therefore be described as those people who:

- start their own business
- manage the business
- identify new products or opportunities
- seize opportunities
- create and innovate
- organise and control resources of capital, labour and materials to realise profit
- have the ability and insight to market, produce and finance a service or product
- have the financial means, or access to finance, to realise the enterprise
- are willing to take calculated risks.

Entrepreneurship is the process of establishing a business, from the identification of a business opportunity and innovation through to planning, start-up, managing and growing the business. Entrepreneurship is, therefore, also acknowledged as a discipline on its own, especially in developed economies.

Entrepreneurs spot opportunities and organise resources to create new businesses. They have the vision, business skills and courage to take risks, and possess the necessary leadership qualities to overcome problems. Entrepreneurs normally have a strong internal locus of control (their destiny and success are determined by their own actions), self-confidence, passion, determination and the management skills to plan and control the entrepreneurial process.

The entrepreneur's role, however, differs from that of the small business manager in that the entrepreneur manages change by, for example, introducing a new product, buying a new business, deciding which risks to take, introducing new management systems and moving into new markets.

NB

Keep in mind that not everyone who starts a new business is actually an entrepreneur. Some might be *enterprising* but a true entrepreneur habitually creates and innovates to build and develop something of recognisable value. Not all SMMEs achieve something new or different, nor do all grow and become successful. Thus, although small businesses create wealth and add value to the economy, not all SMMEs are *entrepreneurial*. Small businesses tend to swing in and out of periods of entrepreneurial change over time, after which periods of consolidation may take place.

2.4 THE RELATIONSHIP BETWEEN ENTREPRENEURSHIP, A SMALL BUSINESS ENTERPRISE AND SMALL BUSINESS MANAGEMENT

Most businesses begin as small or micro enterprises, usually managed by a single person. That person's aim is to grow and develop the business. This can happen continually as long as the entrepreneur retains his or her entrepreneurial mindset (ie continues to innovate and create). However, if the entrepreneur becomes comfortable and satisfied with the level of growth of the enterprise, he or she stops being an entrepreneur and becomes a small business manager, who is averse to risk, change and innovation. Schumpeter (1934) observes that most firms come to settle for non-entrepreneurial stability; Katz and Green (2014:9) confirm this, suggesting that those that do are usually lifestyle or part-time businesses that start and remain small, and contribute to the owner's living costs. They represent approximately 53% of small businesses. According to them, traditional small businesses are very small; operate from a single site and have reached a sufficient level of income: at most, their growth will be inflation related.

Examples of a small business manager who is not an entrepreneur are:

- a person who manages an existing business or franchise such as a Trellidor franchise without ensuring growth
- a person who works full- or part-time in a lifestyle business, such as a bed and breakfast guesthouse that does not generate sufficient income to cover all living expenses
- a person satisfied with a no-growth, 'single-premise' business, for example a boutique in a shopping mall
- a person who inherits a business and runs it in the same way as his or her predecessor, for example a child who inherits a parent's farm and continues farming without expanding or improving it
- a person appointed by the owner of a small business as the manager.

Successful entrepreneurs and small business owners should also be able to manage a business that is in the process of growing and has grown. The danger is that when the business has grown to a certain size, the entrepreneur may lack the skills to manage the business even though he or she may be competent and innovative. An extreme example: in 2007 the successful entrepreneur, Hamdi Ulukaya, started his own business, Chobani Inc, selling Greek yoghurt. By 2015, it had achieved $1 billion in annual sales. But the growth of the business exceeded his ability to manage it, leading to problems that included financial losses, high debt, scattered operations, a lack of purchasing power and inadequate quality control. Mr Ulukaya came to realise that he had to appoint a chief executive officer with management expertise (Gasparro, 2015:10). Many successful entrepreneurs are able to establish and grow their businesses, but are not as competent in managing medium or large businesses. It is essential that the entrepreneur acknowledges this and ensures that a competent business manager is appointed.

A small business manager must therefore be able to:

- plan, organise, lead and control the various business functions
- organise the efficient performance of tasks
- ensure interpersonal and inter-group competence
- facilitate formal communication during scheduled meetings
- compile and implement necessary policies and procedures for the business.

Successful entrepreneurs are not always successful managers. In fast-growth phases this can become a threat to the business. Entrepreneurs should acknowledge their strengths and weaknesses, such as limitations on time, attention and energy. The entrepreneur may have to upgrade his or her management skills, hire a professional manager, or both. Managers have to be managed.

2.5 TYPES OF ENTREPRENEURIAL BUSINESSES

Entrepreneurial businesses can be classified as either informal, micro, very small, small, medium or large. Each type of business has very specific characteristics with specific needs and features. Some of these are discussed in the section below.

The National Small Business Amendment Act 26 of 2003 has set out criteria defining business size in each sector of industry (see Table 2.1 below).

2.5.1 The formal small business

The small and micro business sector

In the National Small Business Amendment Act 26 of 2003, a micro business is defined as a business with five or fewer employees with a turnover of up to R100 000 per annum. A very small business employs between one and ten employees, and a small business between 11 and 50 employees. The upper limit for annual turnover in a small business ranges from R3 million in the agricultural sector to R13 million in the manufacturing and catering, accommodation and other trade sectors, up to a maximum of R32 million in the wholesale trade sector. The upper limits for employment and turnover of small businesses in the various sectors are shown in Table 2.1 below.

Table 2.1: Definition of a small business according to industrial sector, employment and turnover

Sector or subsector in accordance with the Standard Industrial Classification	The total full-time equivalent of paid employees	Total turnover
Agriculture	50	R3 m
Mining and Quarrying	50	R10 m
Manufacturing	50	R13 m
Electricity, Gas and Water	50	R13 m
Construction	50	R6 m
Retail, Motor Trade, and Repair Services	50	R19 m
Wholesale Trade, Commercial Agents and Allied Services	50	R32 m
Catering, Accommodation and other trade	50	R6 m
Transport, Storage and Communications	50	R13 m
Finance and Business Services	50	R13 m
Community, Social and Personal Services	50	R6 m

Source: Adapted from the National Small Business Amendment Act 26 of 2003

2.5.2 Medium business

Often, when it is a truly entrepreneurial business, a small businesses will grow to become a medium business. Medium businesses employ between 50 and 200 employees, with turnover from the upper limit of small businesses as indicated in Table 2.1 above.

Medium businesses are highly formalised and require special professional expertise, management and of course a dedicated entrepreneur or entrepreneurial team.

Successful entrepreneurs inspire and act as role models. We have all heard of exceptional entrepreneurs such as the late Steve Jobs of Apple, Mark Zuckerberg of Facebook and Elon Musk (an ex-South African) of Tesla. The list includes many South Africans such as Richard Maponya of Maponya Mall, Raymond Ackerman of Pick n Pay, Herman Mashaba of Black Like Me, and Jannie Mouton of PSG, a financial services group. But there are many lesser-known people with whom we can more easily identify. Examples of their businesses exist in all economic sectors, and vary from micro businesses in basic products and services to sophisticated IT companies and highly professional practices. Some examples in the small and medium (and growing) business category are as follows:

- Twenty-five years ago, due to changing circumstances and concern about their future, Willie and Pieter Naudé realised that they had to review their situation. Using their experience as fitters and turners and programmers, they started their own very small business in their garage. They began with one turntable then expanded their equipment and premises as needed.

  Over 18 years, their business grew and became successful. In 2012 they sold it, only to start a new and similar enterprise the next year. Their new business, Turn On Engineering, produces machine parts from steel, aluminium, plastic and other materials on a project basis according to the specifications of the client. The business uses the latest Japanese technology and machinery for their industry. For Willie and Pieter quality service and employment creation are priorities, and they are passionate about what they do in their business (Hatting, 2015:12).

- On his 40th birthday, in 2011, Andy Reid decided to spoil himself and buy a Vespa scooter. When he could not find a new one anywhere in South Africa, he went to Italy – and returned with 600 Vespas. Today he is head of Vespa South Africa. According to Reid, the business started very small and started to break even only after seven years.

  Vespa is an iconic, timeless brand. In addition to selling scooters and accessories, Vespa also provides customers with lessons in driving two-wheel vehicles, assists them in acquiring motorbike licences and provides delivery scooters to businesses. Currently, Vespa has branches in Johannesburg, Cape Town and Durban (Jonker, 2015:17).

- Entrepreneurs do not always start a completely new business, but often explore and identify new markets and open businesses to service them. Big Blue, the clothing and lifestyle company of Philip Cronje and James Robertson, started off as a flea-market stall in 1986. The two needed a form of escape from their full-time corporate jobs and decided to go on their own. Fortunately, frequent travelling was part of their respective corporate jobs and exposed them to creative ideas and people.

With limited access to interesting and unusual fabrics, they created and designed their own fabrics for their clothes that eventually became an iconic range of prints, crafts and designs. During 2003, they opened their first store in Centurion. They now own an interesting, quirky and sustainable, proudly South African business with 21 stores selling clothes made from unique fabrics as well as collections of South African memorabilia.

Their range of products includes ladies' and men's clothing, bags, homeware and interesting gifts. Some products are cheap copies and others recycled and produced by crafting groups such as a Hillcrest Aids project, Diepsloot crafters and anyone who produces products that catch their attention. Through Big Blue many entrepreneurs have access to sales. The jobs created and maintained by the company include those of its suppliers and service providers (Viktor, 2015:12; Big Blue, 2018).

- Peter Herrmann, a textile engineer, and his wife, Coba, started Hertex (Herrmann Textiles) in 1987 in a shed in an industrial area of Cape Town with their first fabric showroom. Although the initial product was fabric, they have expanded and their products, primarily for the décor market, now include fabrics for upholstery, curtaining and drapery; floor and wall coverings; throws and cushion inners. Currently, there are 12 Hertex showrooms and Hertex is the largest local company in the industry. In addition, Hertex operates internationally through agents and has a showroom in London.

  The company houses a variety of brands serving different niche markets including Stonehaus, faBella, Couture, Padari and Studio H.

  Hertex is a true entrepreneurial family business as Peter and Coba's three daughters are the operational, sales and human resource directors of the business. The family also owns and successfully operates two farms in the Piketberg area, growing food and proteas for export to international markets (Van der Merwe, 2015:80; Hertex, 2015).

2.5.3 Gazelles and serial entrepreneurs

Gazelles, otherwise known as high growth entrepreneurial businesses, are what the name implies.

Gazelles are entrepreneurs who are focused on growing and developing their businesses at a quick pace. These are the true entrepreneurs who not only establish a business but also have a strategy in place to ensure that the business grows to become a medium or even large business or corporation, becomes more profitable, employs more people and ultimately satisfies the intrinsic entrepreneurial motivation of this type of entrepreneur.

Serial entrepreneurs are entrepreneurs who are always on the lookout for new business ideas. They are adept in start-ups, or starting a new business and growing it to become profitable. Some serial entrepreneurs keep all their businesses, others sell some, and others start a business with the primary aim of selling it and going on to establish a new one. The motivation and expertise of serial entrepreneurs is that they know they are good with idea identification and commercialisation and they enjoy the novelty of a new challenge, but they are not necessarily interested in managing an established business.

2.6 CORPORATE ENTREPRENEURSHIP OR INTRAPRENEURSHIP

Corporate entrepreneurship or intrapreneurship is also a form of entrepreneurship. It occurs when the corporate entrepreneur identifies a specific business opportunity and establishes a new business within the structure of an existing one.

Corporate entrepreneurship (also known as intrapreneurship) is the creation of a business or businesses within an existing large business, using new ideas and exploiting opportunities. The new and relatively small autonomous business unit produces a product or service using the resources of an existing business.

Corporate entrepreneurship makes it possible for large businesses to adapt to changes in the market entrepreneurially, experiment in the market, diversify from the core business, establish new distribution channels, and make profits from new businesses.

An example of corporate entrepreneurship is First National Bank (FNB), which used to be a conventional bank. FNB ventured into new businesses such as Outsurance and Discovery Health.

Outsurance is a short-term insurance company and represents diversification of FNB's core, traditional business. Outsurance itself was innovative in offering direct, short-term insurance to individuals without the traditional intermediary insurance brokers. Outsurance has grown from a small corporate entrepreneurial business to a large insurance business.

Discovery Health is another corporate entrepreneurship venture, established by a corporate entrepreneur, Adrian Gore, within FNB during the 1990s. It grew to become the largest and most innovative independent medical aid group in South Africa, and has expanded internationally.

Another development of a corporate venture is Discovery Bank out of Discovery. Discovery, now a leader in insurance in South Africa, entered retail banking with Discovery Bank in 2018. Discovery's success was built its on its medical insurance business, Discovery Health.

2.6.1 Franchisors and franchisees

Franchising is an arrangement in which an individual or business (the franchisor) grants an independent party (the franchisee) the right to sell the products or services of the business according to guidelines set down by the franchisor.

The franchisor retains control over the conduct of the business and offers the franchisee a comprehensive business package. Examples of franchises are Cash Converters, King Pie, Car Service City, Hot Dog Café, Trellidoor and Placecol Skin Care Clinics.

The franchisor is an entrepreneur, whereas the franchisee should rather be seen as a corporate entrepreneur (or intrapreneur) who innovates within the franchise system.

Franchisees do not have the latitude to experiment, operate and market their business according to their own vision, but must adhere to the plans of the franchisor. However, it has been proved that franchisees do show an entrepreneurial orientation in certain situations, such as multiple-outlet franchisees (Maritz, 2005). Franchisors in many sectors have recognised the benefit of multiple-unit franchisees (Johnson, 2004), and this is seen as an entrepreneurial extension of the franchise trend.

Franchisors usually fall into the medium- to large-business category, because the more successful franchisors manage a large number of franchises in addition to managing the franchising group. In South Africa alone there are 600 different franchise brands, up from only 156 in 1994. There are 31 000 franchise outlets operating in the country and 26% belong to previously disadvantaged groups. Franchises employ about 320 000 people. Approximately 25% of franchises in South Africa are fast-food restaurants and 13% are retail businesses. They are responsible for 28% and 40% respectively of franchise business employment.

Franchisees can fall anywhere between the small to medium categories. Franchises represent a contribution of approximately 10% of GDP. Measured by sustainability, franchises are sound: 75% of franchises exist for more than six years and 44% remain in business for more than 12 (Brand-Jonker, 2015:2).

Nando's, the fast-food business that serves food with a Mozambican/Portuguese theme, is a familiar South African name. This franchise was started by Robert Brozin and Fernando Duarte in Rosettenville, in the south of Johannesburg, in 1987 as a fast-food shop selling spicy, grilled chicken meals. By 2001, Nando's had 343 branches internationally and by 2017 this number had grown to more than 1 000 in 30 countries – a 190% increase – including Britain, Australia, the US, Canada, Singapore, Malaysia, the Middle East and several African countries, including Mauritius. Many of the outlets are owned by Nando's itself (Nando's, 2017).

2.7 KEY SUCCESS FACTORS OF ENTREPRENEURS

Entrepreneurs have distinctive characteristics. This does not mean that all entrepreneurs have the same characteristics or combinations of them. Some are successful because they are prepared to take chances, while others achieve their goals largely because of their innovative skills and flair for management. Each entrepreneur achieves success because of a unique combination of factors. In fact, research (Fillion, 1991; Timmons & Spinelli, 2009) has shown that there is no typical entrepreneur because few – if any – entrepreneurs possess all of the characteristics or skills discussed in this chapter.

The following figure summarises the key success factors that usually contribute to successful entrepreneurship.

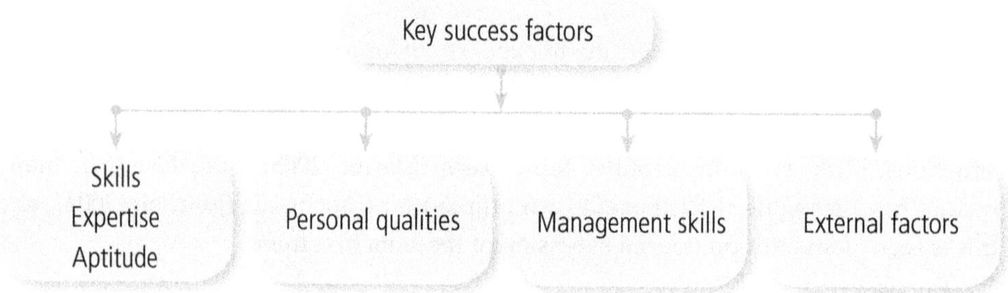

Figure 2.1: Key success factors

It is important for an entrepreneur to analyse their personal strengths and weaknesses. Their strengths can then be constructively applied and their weaknesses can be remedied by one or more of the following:

- personal development
- attending courses
- appointing staff and/or experts to compensate where needed.

2.7.1 The skills, expertise and aptitudes of an entrepreneur

Successful entrepreneurs have particular skills, expertise and aptitudes that can be applied profitably in any business. It is best to start or run a business with something you feel comfortable with and know a lot about (expertise) and/or in which you are skilled. The match between you, as the person starting the business, and the type of business is therefore most important.

Skills usually refer to manual work and can be learned. You can learn to become, for example, an electrician, a hairdresser or a cabinet-maker.

Expertise is based on knowledge you acquire. Expertise and knowledge are obtained by studying and experience. There are experts in fields such as taxation, computer systems and study techniques.

Each person is also born with aptitudes and talents. Some are artistic, some have a talent for communicating and others have a flair for numbers.

The following are examples of ways in which an entrepreneur can use skills, expertise and aptitudes in specific businesses:

Table 2.2: Skills resources required by enterprise type

Skills, expertise or aptitude	Types of enterprise
Technical thinking (aptitude) + Knowledge of antiques (expertise) + Cabinet-maker (skill)	• Draws furniture designs • Restores antique furniture • Designs and installs kitchens and built-in cupboards
Artistic (aptitude) + Experience in jewellery design (expertise) + Apprentice in jewellery manufacture (skill)	• Produces and/or sells art • Designs jewellery • Manufactures jewellery
Analytic, practical thinking (aptitude) + Experience in stock control (expertise) + Knowledge of book retailing and of the need for reliable suppliers (skill)	• Develops computer programs • Develops methods of stock control for enterprises • Provides central distribution service for suppliers of books to retail shops

Usually, your skills, expertise and knowledge are a product of your natural aptitudes, talents and interests. Someone who has a strong verbal aptitude, for example, will learn languages easily and so develop a sound knowledge of languages with further study. People who are artistic can practise art as a career or a hobby. They could, for example, paint or be a graphic designer. Further study would enable them to qualify as an architect or jewellery designer.

The examples above illustrate how important it is for an entrepreneur to consider his or her skills, expertise and aptitudes when planning to start a business.

2.7.2 The important personal characteristics of entrepreneurs

Before discussing the personal characteristics of an entrepreneur, it is important to note that expertise, skills and aptitudes in isolation do not guarantee a successful enterprise. To ensure success in your own enterprise, business aptitude and management skills are indispensable. The following example highlights the range of skills necessary to manage an interior design business.

A successful interior decorator must have a thorough knowledge of materials, furniture styles and the use of space. Knowledge of various manufacturers and their products and services is also essential. Such a person must also be artistic and creative, with a feel for colour and dimensions to be able to furnish a room tastefully. These are the person's expertise and talents. The interior decorator must also maintain sound human relations, because he or she will deal with many different people (clients, employees, suppliers and the public) when the business is marketed.

By staying personally involved in the business, the entrepreneur will use his or her expertise and talents to offer clients the best possible service. This in turn ensures the success of the business.

The following personal characteristics are important to ensure the success of an entrepreneur.

Perseverance

Entrepreneurs have confidence in themselves and their businesses and carry on in spite of setbacks, difficult situations and problems. They are able to take immediate decisions, but can also exercise patience until a task has been completed and a goal reached. They do not lose heart when they make mistakes or fail.

Successful entrepreneurs have an intense determination and a need to overcome obstacles, solve problems and complete a task. They are not intimidated by difficult situations.

Commitment to the business

Entrepreneurs dedicate their skills, expertise and resources to establishing and building the business. They prove their commitment by:

- using their own money to establish the business
- taking a mortgage on a house
- working long hours in order to succeed
- accepting a lower standard of living and possibly earning little or no income from the business until it is successful.

Involvement in the business

Entrepreneurs are personally involved in their business and are aware of everything that is happening on all levels and in all sections of the business. They perform tasks themselves and communicate well with staff and others involved with the business, such as suppliers and clients. The example of the interior decorator reminds us of the importance of personal involvement.

Willingness to take risks

Entrepreneurs take calculated risks. This means that the risk related to a business opportunity must not be too great, for then the chance of success is not in the hands of the entrepreneur. They are not gamblers. The level of risk should not be too low either, for then exploiting the opportunity does not pose a challenge and is usually not as profitable. A risk factor that is too low implies limited profitability. A business opportunity with a low risk factor makes it easy to enter the market, but also increases the risks of competition. In the business world this consideration is called 'barriers to entry'.

Entrepreneurs usually try to reduce risk by finding investors to provide finance, making arrangements with suppliers to provide goods on consignment or persuading suppliers to accept special payment terms, and so forth. The successful entrepreneur will carefully plan and consider each business opportunity.

Sound human relations

Entrepreneurs work closely with other people: they realise they cannot be successful in isolation and therefore motivate their employees. They not only know how to build contacts and long-term relationships to benefit their business, but also how to stay on good terms with suppliers, clients and others involved in the business.

Successful entrepreneurs realise the importance of business relationships. They have good relations with clients, see human relations as an important resource of the enterprise and regard long-term goodwill as more important than short-term benefits. Sound human relations have been identified as one factor that differentiates the 'successful' entrepreneur from the 'average' in developing countries (McClelland, 1986).

Successful and average entrepreneurs maintain good personal relations by, for example, using strategies to develop business contacts and build relationships with influential people to achieve their goals. They are able to persuade people to buy a product or service or to provide financing. They use their capabilities, reliability and other personal or business qualities (McClelland, 1986).

Creativity and innovative ability

Possibly the most important characteristics of successful entrepreneurs are their creativity and ability to innovate. Creativity underlies innovation, which then brings about change in the organisation. Individual creativity is a precursor of the initiation of innovation in organisations. This can involve a new product, service, method, technique or organisation.

Creativity can involve the adjustment or refinement of existing procedures or products or the identification of opportunities and solutions to problems. Basically it involves new ideas. Lateral thinking, decision-making and problem solving are all part of the creative process.

Creativity involves only the generation of ideas and does not imply the actualisation of the idea. When a business idea is actualised it becomes an innovation. It is important to distinguish between creativity and innovation. Creativity is the creation of new ideas, while innovation is the application or implementation of a creative idea into practice. The entrepreneurial application and commercialisation of new ideas is innovation.

Innovation is an introduction of newness and novelty through experimentation and creative processes aimed at developing new products, services or processes for commercialisation and introduction to the market or potential users.

Innovative opportunities are described as the realisation of economic value from a new combination of resources and needs in the market resulting from changes in scientific or technological knowledge, customer preference or interrelationships between economic actors. Innovative opportunities consist of:

- economic value for someone and
- mobilisation of resources to realise the opportunity.
- Some of the economic value generated is appropriated by the person who pursued the opportunity (Holmen, Magnusson & McKelvey, 2007:38).

Innovative opportunities result in innovations. Innovations also include the identification of new market niches, addressing customer needs with innovative approaches, networks and cooperation between organisations (Oksanen & Rilla, 2009:35).

Innovation is the introduction of newness and novelty through experimentation and creativity aimed at developing new products, services or processes for commercialisation and introduction to the market or potential users. Innovation can include technological as well as creative dimensions, but commercialisation is essential as it transforms an invention or bright idea into an innovation. Innovation is crucial to the economy of any country and an essential contributor to the level of performance of organisations. Innovative ability is often identified as the most important leadership and entrepreneurial competency in organisations as innovations can revolutionise industries and can create wealth. Entrepreneurs and leaders such as Steve Jobs of Apple and Jeff Bezos of Amazon, and organisations such as Sasol, the South African company that developed the world's first oil-from-coal process, attest to this.

Innovation can involve a variety of approaches including technological innovation of products, services or processes, product-market innovations, and innovative marketing strategies, or management innovations such as new adminstrative and organisational systems and techniques.

Innovative leadership is essential for the establishment and development of innovative organisations. Innovators can be start-up entrepreneurs, corporate entrepreneurs, product or service innovators, process innovators or management innovators. Innovation comes from leaders and entrepreneurs who understand changes in the macro and market environments of their organisations. The macro environment includes political factors, economic and socio-economic issues, demographics, technology and international change. With regard to the market environment innovation requires the understanding of consumer behaviour and needs, purchasing power, suppliers, intermediaries and competitors. Anticipating customers' needs is an important part of the personal competence of leaders and entrepreneurs. A clear perspective on the strategic assets of the organisation, including its intellectual property, is crucial. Thus innovative leaders and entrepreneurs understand the entire spectrum of the organisation and its environment, which is essential for successful innovation.

Baumol (2011:2) identifies innovation as a significant, if not primary contributor to the high growth rate of per capita income of economies such as the US, Sweden and Japan throughout the 20th century. Innovation, entrepreneurship, performance of organisations and the state of the economy are closely linked, and play important and interactive roles in job creation and wealth creation.

Positive attitude and approach

Entrepreneurs learn from their setbacks and failures. They are realistic and accept that disappointments are inevitable, and are not discouraged when these occur. They are able to identify opportunities even in adverse and difficult situations.

All this indicates that entrepreneurs remain positive despite setbacks, failure and disappointment. This does not mean they do not sometimes feel dispirited when events are not favourable, but on the whole they manage situations well. We often read of entrepreneurs who, having lost everything – sometimes more than once – start afresh. Success is achieved by using negative experiences positively and learning from past mistakes.

Henry Ford, father of the motor car assembly line and the first mass-produced motor car (the Model T Ford), twice started enterprises (both times building racing cars) that proved unsuccessful, before he achieved success.

2.7.3 The important functional management skills of entrepreneurs

The management skills of an entrepreneur are an indication of how well the entrepreneur can perform important tasks or activities. Related activities are grouped, and are known as the eight functions of a business (see Figure 2.2).

The functions are described in more detail in other chapters in this book.

In this section, which is about you, the entrepreneur, your ability to perform specific activities in the enterprise are discussed. Every entrepreneur must be aware of his or her strengths and weaknesses when it comes to management skills in the various business functions, so that they can apply or supplement them to build a successful enterprise.

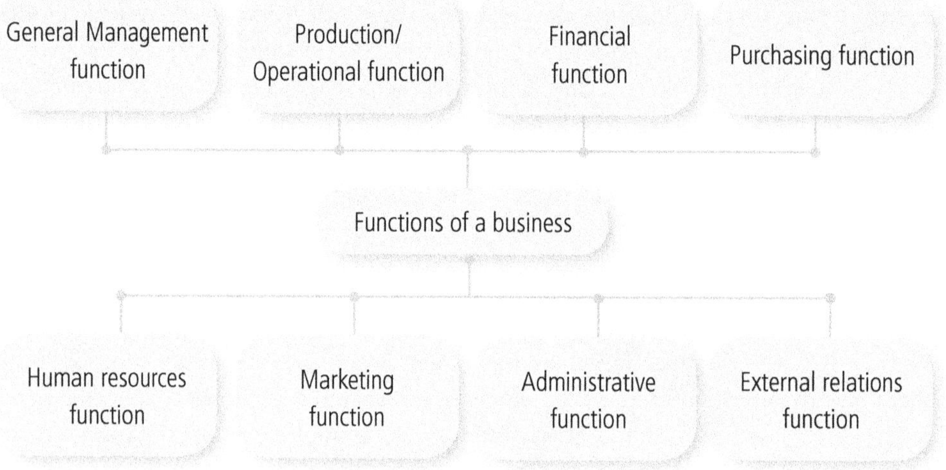

Figure 2.2: The eight functions of a business

If you think back to the example of the interior decorator, it is evident that the success of a business demands specific management skills.

The interior decorator must be market oriented. She must know which target market is to be served. For example:

- the higher income group or corporate clients
- people with modern, traditional or alternative tastes.

The decorator must also be familiar with marketing methods and know how to reach the target market. Managing the income and applying funds are equally essential for the survival and profitability of the business. If the interior decorator cannot manage her finances, she will have to get expert assistance.

According to management consultants, marketing expertise and management expertise are essential for the successful operation of SMMEs. Thus the entrepreneur should have a minimum or particular combination of these management skills.

NB

The following important aspects of management skills will be discussed below:

- planning a business before it is established
- general management skills and the use of advisors
- customer service
- knowledge of competitors
- market orientation
- the importance of quality products or services
- accounting for your own purposes
- insight into expenditure, income, profit and loss
- the ability to use income wisely.

a) Planning a business before it is established

This activity is part of the general management function and involves drawing up the business plan. A well-considered business plan ensures that the business is launched with confidence; a plan shows that the necessary research and planning have been done.

Entrepreneurs often do the planning very informally because there is no time to draw up a formal business plan, or simply because they do not know how to do it. Despite their informal planning, these entrepreneurs can be successful.

NB

Formal planning and drawing up a business plan are desirable activities because they enable the entrepreneur to:

- identify problems early on so that he or she can make wise decisions and fewer mistakes
- consider all the important factors of the intended business and, in so doing, become free of purely instinctive or crisis decisions, thus avoiding stress
- take decisions for the future
- use this planning stage as an ideal opportunity for testing ideas.

b) General management skills and the use of advisors

Entrepreneurs must know what is needed for success in a specific business, and must be intent on developing their skills in these critical areas of performance. If marketing the business's products is the critical area of performance, and a significant determinant of the success of the enterprise, the entrepreneur must know how to carry out this function. If he or she does not have the necessary expertise, trained staff should be appointed. The entrepreneur should also understand the environment in which he or she is competing and be well organised. Know-how is often more important than creativity.

As an entrepreneur, it is logical that you will start a business in which you can use the strengths of expertise and skill. You will also usually be aware of (or soon discover) your weaknesses. Then you can strengthen or supplement your weak areas by:

- using other people, such as employees, consultants, contractors or professional experts
- working on your self-development and consciously remedying deficiencies by learning from others, attending courses, reading or studying.

The interior decorator knows that she is a creative, artistic and stylish person. She realises that her financial knowledge is insufficient for her to do her own accounting, and therefore contracts this out to an accountant. As a good businesswoman she accepts that she must be able to understand financial statements, and therefore takes a course to learn the basic financial terms and principles to inform her proper business decisions. She has identified her weaknesses, and is taking steps to avoid having her enterprise harmed by them.

c) Customer service

This activity is included in the marketing and administrative functions. Entrepreneurs who maintain good human relations are aware of clients' needs, and so provide very good customer service. Examples are after-sales service; attention to detail, such as serving refreshments when a client visits; personal presentability and attractive premises; user-friendliness; and having a neatly ordered shop and clear instructions for using products. Clients remember, support and recommend a business that meets their needs and gives them something extra without making them feel they are paying for it. Little gestures mean a lot: a balloon or sticker for the child; a cup of tea or glass of champagne in the jewellery store; changing an order on short notice; or just friendly, helpful service.

Administrative and technical factors are also crucial to sound customer service. Keep accurate records and an up-to-date filing system for reference and stock control. Use a diary so that you can plan your time and keep appointments, and keep job cards for client information. These are a few examples of methods to ensure effective customer service.

d) Knowledge of competitors

This activity is also part of the marketing function. Successful entrepreneurs know:

- who their competitors are
- how many competitors they have
- the size of their competitors' operations
- which segment of the market their competitors control
- the quality of their competitors' products or services
- how to distinguish themselves from their competitors and so ensure and increase their visibility and thus their share of the market
- how to recognise their competitors' strengths and weaknesses, thus converting a competitor's weakness into an opportunity for their own business.

An entrepreneur sells various artists' work. He knows his competitors and distinguishes his business by going out to visit clients at their homes or places of work rather than expecting them to come to him. He takes along a variety of suitable works of art to make the client's choice easier. His professional knowledge of art, its quality and his taste and flair for colour and style (talent) are presented to the client in a unique fashion. He is successful, because his competitors sell their products from art galleries, shops or at auctions, with no apparent interest in the client's home or place of work.

e) Market orientation

Market orientation also forms part of the marketing function. Successful entrepreneurs are market oriented. They know who or what their target market is; its demands and needs; and how to meet these needs profitably. (The example of the interior decorator illustrates this functional skill.) A market-conscious entrepreneur has developed products and services to satisfy the client's requirements.

A market-conscious entrepreneur is positioned realistically in relation to competitors. This means that the entrepreneur's products and/or services are distinguished (by look, feel, design, packaging, price or delivery mechanism) from competitors' to ensure profitability and a competitive edge. The customer is the focus of the business, with products and services being developed and adapted to meet the client's desires and needs.

Product-oriented entrepreneurs often have problems because they are more concerned with the product than the client, and consequently do not know how to market their products/services successfully.

The following should serve as a warning:

Many aspiring entrepreneurs are so in love with their product–service idea that they ignore the market; they assume their product or service will sell. The market road is strewn with product–service ideas that were heavily, and many times cleverly, advertised and went bust (Burch, 1986:79).

f) The importance of good quality products and services

This activity is part of both the marketing and purchasing functions. Good quality products are not necessarily expensive products. However, the client expects the quality of the product to be consistent with the price charged: value for money is important. A successful entrepreneur aims to offer clients a good quality product while still remaining profitable. Costs must be kept in check without affecting the quality of goods. Good quality products and services contribute to marketing, as they generate new clients through personal recommendations by existing, satisfied clients.

g) Accounting for your own purposes

This activity is part of the administrative and financial function. Successful entrepreneurs realise that they must be able to understand their own accounting systems. Simplicity and usefulness are the most important features of these systems.

A simple system that suits the business is essential. The entrepreneur must understand what has to be done and why, so that the information provided can be properly used. If the size and complexity of an enterprise are such that the accounting cannot be done internally, a qualified person must be appointed for this function. The usefulness of the information provided by the accounting system is of cardinal importance, because it allows the entrepreneur to make decisions on how to improve the management of the enterprise.

h) Insight into expenditure, income, profit and loss

This activity is part of the financial function. Successful entrepreneurs distinguish between income and profit. They realise that income must first be used to buy new stock, to pay creditors, wages, salaries and tax, and for current expenses. Only once this has been done can the entrepreneur determine what portion of the remaining income or profit can be ploughed back into the business and how much can be used for personal remuneration. The entrepreneur knows how to calculate profit and what it means to show a loss. He or she must know which costs are essential and understand the implication of increased expenses. This management skill is closely related to the next skill, namely the ability to use income wisely.

i) The ability to use income wisely

This activity is also part of the financial function. We discussed this management skill in the example of the interior decorator.

The successful entrepreneur exercises financial discipline and understands what to spend on to ensure success. An expensive car may convey an image of success, or it may be a source of resentment or suspicion to the customer. If this will serve the business, the entrepreneur may take the risk of buying the car. On the other hand, a successful entrepreneur will not waste money on unnecessary personal luxuries and status symbols.

Entrepreneurs must constantly take decisions on expenses. They must develop the ability to make the right decisions to ensure growth.

NB

Examples of good decisions are:

- postponing the payment of a debt/creditor for as long as possible to keep cash available for a special offer on necessary stocks, which will enhance profitability
- applying profits to the business instead of spending them on holidays, luxuries or a more expensive house or car
- using money wisely in departments or on products that will result in the greatest profitability for the enterprise.

Remember that, although all management skills are important, few – if any – entrepreneurs have all the management skills necessary to run a successful business.

2.8 DEALING WITH EXTERNAL FACTORS THAT AFFECT ENTREPRENEURSHIP

External factors and circumstances also influence the way an entrepreneur may be able to exploit his or her potential. How you accommodate, deal with and even exploit external factors to your personal advantage is a measure of your entrepreneurship.

NB

As an entrepreneur you must be aware of the following external factors:

- economic conditions

The entrepreneur must know how to adapt to fluctuating interest rates or declining levels of customer spending power.

- technological changes

The entrepreneur must keep up with technological developments and know how to exploit them to the benefit of his or her business.

- social and cultural forces

The entrepreneur must be able to identify opportunities for growth in market share, given the fact that large sectors of the population are now better educated.

- political and legislative variables

The entrepreneur must realise the opportunities that arise after political adjustments and events.

- physical variables

The entrepreneur must keep abreast of the availability and price of resources, such as considering the use of alternative raw materials if prices rise.

- international forces

The entrepreneur who uses technologically advanced communication channels can, for example, expand to and even establish a business in another country.

Skills, expertise, aptitude, personal characteristics and management skills determine how a person will handle external factors. The relationship between a person's inherent attributes and external factors is crucial to successful entrepreneurship.

2.9 SUMMARY

The importance of entrepreneurial business at all levels is essential to a country's economic development, wealth and employment creation. Entrepreneurship was identified as a specialised discipline that can be taught and learned. Entrepreneurial development is the origin of successful entrepreneurial activity, and although some are born entrepreneurs, it is possible to develop individuals to become entrepreneurs. This is where entrepreneurial education and training plays an important role.

The entrepreneur who applies certain talents, skills and expertise in the start-up, development and growth of a business was introduced as a person who continuously creates and innovates to build and develop a business of recognisable value.

Many entrepreneurs start small businesses, but then prefer to remain small due to lifestyle preferences. Small businesses are usually owner-managed with few employees, but although not entrepreneurial, they are also very valuable contributors to the economy of a country.

Entrepreneurs are found in a variety of types of businesses including formal small, micro and medium businesses, as franchisors or franchisees or within other businesses as corporate entrepreneurs.

All the success factors, including the skills, expertise, aptitude, personal qualities, management skills and external factors, that have been discussed must be analysed in personal terms. This may discourage some potential entrepreneurs, but it is vital that the aspiring businessperson be aware of all the important aspects. Remember that a successful entrepreneur is self-critical, but optimistic about solving problems. The entrepreneur will, therefore, see which adjustments must be made or what can be done to start an enterprise that has been a dream. Thus, the entrepreneur has a vision. He or she realises that it is essential to evaluate realistically personal strengths and weaknesses in order to achieve goals.

Finally, the entrepreneur should be aware of the external factors such as economic conditions, technological changes, social and cultural forces, political and legislative variables, physical variables and international forces that influence a business.

2.10 CASE STUDY

South African-born Elon Musk is an example of an exceptional entrepreneur who has established and grown multiple successful businesses starting from nothing. In his early twenties he left South Africa to pursue his American dream. With his brother Kimbal as partner he started his first business, Zip2, and later sold it to Compaq for $300 million. After that he co-founded X.com, also with his brother. That company later became the well-known PayPal online payment system. Eventually, PayPal was sold to eBay for $1.5 billion.

Musk went on and used most of the money that he made from these sales plus a lot more that he borrowed, to start, establish and grow two new businesses, SpaceX and Tesla. SpaceX is a company that produces rockets and Tesla is a luxury electric car manufacturer. These companies are both extremely idealistic and are now very high-level businesses in the aeronautical and motor industries. Musk's business goals were to make humankind an interplanetary species and to make the world independent of fossil fuel.

Musk's close friends and associates have noted that he works very hard, that he handles extreme stress very well and is able to make clear long-term decisions because of that.

His passion and interest was to explore space and go to Mars. In 2001 he started investigating the purchase of a rocket for sending a plant or mice to Mars. After negotiations with various Russian companies, joining the Mars Society and investing heavily in SpaceX, he and his team of experts started the process of building his first rocket. That rocket specialised in carrying smaller satellites and research payloads into space. SpaceX built its own engines, rocket bodies and capsules. It also designed its own motherboards, circuits, flight computers and solar panels.

After many trials and setbacks and the spending of billions of dollars, SpaceX successfully launched the first privately built rocket in 2008. However, the exorbitant financial needs ➠

of a business that builds rockets became a major problem and SpaceX nearly went broke. But after a lot of planning and negotiations, SpaceX won a $1.6 billion contract from National Aeronautics and Space Administration (NASA) late in 2008.

Despite high levels of stress and a serious shortage of cash, Musk managed to evade bankruptcy in 2008 and gained sufficient loans and investors to build his other dream: Tesla. Tesla Motors subsequently delivered an all-electric sedan, the Model S, that greatly impressed everyone in the motor industry.

By 2015 SpaceX was well established and had become profitable. Almost every month it sends up a rocket that carries satellites for Canadian, European and Asian companies. At $60 million per launch, SpaceX's prices are well below those of competitors such as Boeing and Orbital Sciences. In addition, SpaceX does not rely on other producers and countries such as Russia for parts, as its rockets are built from scratch in the US.

SpaceX now has an estimated worth of about $12 billion and is still privately owned, with Musk as the majority shareholder. NASA continues to award SpaceX various contracts, including a Commercial Crew Program to transport American astronauts into space; delivering cargo to and from the International Space Station under Commercial Resupply Services contracts; and carrying out commercial and government satellite launches. By 2017 SpaceX employed 7 000 people.

By February 2018 Tesla had produced more than 300 000 vehicles. Musk's goal is to make available an affordable mass-market electric car that will replace petrol-driven cars. In addition to vehicles, Tesla also specialises in producing energy storage batteries and solar panels. Tesla, established in 2003, employed 37 500 people by 2017.

'SpaceX designs, manufactures and launches advanced rockets and spacecraft. The company was founded in 2002 to revolutionize space technology, with the ultimate goal of enabling people to live on other planets.'

Sources: Tesla's Not as Disruptive as You Might Think (2015:22–23); Meintjies (2015); Vance (2015); SpaceX.com (2018), Tesla.com (2018)

Case study questions

1. What type of entrepreneur is Elon Musk?
2. Explain why you identified him as the type of entrepreneur in question 1.
3. Name and discuss the three most important entrepreneurial characteristics that Elon Musk exhibits in this case study.
4. How do Elon Musk and his companies contribute to the economy of his country? Identify and discuss at least three factors.

Self-evaluation questions

1. Identify an entrepreneur and a small business owner in your community or reported on in the media. Describe both and indicate how the entrepreneur differs from the small business owner.
2. Can entrepreneurship be taught? Justify your answer.
3. Describe how entrepreneurs contribute to the national economy.
4. Using the example of the entrepreneur identified in question 1 (or identifying another), describe what his or her business entails, and why you regard the person as an entrepreneur. Also indicate whether you regard the business as a micro, small or medium enterprise. Justify your classification.
5. Determine how a medium business differs from a small business.
6. Discuss the importance of the skills, expertise and aptitudes of an entrepreneur and determine your own skills, expertise and aptitudes.
7. List the seven personal characteristics that may contribute to successful entrepreneurship.
8. List and briefly describe the eight functional management skills of successful entrepreneurs.

REFERENCES AND FURTHER READING

Baumol, W. 2011. Innovation: Meager private gains, enormous social gains. *Advancing Research on Innovation and Entrepreneurship*. 1(4):1–5.

Big Blue. About Big Blue. Available from: http://www.bigblue.co.za/about-us. Date accessed: 23 July 2018.

Bird, B.J. 1989. *Entrepreneurial Behavior*. Glenview, IL: Scott, Foresman and Company.

Brand-Jonker, N. 2015. Franchises in Suid-Afrika. *Rapport*, 8 February 2015:2.

Brand South Africa. 2017. *State of entrepreneurship in South Africa*. Available from: https://www.brandsouthafrica.com/investments-immigration/state-of-entrepreneurshipin-southafrica. Date accessed: 31 May 2018.

Burch, J.G. 1986. *Entrepreneurship*. New York: John Wiley and Sons.

FASA. Franchise Association South Africa. 2015.

Filion, L.J. 1991. From entrepreneurship to entreprenology: The emergence of a new discipline. *Journal of Enterprising Culture*, 6(1):1–24.

Gasparro, A. For Greek yogurt king, path isn't always smooth. *The Wall Street Journal*, 19 May 2015:10—11.

Global Entrepreneurship Monitor (GEM). 2018. Available from https://www.gemconsortium.org/report/50012. Date accessed: 23 July 2018.

Hatting, T. Onderneming pas en draai suksesvol. *SakeNuus*, 4 Mei 2015: 12.

Hertex. Available from http://www.hertex.co.za. Date accessed: 23 July 2018.

Johnson, D.M. 2004. In the mainstream, multi-unit and multi-concept franchising. *Franchising World*. 36(3):3.

Jonker, S. Ikoniese bromponie stewig in die SA saal. *SakeNuus*, 15 April 2015.

Katz, J. & Green, R. 2014. *Entrepreneurial Small Business*. New York: McGraw-Hill Irwin.

Kelly, J.D. 2010. Seeing Red: Mao fetishism, Pax Americana, and the moral economy of war. In Kelly, J.D., with Jaureguim, B., Mitchell, S.T. & Walton, J. (editors). *Anthropology and Global Counterinsurgency*. Chicago: University of Chicago Press, 2010: 67–83.

Kerstiens, T. Pick a color: Children of mixed race struggle to find identity. *Bellingham Herald*, 10 January 1999: sc. C1.

Kongolo, M. 2010. Job creation versus job shedding and the role of small and medium enterprises in economic development. *African Journal of Business Management*. 4(11):2288–2295.

Kuratko, D.F. 2014. *Entrepreneurship: Theory, Process, Practice*. (9th edition). Mason, Ohio: South-Western Cengage Learning.

Maritz, P.A. 2005. *Entrepreneurial service vision in a franchised home entertainment system*. Unpublished DCom thesis (Business Management). Pretoria: University of Pretoria.

McClelland, D.C. 1961. *The Achieving Society*. Princeton, N.J.: Van Nostrand.

McClelland, D.C. 1986. Characteristics of successful entrepreneurs. *Journal of Creative Behavior*. 21(3):219–233.

Meintjies, M. 2015. How a bullied boy became a man who can change the world. *Sunday Times*, 31 May 2015.

Nando's, 2017. *Explore the Nando's world*. Available from: https://www.nandos.com/worldwide/. Date accessed: 6 August 2018.

Nieuwenhuizen, C. & Kroon, J. 2002. Creating wealth by financing small and medium enterprises of owners who possess entrepreneurial skills. *Management Dynamics: Contemporary Research*. 11(1).

Schumpeter, J.A. 1934. *The Theory of Economic Development*. Translated by R. Opic. Cambridge, Mass.: Harvard University Press.

Shevel, A. 2015. Seat at top table for Steinhoff after years out in the cold. *Sunday Times Business*, 24 May 2015: 3.

SpaceX.com. Date accessed: 28 May 2018.

Tesla.com. Date accessed: 28 May 2018.

Tesla's not as disruptive as you might think. 2015. *Harvard Business Review*. May: 22–23.

Timmons, J.A. & Spinelli, S. 2003. *New Venture Creation and Entrepreneurship.* (9th edition). Burr Ridge: Irwin.

Van der Merwe, L. Als in die familie. *Sarie*, April 2015.

Vance, A. 2015. *Elon Musk: Tesla, SpaceX, and the Quest for a Fantastic Future*. New York: HarperCollins Ecco.

Viktor, A. Koel kurators en die konings van rondsnuffel. *Beeld*, 6 March 2015.

Weinstein, J.I. 2009. The market in Plato's Republic. *Classical Philology*. 104:439–458.

World Economic Forum. 2017. *The Global Competitiveness Report* 2017–2018. Schwab, K. (editor). Geneva: World Economic Forum.

Legislation

National Small Business Amendment Act 26 of 2003.

Chapter 3 Identifying feasible business ideas

3.1 LEARNING OUTCOMES

After you have studied this chapter, you should be able to:

- identify and explain the stages of setting up a business
- explain the cultivation of an entrepreneur's creative attitude
- explain the generation of business ideas
- discuss the development of business ideas
- evaluate the feasibility of business ideas.

Example 3.1 is an example of a feasible business idea.

Example 3.1 – Farmer Angus

Over the years farming has evolved much to keep up with the demands of modern day living. Driven by the desire to have a non-corporatised, non-mechanised relationship with the earth and animals, Angus McIntosh bought a 126-hectare farm in the Western Cape. He named the farm Ezibusisweni, meaning the place of blessings in Zulu. What started out as a way for Angus to live off the land to feed himself and his family ended up evolving into something much greater than he could have ever imagined. The family set out to build a home that could function entirely off the grid and farm the land to provide the family with organic fruit and vegetables. However, after reading Michael Pollan's, the 'Omnivore's Dilemma', Angus became inspired to start livestock farming and so in 2008, the 'Farmer Angus' brand was born.

They farm with beef, pork, chicken and eggs. With no formal training as a farmer Angus sought out the guidance of another regenerative farmer, who mentored him for the first three years. Angus also devoted much of his time to studying permaculture and chose to apply biodynamic and regenerative farming practices and principles. He is dedicated to reviving the way farming used to be before the days of chemical fertilisers and herbicides.

Farmer Angus meat is like no other and it has a lot to do with the way Angus raises his animals. The cows eat only grass and, like the pigs and chickens, are moved regularly to different grazing areas on the farm. Constantly moving them not only prevents overgrazing but also over-fertilisation. Because the manure and urine from the animals is the only fertiliser Angus uses on his pastures, it's essential it doesn't become over-saturated.

None of Farmer Angus' meat contains gluten, MSG, GMO, nitrites, nitrates, antibiotics or hormones. You can be sure you are eating a product that is of the earth in its most natural and nutritious state. As Angus says: '*Regenerative artisanal farming is the only future of agriculture as it is the only form of agriculture that provides nourishing food, heals the earth and provides dignified employment.*'

Source: 'Revival of the artisan farmer' in *Entrepreneur Magazine*

3.2 INTRODUCTION

Setting up a business can be divided into three main stages, namely:

- identifying a feasible business idea (the idea stage)
- investigating the profitability of the feasible idea (the viability study) and the drawing up a business plan (the planning stage)
- implementing the business plan (the implementation stage).

Figure 3.1 illustrates the three-stage process.

These three stages form the theme of the rest of the book. In this chapter we will discuss the first stage, namely the identification of feasible business ideas. Chapters 4 and 5 deal with the planning stage and Chapter 6 looks at the implementation stage.

The identification of business ideas is a creative process. A prospective entrepreneur must, therefore, be able to cultivate a creative attitude. Everyone has the potential to think creatively. In this chapter, certain techniques will be introduced that can be used to improve the creative mindset of an entrepreneur.

Although it is important to think of as many business ideas as possible, only one idea can eventually be converted to a business enterprise. This chapter will assist in identifying a suitable idea (i.e. a feasible business idea).

3.3 CULTIVATING A CREATIVE ATTITUDE

Chapter 2 explained that the capacity to act creatively and innovatively is one of the characteristics of an entrepreneur. Although an innovative business idea can give you an advantage, there are also disadvantages to being a first mover, i.e. being the first in offering a product or service. Being first, you have to convince others that there is a need for your product or service. Being second or third means that you can learn from the mistakes of those who went before you.

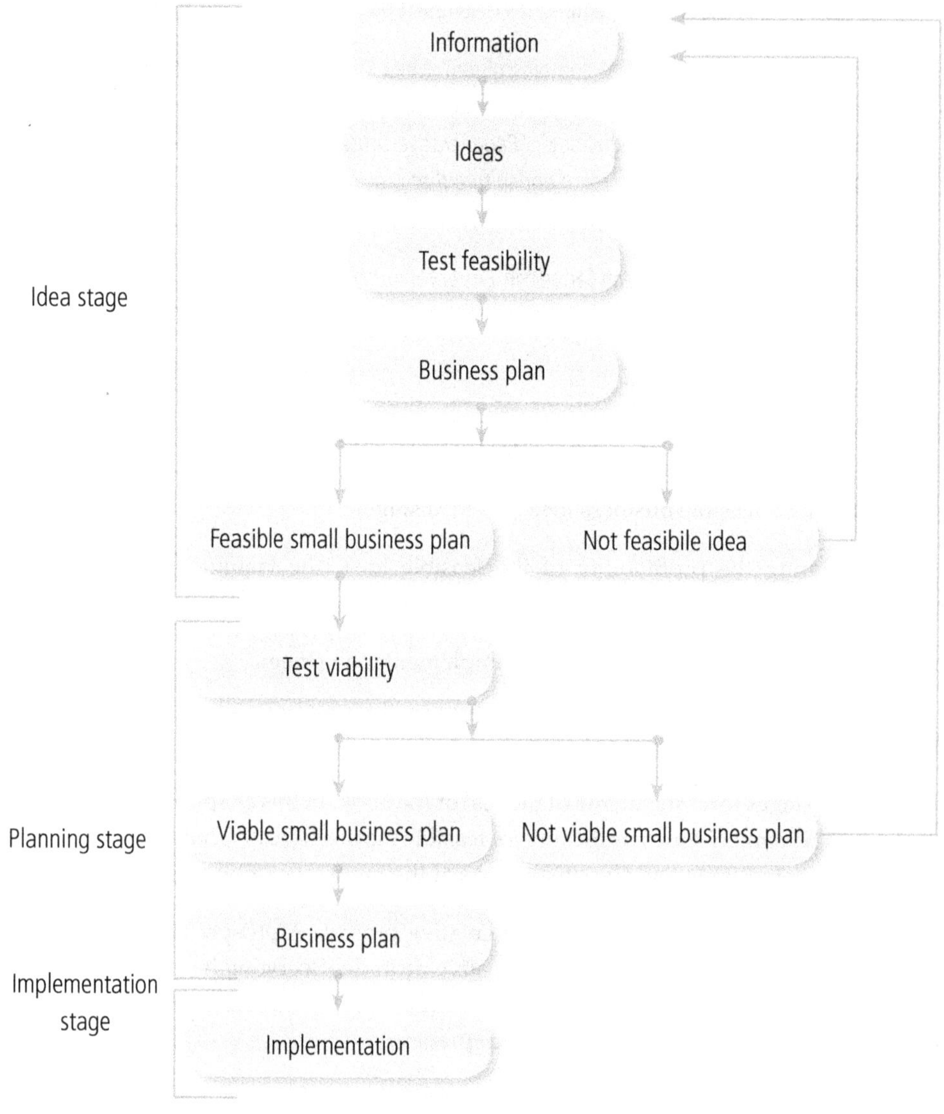

Figure 3.1: The three stages of setting up a business

This does not, however, imply that others' ideas should be imitated and offered to the market. An entrepreneur should try to provide specialised or unique products or services. Think of an idea or ideas that will distinguish your business from competing businesses. To do this, one must think and act creatively.

3.3.1 What is creativity?

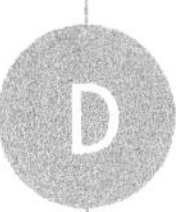

Creativity is defined as the tendency to generate or recognise ideas, alternatives, or possibilities that may be useful in solving problems, communicating with others, and entertaining ourselves and others (Fanken, 2006).

In order to be creative, you need to be able to view things in new ways or from different perspectives. Among other things, you must be able to generate new possibilities or new alternatives. Being creative is not only about the number of alternatives that can be generated, but about the uniqueness of these ideas.

3.3.2 Am I creative?

How does one recognise creativity? Think of half a dozen people you believe to be creative. They could include those around you or perhaps famous South African inventors, such as Mark Shuttleworth, who invented an electronic security system, and Chris Barnard, who developed surgical procedures for organ transplants, invented new heart valves and performed the first human heart transplant, or Elon Musk who co-founded PayPal, or George Pratley who invented Pratley's Putty, which had a part in the success of the first moon landing.

Which characteristics or abilities do these people have in common that make them creative? Obvious abilities with which you could start your list might include:

- solving problems in a different way
- thinking imaginatively
- seeing possibilities others have not seen
- initiating change

The creative person usually enjoys problem-solving and tends to bring fresh perspectives to old problems. Example 3.2 provides some fun problems to stimulate creativity.

Example 3.2

Question: You are participating in a race. You overtake the second person. What position are you in?

Answer: If you answered that you are first, then you are absolutely wrong! If you overtake the second person and you take his place, you are second!

Question: If you overtake the last person, then you are…?

Answer: If you answered that you are second to last, then you are wrong again. Explain how you can overtake the last person?

Question: Two South Africans walk down a street in Soweto. One South African is the mother of the other South African's son. How are they related?

Answer: They are husband and wife (the father and mother of the son)

Question: Join these nine dots (3 x 3) with not more than three lines.

• • •

• • •

• • •

Answer: There is often more than one right answer to a problem. This problem can be solved in, among others, the following ways:

- If you take a thick pencil, you could join the dots with just three lines.
- If you take a very thick pencil, you can do the job with just one line!
- By rolling the paper into a cylinder, you could draw one long line which encircles the cylinder.
- You can fold the paper in three, so the rows of dots all line up, and fold it again and poke the pencil through.

Question: Make four triangles, all the same size with only six matches.

Answer:

Creative thought can be divided into divergent and convergent reasoning.

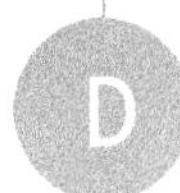

Divergent thinking is the intellectual ability to think of many original, diverse and elaborate ideas.

Convergent thinking is the intellectual ability to logically evaluate, critique and choose the best idea from a selection of ideas.

Divergent and convergent reasoning are both necessary for creative output. Divergent thinking, also referred to as lateral thinking, is a thought process used to generate ideas by exploring many possible solutions related to a problem, such as brainstorming. On the other hand, convergent thinking is a thought process used to organise and structure the many solutions to arrive at a single best solution to a problem, such as a multiple-choice test.

Research has shown that divergent (creative) thinking is natural for right-brain dominant people, whereas convergent (logical) thinking is natural for left-brain dominant people. The right brain processes data in a rapid, complex, whole-pattern and perceptual manner, while the left brain operates in a more verbal, analytical mode.

Brain hemispheric dominance can therefore be an indication of creative ability. Why don't you test your brain dominance with one or more of the online brain dominance tests? Try the one at https://personalitymax.com/left-right-brain-test/.

Although some people are born with the gift of creativity, it is possible for everyone to develop and improve their creative abilities. It is important to understand that creativity is just as much an attitude as a manner of thinking. It is thus possible to think of new ideas by attuning yourself to creativity. The following methods can be used to improve creativity:

(a) **Actively seek ideas:** You can learn to seek ideas actively by judging everything that you read or observe on the strength of the ideas that can be developed from it. If you think in this way regularly, it will become a habit and ideas will come to you more easily.

(b) **Write your ideas down:** Make a habit of writing down an idea as soon as you have one, even if you feel it is not a good idea. Read through the ideas regularly. Review them and perhaps combine them in a new concept.

(c) **View a topic from another person's perspective:** Put yourself in somebody else's position to get a different view of a topic. With a better understanding of others' points of view, you will gain new insights and ideas. By asking yourself, for example, what the mother of a pre-school child thinks of the concept 'to see red', and then looking at the same idea from the perspective of a busy businesswoman or a widowed grandmother, you can generate totally new ideas.

(d) **Break your routine:** A good way of stimulating your thoughts is to break your routine. Here are a few suggestions:

- Note how you perform everyday actions, such as washing dishes, and then do them differently.
- Spend a whole day without something that is a part of a daily routine, for example your cellular phone.
- Browse the web on a subject that you know nothing about.
- Start a conversation with a stranger or someone you would not normally speak to.
- Do something you have never done before, such as going to the theatre, riding a horse or starting a new hobby or sport. In other words, broaden your horizons.

(e) **Explore the grey areas:** If you tend to see only the right and wrong sides of a case, it is time to explore the grey areas between right and wrong. Make a habit of looking for different solutions and possibilities. Start by completing the following incomplete questions. See how many solutions you can find to each in ten minutes.

- What will happen if I ...?
- In what different way can I ...?
- Who will benefit by ...?

(f) **Use a creativity tool:** The SCAMPER technique developed by educational expert Bob Eberle is such a tool. Each letter of the acronym represents a different way you can play with new ideas (Mansfield, 2018):

- Substitute: What happens if we switch two things around?
- Combine: What if we add these two things together?
- Adapt: Is there another use? Can we invent one?
- Modify: What can you emphasise, hide or change?
- Put to other use: A shoe can be a doorstop. A brick can be a paperweight.
- Eliminate: What can we delete – and what does that do?
- Rearrange (or Reverse): Why not turn it upside down?

Before you start looking for business ideas, take some time to adjust your mind to creativity. This mindset will eventually help you to identify new or better business ideas.

Team creativity

There are at least 200 different techniques and tools to enhance the creativity of teams, for example:

- Brain sketching
- Card storyboards
- Bunches of Bananas
- Brainstorming
- Creative problem-solving (CPS)
- Idea advocate

- Pin cards
- Trigger sessions
- Rotating roles
- Superheroes
- Visualising a goal
- Six thinking hats

Some of the tools and techniques listed are discussed below:

a) Brain sketching

Brain sketching involves passing evolving sketches around the group. Limited facilitation skills are required. Brain sketching is typically conducted in the following manner:

- A group of between four and eight people sit around a table or in a circle. They need to be far enough apart to have some privacy. The problem statement is agreed to and discussed until it is understood.
- Each participant privately draws one or more sketches (each on separate sheets of paper) of how the problem might be solved, passing each sketch on to the person on their right when it is finished. The facilitator suggests that sketches should not take more than five minutes to draw.
- Participants take the sketches passed to them and either develop or annotate them or use them to stimulate new sketches of their own, passing the amended original and/or any new sketches on to their neighbour to the right when ready.
- After the process has been running for a suitable period or energy is running down, the sketches can be collected.
- It will probably help to display all the sketches and discuss them in turn for clarification and comments.
- The team then moves on to a categorisation, evaluation and selection process.

b) Bunches of Bananas

The 'Bunches of Bananas' technique requires lateral thinking, reducing excessive left-brain attention. Provocative statements or ideas are voiced on purpose to create a reaction, symbolically like 'throwing in a bunch of bananas'. Here are some tips:

- Consider the mood and atmosphere: Are there signs of the group being stuck in a rut, sluggish or showing inertia?
- Think of what you could say or do to move the group out of this state of inertia? Create 'bunches of bananas' to suit your own character and style.
- Bear in mind that you are engaging in a 'whole-brain' activity. Just as with a comedian, it is as much the delivery as the idea that brings about the effect.

- If the group is inexperienced, the approach may have to be appropriately signalled: 'I know this is going to sound a little crazy, but bear with me a minute or so. Sometimes you can get out of a rut in the most unexpected ways ...'.
- 'Bunches of Bananas' can come in a variety of forms – any well-placed joke or image that captures attention when appropriate.

c) Superheroes

Superheroes is a fantasy-based technique. Participants pretend to be a fictional (or real) superhero (like Superman, Thor, Batman, Ironman, Invisible Woman, Sherlock Holmes or Spider-Man) and use their 'superpowers' to trigger ideas.

This technique is good for creating an atmosphere of light-hearted fun in which energy is high and fantasy and metaphor acceptable. All superheroes have skills and capacities that are outside 'normal' life. This means that people tend to think outside of the norm and they play a role that allows them to express more unusual ideas than they might normally.

Superhero stories also have strong elements of wish-fulfilment and can therefore help people to express wishes. The stories may not be suitable for serious or introverted groups, or groups without a level of trust. Here is how you can facilitate this technique:

- Prepare some general information on each superhero. This might include their name, special powers, weaknesses, background and a picture. You can also provide props if you have an extrovert in the group.
- Display and discuss the problem to ensure everyone understands the issue. It can be useful to brainstorm in order to list the more obvious ideas. (Brainstorming is a technique to build on others' ideas. Members of the group put forward ideas without interruption or evaluation from the others.)
- Select a superhero for each participant. (Each could also choose one for themselves or take one from the faciliator's information pack.) Give them time to think a little about that superhero and talk to them about what life is like as a superhero in order to help them get into the role.
- The superhero characters are then used as the basis of an excursion. The extrovert groups will get into the role – 'I will heat the chemicals instantly with my laser eyes while freezing the container with my breath' – whereas the more introverted groups will tend to be happier talking in the third person ('Super-Man could heat the chemicals with his laser eyes ...').
- Start by getting each superhero to voice a few ideas.
- Allow the group members to bounce off each other's ideas. Perhaps if Super-Man and Invisible Woman worked together they could produce an improved solution?
- When you have sufficient ideas, evaluate them.

d) Trigger sessions

Trigger sessions are a good way of getting lots of ideas from untrained resources and are carried out as follows:

- The person with the problem explains and defines it.
- Each member in the group writes down his or her ideas quickly (two minutes only).
- One member reads out their list – others silently cross out ideas that are similar and write down ideas that are 'hitch-hiked' (i.e. triggered by ideas that have been read out).
- The second member reads out their list of ideas not covered in the first person's list, followed in turn by other members.
- The last member reads out his original list plus his 'hitch-hiked' list. The procedure is then repeated, reversing the original order (for example, if there are six members, the order is: member 1, 2, 3, 4, 5, 6, then 5, 4, 3, 2, 1, then 2, 3, 4, 5, 6 and so on).

A good group will be able to manage several passes. Everyone's paper is then collected and can be typed up into a single list of ideas – all duplicates should have been crossed out during the session.

3.4 GENERATING BUSINESS IDEAS

A good business idea seldom comes out of the blue or as an inspiration. A prospective entrepreneur must look deliberately and think creatively about ideas that can be transformed into a business.

In your search for ideas, you can make use of certain structured techniques. The techniques for the generation of business ideas proposed in this book can be divided into five broad approaches, as illustrated in Figure 3.2:

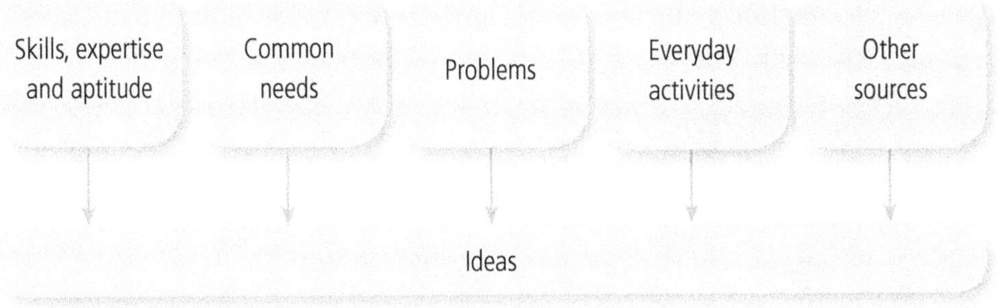

Figure 3.2: Generating business ideas

These approaches have been tested successfully and promise to produce positive results and will be discussed in the sections that follow.

3.4.1 Generating ideas from the entrepreneur's skills, expertise and aptitude

Everyone has certain skills. An entrepreneur's skills, expertise and aptitudes are among key factors for success, as discussed in Chapter 1.

In addition to these key factors, consider the following:

- Formal training does not necessarily guarantee success in a business enterprise. This does not mean that your qualifications are useless: through your studies you can obtain certain knowledge that can lead to a business idea. An engineering student, for example, has gained certain technical knowledge that could give him or her the idea and ability to start a specific manufacturing business.
- Skills can also be gained from working experience. As an employee, you are responsible for certain activities. Your knowledge of them can enable you to start a business of your own involving these activities. For example, the fact that you worked as a telemarketer can be the reason why you consider starting a direct sales business.
- Have you developed any skills through your hobbies or other non-career activities that could be used as ideas to start your own business? For example, the fact that you collect antiques and know how to negotiate to get the best swap or price for your items, means you have learned certain purchasing or negotiating skills.

- Draw up a profile of your own abilities. List your skills. For example, can you do programming or create designs using a computer program? Identify your expertise.
- List your formal qualifications (e.g. diplomas or certificates) and experience gained (eg problem-solving capabilities).
- Write down your natural aptitudes or talents and interests. For example, you may be an attentive listener (this is an aptitude). Your interest may be in working with children or writing creatively.

This list of skills, expertise and aptitudes can now be used to identify business ideas. To show you how this can be done, consider the following example:

Example 3.3

Amahle Nkosi has a Linguistics degree and is fluent in most of the official languages in South Africa. With this skill, she can provide a service or create a product for individuals or organisations.

You can identify many business ideas by thinking of how to provide products or services to individuals or organisations, and what types of products or services they might need.

Looking at Example 3.4, you can see how many ideas Amahle, with her single skill, could identify. Now take one of your skills and do a similar exercise.

Example 3.4

3.4.2 Generating ideas from common needs

Everyone has needs. However, not everyone's needs are the same. The business idea should satisfy a need among a range of people for the same product or service. In other words, the entrepreneur must try to satisfy a common or shared need.

Individuals with common needs can usually be grouped together; for example, all mothers with small children, all members of a soccer team and all prospective homeowners.

You can also identify groups of organisations that have the same need; for example, businesses that need catering on a regular basis, or businesses that need a complete maintenance service.

Think of examples of interest groups and their needs and write them down. By concentrating on the needs of only one interest group, you will find that many business ideas will cross your mind. Example 3.6 illustrates a technique developed by Richardson and Clark (1990) for generating business ideas from the needs that groups experience – in this case the needs of cyclists.

3.4.3 Generating ideas from existing problems

Instead of thinking of unfulfilled needs, you can think of existing, unsolved problems. Think of things that irritate you. Now think of ways of removing those irritations.

Example 3.5

One-person small business owners know how tough it is to work alone. They enjoy pushing for something they care about deeply and have total creative autonomy in something. But having people around is critical to harnessing the energy required for good work, and it prevents myopic thinking too. An entrepreneur could solve this problem by offering co-working spaces. This can help to mitigate the problem.

Knowing these problems enables the prospective entrepreneur to find the initial idea for a business that is based on the solution of a specific problem. Example 3.7 illustrates a technique developed by Richardson and Clark (1990) for generating business ideas from everyday problems. This example uses the general problem of traffic jams to illustrate the technique.

Example 3.6

Suppose we regard cyclists as a group – those who ride bicycles for recreation. Write down the group's needs as you answer the questions in the diagram. You can use the answers to develop new business ideas.

Source: Adapted from Richardson and Clarke (1990)

eg

Example 3.7

Suppose 'traffic problems' is a major problem in your community. What business ideas can this problem offer? Think of solutions to alleviate the problem as suggested and generate specific product or service ideas from these.

3.4.4 Generating ideas from everyday activities

Many business ideas can be identified merely by awareness of everyday activities. The entrepreneur can use the following methods to identify new business ideas:

- **Use print or electronic media:** Think of the products that are advertised on television, in magazines and in newspapers. Ask yourself whether they can be improved, distributed or marketed differently.
- **Look in other places:** Come up with business ideas by looking in unlikely places. The following questions may help:
  - What ideas can you get at an airport, a movie theatre or a church?
  - What ideas can you bring back from a sports meeting, a funfair or a doctor's consulting room?
- **Explore your surroundings:** Explore a part of your city or town that you have not seen before. What do you notice?
- **Observe other cultures:** Take note of the novelties and different ways of doing things at places where you go on holiday.
- **Talk to other people:** Have conversations with your family, friends, colleagues and businesspeople and find out if they have come across possible business ideas. The problem of obtaining holiday accommodation at short notice could, for example, lead to an enterprise that specialises in finding and allocating unused and cancelled holiday accommodation.
- **At work:** Ask yourself if the products and services at your place of work could be improved upon.
- **Go shopping:** Examine some of the products on your next visit to the shops. Remember that no product or service is perfect. By asking questions about the products, new ideas can emerge. Here are some questions to ask yourself:
  - What problems are there with this product?
  - Could the product be improved in any way?
  - Is there a better way for the product to be packaged?
  - Can any new product be added to the present range of products?
  - Can the product be aimed at another market?

Example 3.8

Cell phones have become a part of everyday life. The market for cell phone accessories is growing at a rapid pace and shows no signs of slowing down. Selling handmade cases has the potential to generate large sums of money.

- **Changes in your immediate area:** By noting changes or important events that take place around you, new business ideas can be identified.

Example 3.9

If you're looking for something bigger than wedding planning, event planning might be right for you. Event planners manage seminars, workshops, baptisms, birthdays, concerts, conferences, and several other events.

3.4.5 Generating ideas from other sources

Apart from taking note of everyday activities, ideas can also be found by consulting other reference sources. Figure 3.3 summarises some examples:

Figure 3.3: Other sources to generate ideas from

- **Online business directories:** In the digital age, searching online for business ideas based on what products and services are already on offer is a fitting option. Accessing detailed information and even online reviews, is possible. Some of the free business directories in South Africa are Hotfrog, Entrepo, Activeweb, Cylex Business Directory, Yellosa, Citylist, Rateitall, FoxList and Snupit.
- **Consult business publications:** Magazines such as *Forbes Africa* and *SA Franchise Warehouse Magazine* can be valuable sources of ideas. *Entrepreneur Magazine* carries up-to-date success stories on successful entrepreneurs in South Africa.

- **Contact an inventors' association:** This can be a rich source of ideas. For example, you might be able to collaborate with an inventor to produce and market their invention. An association that might be useful to contact is the Institute of Inventors and Innovators.
- **Examine patents that have expired:** Expired patents are public property. There can be various reasons why a patent has not been exploited, and it may now be ready for the market. These reasons could include:
  - bigger markets for the product have arisen in the interim
  - the product can now be used with other products that were previously unavailable
  - the product can be manufactured using new technology, which now makes it technically feasible and commercially viable
  - a new use for the product has arisen.

An example of an expired patent is antibiotics and pills to alleviate muscular injuries. Lennon sells a product called Panamor that is comparable to the well-known product Voltaren. Panamor originated on the expiry of a patent on the original product.

- **Investigate advertisements for business opportunities:** Newspapers and magazines often carry advertisements for business opportunities. Although many of these must be investigated with caution, there are real opportunities that can serve as sources of new business ideas. Note, for example, how many franchising opportunities are advertised in the newspapers.
- **Visit trade shows:** Trade shows are a good source of ideas. You also get the opportunity to see the physical product and to talk to the exhibitors about the potential market, product features, new technology and even the possibility of doing business together. Examples are the annual Design Indaba in Cape Town, the Grand Designs Live show in Johannesburg, the My Business Expo Durban, and the Small Business Expo in Johannesburg.
- **Examine overseas products:** Products that are not yet available in South Africa are often imported, imitated or adapted for the South African market. Chicken Licken is an example of a South African business that originated from a business idea obtained abroad, and which has been developed into the biggest fried chicken franchised brand outside the USA.

3.5 DEVELOPING AND EVALUATING BUSINESS IDEAS

In the previous section, you were encouraged not to limit your creativity but to think about all possible business ideas. However, most of these ideas will not work. The initial sifting of ideas is performed by relying on your personal judgement and intuition.

Only one of the ideas can be chosen and converted into a business on its own or in combination with one or more of the other ideas on the list. To choose the correct business idea, the potential entrepreneur must evaluate each idea on the list.

Although there are examples of entrepreneurs who have converted an idea into a successful business opportunity merely on the strength of their intuition, this is not the best way. (Henry Ford, the creator of the Model T Ford, is the exception: he followed his intuition and made millions from it (thehenryford.org, 2018).)

Business ideas can be evaluated primarily by means of two methods, namely a feasibility study and a viability study.

A feasibility study is a general examination of the potential of the idea to be converted into a business enterprise. This study focuses largely on the ability of the entrepreneur to convert the idea into a business enterprise.

A viability study is an in-depth investigation into the profitability of the idea that is to be converted into a business enterprise.

Before evaluating the ideas, you should first be clear about what each of these ideas suggests. In particular, two things must be clear:

1. What will be the chief activities of the business?
2. Who will the customers be?

The activities of the business will consist of two or more of the following:

1. the manufacture of a product
2. the provision of a service
3. the sale of other people's products and/or services.

Your customers will consist of:

- individuals and/or
- organisations.

The 'bow-tie' diagram in Figure 3.4 illustrates these elements:

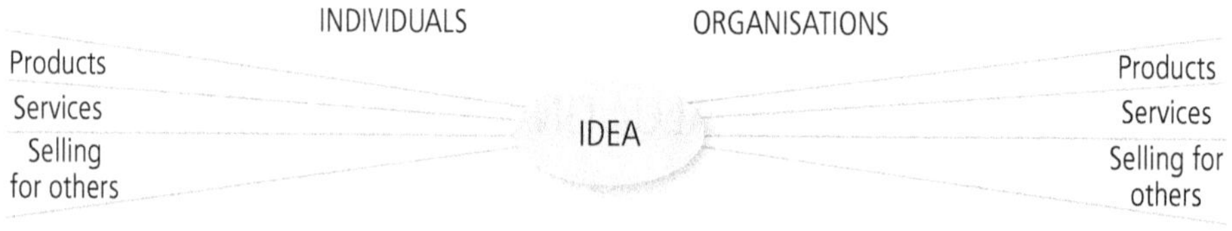

Figure 3.4: Bow-tie diagram

Source: Adapted from Richardson and Clarke (1990)

Figure 3.4 provides six options for your business, namely:

1. the manufacture of products for individuals
2. providing services for individuals
3. the sale of other people's products and/or services to individuals
4. the manufacture of products for organisations
5. providing services for organisations
6. selling others' products and/or services to organisations.

3.5.1 The development of your business ideas

The bow-tie diagram can also be used to develop your business idea in terms of:

- the essence of the idea
- the possible combination of ideas
- the possibility of taking a new direction with the idea.

In the following example, the idea is 'to bake cakes'; it shows all the business ideas that might emerge from this one idea.

Example 3.10

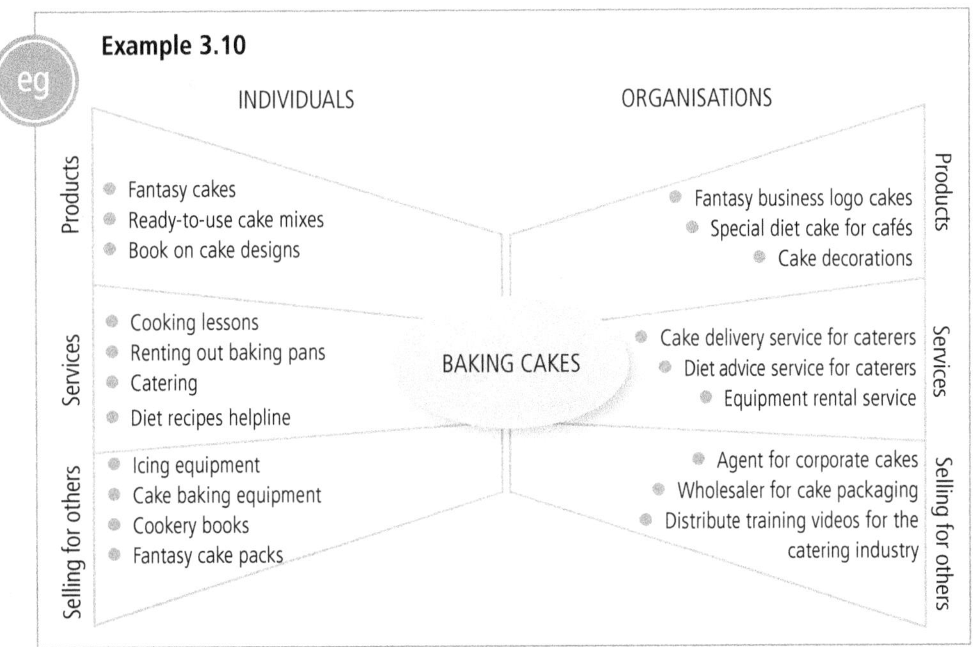

Source: Adapted from Richardson and Clarke (1990)

From this example, you can see that the idea 'to bake cakes' can be developed further. Here are some examples:

- baking decorative cakes (the essence of the idea)
- making cakes and making and selling cake decorations to bakeries (the combination of ideas)
- producing training DVDs for the catering industry (taking a new direction with the idea).

3.5.2 Feasibility of your business ideas

To determine whether the business idea is feasible, the entrepreneur must be able to answer the following four questions satisfactorily:

1. Do you want to do what the idea suggests?
2. Is there a market for your idea?
3. Can you meet the needs of your customers?
4. Can you advertise the idea to your customers?

To determine the feasibility of your business idea, answer the following questions, by filling in a tick (✓) or a question mark (?) in the block alongside each question:

NB

1. Do you want to do what the idea suggests?

- Is the idea really something that you want to pursue? ☐
- Do you want to do business with the types of people who will be your customers? ☐
- Do you have the health, energy and personality to pursue your idea? ☐
- Can you cope with the long hours, few, if any, holidays, etc associated with this idea? ☐
- Will you sacrifice the things that are important to you in order to make a successful enterprise out of this idea? ☐
- Does your family understand the full implications of your decision to start a business? ☐
- Do you have the support of your family and are they willing to help? ☐
- Is this idea more important to you than any other idea that you have identified? ☐

Source: Adapted from Richardson and Clarke (1990)

If you filled in any question marks (?) in the blocks, you must ask yourself whether you really want to pursue this specific idea. In other words, do you have the motivation to achieve success with it? Think of ways to change the question marks (?) into ticks (✓) and how, for example, you can justify the ticks (✓) to your bank manager.

NB

2. Is there a market for your idea?

- Do you know who your customers will be?
- Will they pay you for your product and/or service?
- Do you think there are many customers for your idea? Estimate how many.
- Will people prefer your product and/or service to those of your competitors?
- Do you think you will gain more customers in the future?
- What are three advantages you have over your competitors?
- Can you prevent other people from copying your idea?

Source: Adapted from Richardson and Clarke (1990)

If you filled in any question marks (?) in the blocks, you must ask yourself whether you have a market for this specific idea. Think of ways to change the question marks (?) into ticks (✓) and how, for example, you can justify the ticks (✓) to someone like your bank manager.

NB

3. Can you meet the needs of your customers?

- Do you have, or can you develop, the skills to manufacture your product and/or to provide your service?
- Can you provide the quantity and quality of products or give the level of service that your customers expect?
- Do you know how much money you can charge for your product or service?
- If you need someone to help you provide your product or service, do you know anyone who would be willing to do it?
- Do you know more or less how much money you will need to start your business?
- Do you know how much money you will need in the first year to run your business?
- Do you personally have the money to start and run your business? How much do you still need? Where will you get the rest of the money?

Source: Adapted from Richardson and Clarke (1990)

If you filled in any question marks (?) in the list, you must ask yourself if you can pursue this idea. Think of ways to change the question marks (?) into ticks (✓), and how, for example, you can justify the ticks (✓) to someone like your bank manager.

NB

4. Can you advertise the idea to your customers?

- Do you know how your customers buy this product and/or service?
- Is there a special magazine, newspaper or blog that your customers read? What is it?
- Do you know of any agents or intermediaries who are currently selling to your customers? Who are they?
- Do you know of any businesses or organisations that are currently doing business with your customers? Where are they?
- Will these businesses or organisations be prepared to promote your idea?
- Can you get the names and addresses of a large number of potential customers? About how many?
- Do you already have various customers who have indicated that they will buy from you? How many?

Source: Adapted from Richardson and Clarke (1990)

Question marks (?) in the questionnaire are less important than the ticks (✓). If you have no ticks (✓), or only one or two, you must ask yourself if you should pursue this idea. Think of how you can turn the question marks (?) into ticks (✓) to someone like your bank manager.

How do you feel about your business idea now that you have answered all the questions? Complete the rating scale in Table 3.1 by circling the number that represents your choice.

Table 3.1: Rating scale

	Level of conviction			
	Very high	High	Average	Low
• Do you want to follow the idea?	4	3	2	1
• Is there a market for your idea?	4	3	2	1
• Can you meet your customer's needs?	4	3	2	1
• Can you advertise the idea to your customers?	4	3	2	1

Source: Adapted from Richardson and Clarke (1990)

By counting the numbers circled, you can reach the following conclusions from your results:

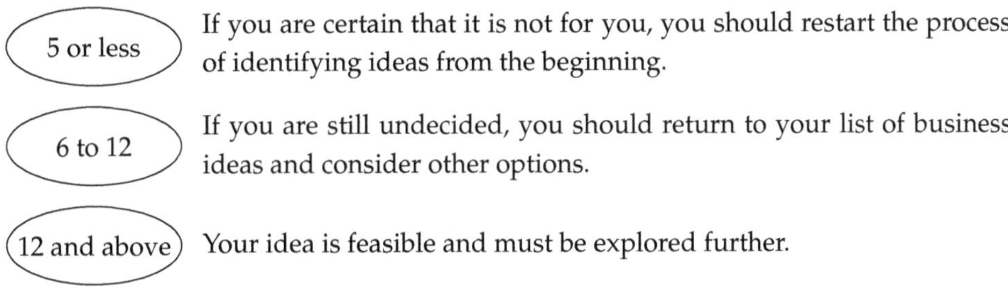

If you have learned from the results that your business idea is in fact feasible, you should investigate its viability. Since a formal viability study is expensive in terms of both time and money, it is important first to do the feasibility study as shown. The next chapter gives a step-by-step description of investigating the viability of a business idea.

3.6 SUMMARY

In this chapter, the first step in setting up a business was discussed, namely to identify a feasible business idea. The planning and implementation phases were also mentioned; however, these phases are discussed in greater detail in the chapters that follow.

A business idea does not always have to be innovative, but it must stand out from other comparable and competitive products or services in some way. This means that the entrepreneur must be able to think and act creatively. The creative abilities of prospective entrepreneurs can be improved in various ways, such as thinking unconventionally, breaking the routine, viewing a matter from another person's perspective or using one of the various team creativity techniques.

The techniques for generating business ideas were discussed. These techniques can be divided into five broad approaches. The entrepreneur can generate a business idea from their skills, expertise and aptitudes; from common needs; from existing problems; from everyday activities; and from various other sources as well. These approaches can be adopted separately or in combination to come up with a unique idea.

A business idea should be defined in terms of its business activity and customer profile before it is evaluated and developed. This can be done through a feasibility study of the idea by matching the business ideas with questions on how the prospective entrepreneur feels about the specific idea. The viability of business ideas will be discussed in the next chapter.

Self-evaluation questions

1. Discuss the three stages of setting up a business.
2. Define 'creativity'.
3. What characteristics or abilities do creative people have in common?
4. Distinguish between 'divergent' and 'convergent' thinking.
5. Perform an online brain dominance test. What is the result of the test and how does it relate to your inclination for creativity?
6. Name and discuss the methods you can use to improve your creativity.
7. Suppose two friends and you want to start a business. Explain two creativity techniques to help you generate business ideas (use one of the techniques explained in this chapter and one technique that you have researched on your own).
8. Generate one business idea from your skills, one from your expertise and one from your aptitude by using the method in this chapter.
9. Generate a business idea from a common need of people in your neighbourhood by using the method proposed in this chapter.
10. Generate a business idea from an existing problem in your area by using the method proposed in this chapter.
11. Generate a business idea from everyday activities by using the method proposed in this chapter.
12. Name and discuss the other reference sources that can be consulted about generating ideas.
13. Generate business ideas from other sources by using the method proposed in this chapter.
14. Distinguish between a feasibility and a viability study.
15. Discuss the bow-tie diagram by mentioning what it provides and what it can be used for.
16. Take one of the business ideas generated in questions 8 to 11 and develop it by using the proposed bow-tie diagram.

17. Determine the feasibility of one of your business ideas by answering the following four broad questions: (a) Do you want to do what the idea suggests? (b) Is there a market for your idea? (c) Can you meet the needs of your customers? (d) Can you advertise the idea to your customers? (Justify your answers and final conclusion.)
18. No commonly agreed, single definition of creativity exists. Discuss different views on creativity.
19. Discuss various uses for creativity techniques.
20. Business ideas can be discovered by accident. Debate the pros of this statement versus the pros of a more structured approach to finding business ideas.
21. Discuss the need for both a feasibility and a viability study in setting up a business.

REFERENCES AND FURTHER READING

Amabile, T.M. & Mueller, J.S. 2008. Studying creativity, its processes, and its antecedents. An exploration of the componential theory of creativity. Zhou, J. and Franken, R.E. 2006. *Human Motivation*. (6th edition) Belmont: Wadsworth.

Nieman, G. & Nieuwenhuizen, C. (eds.). 2018. *Entrepreneurship: A South African Perspective*. 4th edition. Pretoria: Van Schaik.

Richardson, P. & Clarke. L. 1990. *Good Ideas Don't Come Out of the Blue – You Have to Work at Them*. The Scottish Enterprise Foundation for the Training Agency: Crown.

Shalley, C.E. (eds.). *Handbook of Organizational Creativity*. New York: Lawrence Erlbaum.

Sparks, G. 2019. Revival of the artisan farmer. *Entrepreneur Magazine*. Available from: https://www.experthub.info/success/success-stories/entrepreneur-profiles/revival-of-the-artisan-farmer/ Date accessed: 25 July 2019.

Thehenryford.org. 2018. Henry Ford, Founder, Ford Motor Company. https://www.thehenryford.org/explore/stories-of-innovation/visionaries/henry-ford/ Date accessed: 31 July 2019.

Chapter 4

The viability of a business idea

4.1 LEARNING OUTCOMES

After you have studied this chapter, you should be able to perform a viability study for a proposed business idea by doing the following:

- establish if there is a need for a product or service
- formulate the mission and objectives of the business
- calculate the market share of the product or service
- calculate the income that can be derived from the product or service
- determine the break-even point for the business
- determine whether a sustainable profit can be made
- draw up a cash budget to determine whether the business can service its financial obligations as they occur.

4.2 INTRODUCTION

The previous sections focused on the generation of ideas and studying feasible business ideas. In this chapter we will focus on exploring the planning phase of a business. Many entrepreneurs, however, fail to spend sufficient time in planning their business before starting up their businesses. Planning the business may well be the most crucial element of the business to ensure its success.

Business planning usually has two phases. The first is to establish whether a business idea is viable: this is known as the viability study. For an idea to be a viable business idea, you must be able to market it and manage your business at a sustainable profit.

Only if you find that the idea is viable do you continue to the second phase namely the drawing up of a business plan. The business plan summarises the conclusions drawn from the viability study. It can then be used to make the idea known to other people, and to obtain financing to implement the business idea.

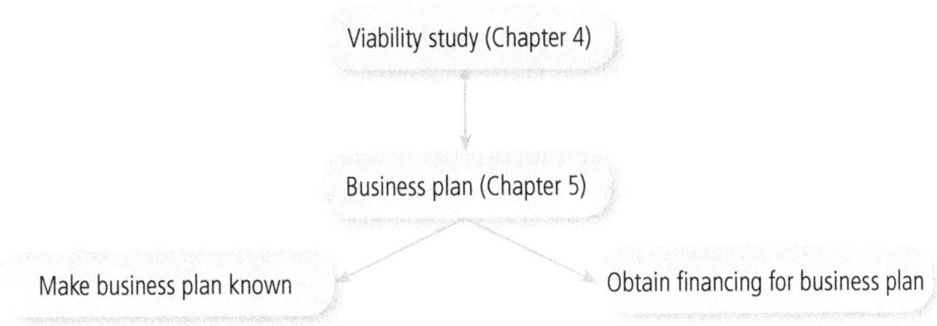

Figure 4.1: The planning stage in establishing a business

An idea is viable if you can market it and manage a business over time at a sustainable profit. The viability of an idea must be tested, based on certain assumptions and on research that has to be conducted. The viability study must also make provision for unforeseen circumstances.

Imagine you start your business and as you are just starting up, you realise that the demand is bigger than anticipated? Or that customers expect to pay in 60 days and not cash? Or that your product is suddenly more expensive due to cheaper imports?

In order for an idea to be viable it must be managed over a period of time, usually at least two to five years, and at a sustainable profit.

4.3 THE VIABILITY STUDY

The purpose of a viability study is to establish the level of interest in the offerings of the business, what the estimated sales per unit and rand value would be, the price of the product, the cost and profit per unit, the most suitable distribution channel and marketing channels, strengths and weaknesses of the business, and so forth.

Before you can begin work on the viability study, you will have to do some market research and gather various facts and figures to estimate the size of the market. A mistake that many entrepreneurs make is to be overly optimistic and in the process inflate expected sales and underestimate costs, and to overestimate the size of the market. It is better to be more conservative and be more realistic in these estimations.

Typical questions that need to be asked are as follows:

- Does a big enough number of people want my product or service? (needs analysis)
- What is the profile of these potential buyers – do they have the money, are they men or woman, where do they live? (customer profile and characteristics)
- How many of these products do I expect to sell? Will there be repeat sales? How does the competition look? (market share)
- What are people prepared to pay for it? (price analysis)

Based on the information received from the market research, you can make some assumptions, such as:

- the estimated number of units that will be sold – per day, week, month
- the acceptable price that the market will be prepared to pay for the product or service
- the cash flow requirements for the business.

It is therefore essential that a proper needs analysis of the market is done as well as the profile and characteristics of the market. The section below explains how to do this.

4.4 THE NEEDS ANALYSIS AND CHARACTERISTICS OF CUSTOMERS

As an entrepreneur, the very first thing you should do is find out exactly who your potential customers are, what their needs are and how they make their buying decisions. The key to success is to make sure that the product or service you offer is what the customer wants and not just what you want to sell. Many entrepreneurs make the mistake of thinking because they like the product the market will also like it.

In order to be able to make a decision on the viability of your idea or business, you must have information on the characteristics, needs and purchasing patterns of the customers. Given the intense competition in the market today, reliable information is the key to a successful business.

In Chapter 1 we explained that people buy products and/or services in order to satisfy a need. However, this concept of buying to satisfy a need is not that clear or straightforward. On the one hand, a need can be very strongly felt but not easily defined but, on the other hand, there can be various options for satisfying that specific need. There is generally a distinct difference between the physical product that customers buy and the image customers have of the product. When you are about to provide a product or service to the market, you must determine which need that product or service will satisfy.

To do this, you need to be very specific about who your customers are and be able to develop a customer profile. A customer profile is nothing more than a description of your potential customers. You must be able to determine their distinguishing characteristics and then look for information about their location and numbers.

eg

An example of a customer profile would be:

Age:	Between 18 and 25
Family status:	Single
Income:	Low to moderate income range
Geographic region:	Western Cape

Once you are aware of the needs of your customers can a market strategy be formulated. It is one thing to determine what customers want, but another matter altogether to meet that need profitably. Therefore it is important that you establish how you can provide the right product or service at the right price so that you can make a profit. If you cannot make a profit within a certain time period, there is no sense in entering that market.

To establish if there is a need for a product or service, you must define the market in terms of its total size, that is, the group or groups of potential customers you will be marketing your business to. You should also identify the market where your products or service will be most widely accepted.

NB

To establish if there is a need for a particular product or service, you can ask these questions to conduct your market research.

(a) **List the features of the product or service:** This will help you to focus on each aspect of your product or service and decide whether it meets the needs of the market. For example, my product is colourful, enamel cast iron casseroles and cookware. The features of the casserole are that it has excellent heat retention when cooking; it is a very durable product with a lifetime guarantee; it is aesthetically pleasing and comes in a range of colours; it can be used for cooking as well as serving and dishing up at dinner parties.

(b) **Determine who the major competitors are and who the industry leaders are, as well as suppliers and other major role-players in this market:** This section is very important as it forces you to examine the industry as a whole, in order to determine its place in the market. You need to look at the size of your competitors and how they compete in the marketplace. If, for example, competition is largely on price, you may want to stay out of the market as customer loyalty will be low in such a market. Not only must you look at direct competition (other cast iron cookware manufacturers) but you also need to look at indirect competition (customers might prefer to spend their money on other kitchen aids and appliances). In a similar way, you should identify and evaluate your suppliers. Suppliers vary, some are reliable and deliver the right product on time at a good price, and others do not.

(c) **Identify the possible customers and segment the market:** To do this, you need to define the market in terms of its total size and target market. Each market must be examined carefully as to overall size, demand and potential profitability. It is not possible to try and satisfy all segments so it is better to focus on that part that is most likely to buy your product. Determining which market segments are most attractive is called market segmentation. Market research will be crucial to obtain this information.

(d) **Draw up a final list.** This should include:

- the features of your product or service
- the needs of the customers that the product or service will meet
- a profile of your customers
- the potential number of customers.

Say for example that the market research shows that younger men between the ages of 24 and 35 years have an interest in growing and grooming their beards, it is logical that the focus will be on men in that age group. It may even be further refined to focus on a specific race group if the research covers this.

Once you have this information, you can determine what kind of business you wish to start. You can then also define your business and determine its objectives.

4.5 THE MISSION STATEMENT AND OBJECTIVES OF THE BUSINESS

In Chapter 1, the mission statement and objectives of the business were broadly described as 'what you want to achieve ... and how you will achieve it'. In this section we will look at these in more detail. By this stage, you probably know what type of business you would like to run. It is therefore possible to move on to defining the mission statement and objectives. This is an important task and deserves some time and thought.

It is usual to define a business according to the product or service that you wish to sell, as well as by the customer profile. The definition must not be too narrow or too broad.

If it is too narrow, it might exclude possible opportunities, but a definition that is too general can cause a lack of focus. The following questions will help you define your business:

- Who are the customers of the business?
- Which customer needs will the business satisfy?
- How will the business satisfy these needs?

By following the steps outlined on page 75, you have already collected the information to answer these questions. You can now proceed to defining the mission statement.

4.5.1 Mission statement

A business is defined by its mission statement. Only a clear definition of the mission and purpose of the business makes it possible for clear and realistic objectives. Most companies have their mission statement on their websites. For example, Estee Lauder's mission statement, which is 'bringing the best to everyone we touch' clearly describes what they want to achieve.

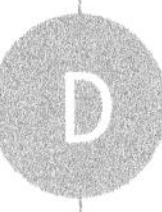

A mission statement defines the fundamental and unique purpose of a business and identifies its products or services, as well as its customers. The mission of a business is defined by customers' satisfaction with its products and services.

Questions that need to be answered when formulating the mission statement are:

- Who are the customers?
- Why do they buy?
- What do they buy?
- How do they buy?
- Where are they located?
- How can the customers be reached?
- What, in the opinion of the customer, is value for money?

An example of a mission statement for a jewellery outlet may be as follows:

'We make dreams come true through the offering of products and services of a personal nature that exceeds the expectations and wildest dreams of people who have an interest in the finer things in life and who have an appreciation for the unusual and exceptional at a price that is affordable'.

After you have set the mission statement, you can now formulate objectives for your business. The objectives must be measurable, realistic, clear, attainable and within a set timeframe.

An objective is something the business wants to achieve over a set period of time.

An entrepreneur may set an objective of increasing its awareness of its products in the market from 3% to 8% over a six-month period.

Objectives are necessary so that you have something to measure progress against. They are usually adjusted over time, based on changes that take place in the industry and environment.

Defining your mission statement and objectives clarifies what your business is all about. It will also help you calculate your market share, so that you can work out if your product or service can be marketed profitably. You must make realistic predictions. Whatever you do, do not be too optimistic; it does not help to mislead yourself. If you are too optimistic, it could lead to failure.

4.6 CALCULATING THE EXPECTED MARKET SHARE

The next step in the planning process is to determine the expected market share for your product or service. This is not an easy task but is important in order to assist you in being realistic and to know your market. It is important to calculate this as accurately as possible, because this share will be used as a basis to estimate the potential income of your business. Again, we must stress that you should not overestimate the potential market as this will give you a false sense of what your income could be.

To calculate the expected market share you need to:

- estimate the total potential market for your product or service
- estimate what portion of the market is occupied by your competitors
- estimate what portion you can expect to sell to (this is known as your target market).

A method for calculating these figures follows to help you calculate your expected market share.

4.6.1 Calculating the potential market

It is not easy to estimate a potential market. Most entrepreneurs work with unquantified information and must make many assumptions. However, when you identified the need for your product, you collected much of the information needed to segment your market.

When trying to establish the potential market, you should begin by dividing it into various market segments.

A boutique dessert shop in George, Western Cape cannot cater for all the needs and tastes in the dessert and sweet market. The owner must therefore select a specific segment of the total market to service. For instance, the owner must sell either ice cream and frozen desserts or baked goods like confectionery, biscuits, cakes, pastries and puddings. The chosen segment is then called the target market and consists of customers with similar needs and tastes.

Establishing your target market consists of three steps:

- market segmentation
- evaluation and the target-market decision
- market positioning.

(a) Market segmentation

Market segmentation is the process whereby the total market is identified and divided into sub-groups or segments with similar needs. The market can be sub-divided as follows:

- **Demographic segmentation:** Demographic features such as age, gender and race are useful for describing customers with similar needs.

You may for example decide on your target market as men in the 24 to 35 age group, black, and in the middle-income group, as this is a fast growing segment.

- **Geographical segmentation:** Because you cannot cater for all the young men in the 24 to 35 age group country wide you may decide to focus on Johannesburg or Soweto as a start.
- **Psychographic segmentation:** Customers can be grouped on the basis of their personality or lifestyle, for instance those who are independent and conservative.
- **Behaviouristic segmentation:** Some people may be single, socially active and prefer smaller groups to larger groups. You should note that customer behaviour differs.

Because there are various ways to segment the market, you must select appropriate criteria for your product or service. Table 4.1 gives some examples.

Table 4.1: Different ways to segment the market

Product or service	Characteristics	Segmentation
Alarm system	Cares for the family, needs protection while on holiday	Psychographic
Golf club and tennis racquets	Used for exercise and entertainment	Demographic and psychographic
Cinemas	Visited for entertainment	Behaviouristic

(b) Evaluation and the target-market decision

After you have grouped the total market into segments, you must select one segment as your target market and focus your marketing campaigns on that specific segment. The choice of your segment should be governed by things such as accessibility (for advertising purposes) and size (to generate enough profits).

If most single elderly customers (size) in an area prefer eating alone at home every night and there is no prepared meals service provider or delivery service in the area, it is logical to cater for prepared meals (accessibility) as this will generate more sales and profits.

(c) Market positioning

If you choose more than one segment as your target market, you must design a different marketing campaign for each segment. For example, one market segment prefers having prepared meals at home and the other segment prefers family dining; advertising for these segments will differ.

It is usually impossible for any one entrepreneur to focus on the total market. It is usually preferable and realistic to focus on one segment only. We call this the target-market decision. Successful entrepreneurs go for a large share in one segment, rather than a small share in the total market.

4.6.2 Calculating the size of the market

Here is the traditional method for estimating the market size of your target market.

- Number of customer units (a)
- Average annual gross income per unit (b)
- Total income for area (a × b = c)

- Percentage (%) of income spent on item (d)
- Potential rand value for item ($c \times d = e$)
- Realistic percentage (%) of entrepreneur's market share (f)
- Rand value of entrepreneur's market share ($e \times f = g$)

Maria wants to sell homemade rusks, biscuits and desserts in the university hostel where she lives and studies. There are 400 students living in the hostel and the average annual income per person is R12 000. On average the students spend 10% of their income on snacks like rusks, biscuits and desserts during the year. Maria is convinced that she will attract 7% market share, as students already buy rusks and biscuits from the local home industry and also other competitors where the students buy their groceries. What is the potential rand value of this market?

Answer:

1. Number of customer units	400
2. Average annual gross income	R12 000
3. Total income of students	R4 800 000
4. Percentage spent on items	10%
5. Potential rand value of market	R480 000
6. Realistic percentage of market share	7%
7. Rand value of Maria's market share	R33 600

The rand value of Maria's sales amounts to R33 600 a year. This is not her profit, but her turnover. This rough estimate gives the entrepreneur an idea of the market potential. *Be careful not to be over-optimistic of your potential market share.*

If Maria is happy with her rand value, she can continue with her business plans. If she is unhappy with the market share, she should research another business idea.

If you want to maintain your share of the market, increase it or to even just protect it the entrepreneur should constantly look at ways and means to keep existing customers happy, or to attract new customers to their offering.

How do we determine the number of units, average income, percentage spent on items, etc? This information can be found in reports in newspapers, from government departments, municipalities and research bureaus of universities.

4.6.3 Calculating the expected market share

There may be times when a business cannot satisfy the demand for a product or service because its capacity restricts the number of products that it can produce. At other times, the economy may be in decline and customers may not be able to satisfy their need for the product because they do not have the necessary money or credit to buy it. Because the economy and external environment changes, you should determine what your expected market share would be under these varying circumstances.

The expected market share is that part of the target market that a business will be able to serve on the basis of its production capacity and the state of the economy.

Figure 4.2: Expected market share

It is not easy to estimate the expected market share but it is important to do this as accurately as possible in order to calculate a realistic potential income. In order to be realistic and to reduce risk, you should calculate three scenarios:

- a very prosperous one
- a very conservative one, and
- a most likely one.

The average of the three scenarios could be taken as the one to work from. (Remember that if you 'manipulate' or inflate the figures, you will only be fooling yourself!)

You should then calculate the profit for each scenario and judge from that whether it is worth going ahead with the business idea. (See page 98 for an explanation of how to calculate your profit.) This kind of calculation is imperative if you intend to obtain financing from a source such as a bank.

Table 4.2 illustrates the steps needed to test a business idea's feasibility.

Table 4.2: Judging the business idea

Step	Action
1	Estimate expected market share
2	Estimate profit for each scenario
3	Decide if the business idea is worthwhile or not

4.7 CALCULATING THE INCOME

To calculate the potential income for your business, you have to work out the selling price of your product or service. To do this, you must establish exactly what costs will be incurred to manufacture and sell the product. You must first know what the total cost per unit (cost price) will be before you can calculate the selling price (see 4.7.1).

The selling price must at least cover all the costs. If the costs are not covered, the business will show a loss from the start and will not survive. After the costs per unit have been established, the next step in calculating the selling price is to add a percentage profit (markup) to the cost price (cost price + profit = selling price). If you add a markup of 30% and the cost price of the product is R20, the product will sell at 130/100 × R20 = R26.00.

To calculate the selling price by adding a markup to the cost price, you must add the percentage markup to 100 and then divide it by 100. You then multiply the answer by the cost price of the product.

If you have a 30% markup and the cost price of the product is R20, the selling price will be:

30 + 100 = 130

$\frac{130}{100} = 1{,}30$

1,30 x 20 = R26.00 (selling price)

Put differently, the selling price would be R20 plus R6 = R26.00.

If you have a 50% markup and the cost price of the product is R30, the selling price will be:

50 + 100 = 150

$\frac{150}{100} = 1{,}50$

1,50 x 30 = R45.00 (selling price)

When deciding what the markup and selling price should be, you need to look at what the market price is (what your competitors are charging for the same product). If your market analysis has shown that the market is price sensitive, you must charge a price that is competitive. If the market is not price sensitive, then you may get away with charging a higher price if the product can be differentiated.

4.7.1 Calculating the total costs per unit of the product (cost price of the product)

When calculating the cost price it is important to classify the costs as either:

- variable and fixed costs, or
- direct and indirect costs.

Variable costs are costs that are fixed per unit, but variable in total. This means that the costs rise in relation to the number of units manufactured (see graph below). For example, if the raw materials in a product cost R2 and 20 products are manufactured, the total variable cost is R40. If 30 products are manufactured, the total variable cost is R60, but it is still R2 for one product.

Figure 4.3 shows variable costs on a graph.

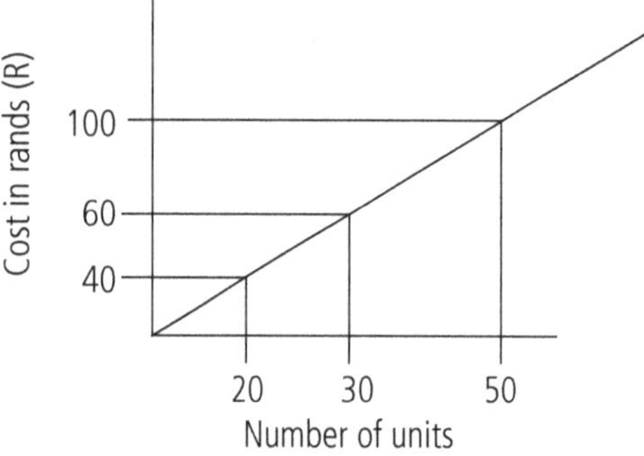

Figure 4.3: Variable costs

Fixed costs are the costs that are fixed in total, but variable per unit. Look at the following graph. The rent on a factory is R100. This means that if you make 10 units of your product, each one costs R10 to make (point A). If 20 products are manufactured (point B), the total fixed cost is still R100, but each unit costs R5. Figure 4.4 illustrates fixed costs on a graph.

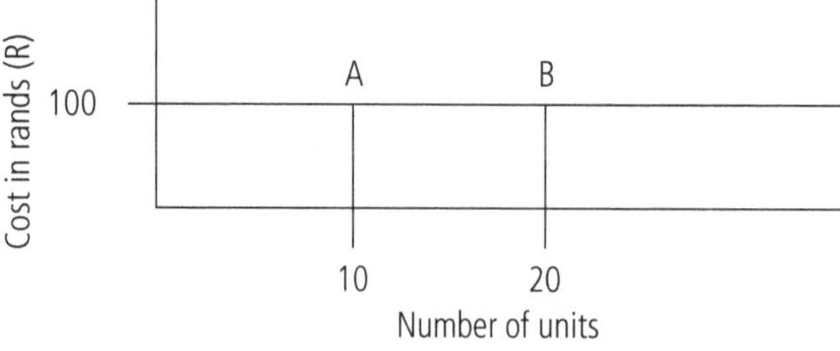

Figure 4.4: Fixed costs

Direct costs are costs that can be allocated directly to the manufacture of the product. Examples of direct costs are the raw materials used for the manufacture of a product, and wages of labourers who are directly involved in manufacturing the product.

Indirect costs (also called overheads) are costs that cannot be allocated directly to a product. Examples of these are rent on the factory, electricity, water, depreciation and indirect wages (like the salary of the owner).

Figure 4.5: Calculating total costs

The way the cost of a product is calculated depends on the type of business. There are different ways of calculating costs in different types of businesses. These are discussed below.

(a) Calculating the total costs per unit of a product for a manufacturing business

The total costs of a product in a manufacturing business consist of manufacturing costs plus commercial overhead costs.

- **Manufacturing costs** consist of direct labour costs (the wages of the factory workers), direct material costs (the costs of raw materials) and manufacturing overhead costs (indirect costs).

Figure 4.6: Calculating manufacturing costs

- **Commercial overhead costs** consist of administrative overheads and marketing overheads. The administrative overhead costs are all costs related to the administration of the business functions, such as human resources, finance and management. **Marketing costs** are all the costs incurred in marketing the product, such as advertising.

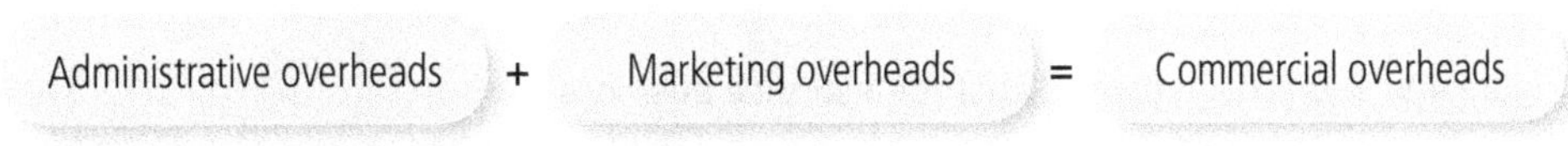

Figure 4.7: Calculating commercial overheads

Follow these steps to calculate the total costs of one unit of a product.

- Calculate the direct costs of the materials that are used to manufacture one unit of a product.
- Calculate the direct labour costs needed to manufacture one unit of a product.
- Calculate the indirect costs per unit of the product. (Add the manufacturing overheads, marketing overheads and administrative overheads together and divide this total by the number of products that was manufactured in the same period the costs were incurred – for example, one month.)
- Add the costs together to get the total costs per unit.

Figure 4.8: Costs per unit for a manufacturing business

(b) Calculating the total costs per hour for a service business

In a service business, the product that is for sale is knowledge and skill. An example of this type of enterprise would be a business that repairs computer equipment. In this kind of business, an hourly rate for labour must be calculated.

Follow these steps to calculate the total costs of one unit of 'product'.

- Calculate the number of business hours per month. (This is the number of hours the business operates.) For example, daily from 07:00 to 16:00, in other words:

  9 hours a day × 6 days a week = 54 hours a week × 52 weeks = 2 808 hours a year ÷ 12 months = 234 hours a month.
- Calculate the cost per hour. To do this, calculate the total expenses for a month, for example rent on the building, salaries, rental on office equipment. Suppose it is R10 000 a month. Divide the total costs by the number of working hours per month: R10 000 ÷ 234 hours = R42,73 an hour. This means that you cannot charge less than R42,73 an hour for your services.

Figure 4.9: Total costs of a product for a service business

(c) Calculating the total costs per product for a commercial business

A commercial business does not manufacture products. It buys finished products and then sells them again at a higher price. The total costs for a product in a commercial business are made up of the purchasing costs of the product to be sold (the cost of sales) plus the commercial overhead costs.

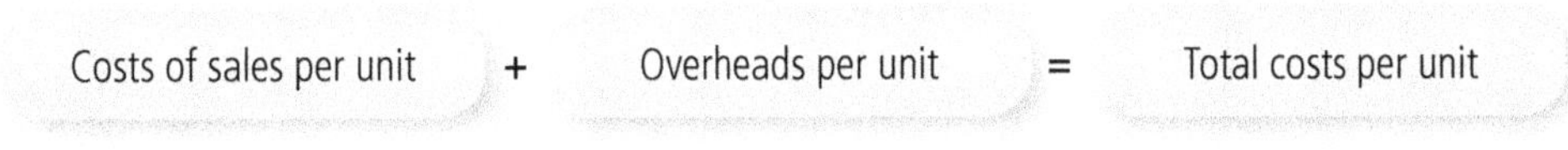

Figure 4.10: Total costs of a product for a commercial business

4.7.2 Calculating the selling price

Entrepreneurs need to be aware of the fact that they cannot always charge the price they want to, or even the price based on the actual cost of producing the product or service. Customers compare prices and if the entrepreneur cannot produce the product or service at a competitive price they will never be in the game and the business will fail even before it started. The price you can charge for your product or service is directly influenced by the price that your competitors charge for the same kind of product or service. If your product or service is much more expensive than that of your competitors, you will lose customers. Your product or service can only be more expensive than that of your competitors if you offer more benefits than your competitors – this means that the market must perceive that they are getting more value for money.

To determine what you can charge for your product, make a list of your products and then establish what your competitors charge for similar products. Next list the competitors' strengths and weaknesses, as well as your business's strengths and weaknesses and compare them with those of the competitors. Table 4.3 provides a template for this activity.

Table 4.3: Comparing your products and services to the competition

Your own business		Competitor's business	
List of products and prices		List of products and prices	
1.	R	1.	R ....
2.	R	2.	R ....
3.	R	3.	R ....

You can now establish what the highest and lowest prices are and also what price range (the prices charged for the product or service in general) apply to the product or service. If a business has exceptional strengths, this can justify higher prices. The opposite is also true: if the business has many weaknesses it will be obliged to charge lower prices than its competitors.

After you have made the comparison, you can decide what you can charge for your product or service. Remember that you may never charge less than the total cost of a product or service unless such a product is used as a loss leader to bring customers in the store.

Once the selling price has been established, the potential income and net profit from the sale of the product can be calculated.

4.7.3 Calculating the expected net profit

After establishing the costs and markup for your product, you are now ready to test the viability of the business. To be viable, the business idea must be profitable. To establish whether the business is going to be profitable, the expected unit sales must be multiplied by the expected selling price to arrive at the turnover. From this figure, deduct the expected costs. The difference will be the profit. If the income exceeds the expenses, you will be making a profit. If, on the other hand, your expenses exceed your income, you will be making a loss.

The net profit is calculated by drawing up a pro forma income statement.

A pro forma income statement is one that is drawn up using estimated figures.

You can calculate the net profit using the figures you arrived at for the various scenarios discussed under Section 4.6.3.

Here is an example of an income statement.

Happy Traders Limited

Income statement for the year ended 28 February 20xx.

		R
Revenue		970 000
Less	Cost of sales	701 000
	Inventory: 1 March 20xx	90 000
	Add: Purchases	700 000
	Freight on purchases	6 000
	Inventory: 28 Feburary 20xx	796 000

	Gross profit (970 000 – 701 000)	269 000
	Add (Discount received):	4 000
	Total	273 000
	Less: Selling administrative and general expenses	178 450
	Freight on sales	4 000
	Discount allowed	3 000
	Commission to sales personnel	9 000
	Salaries and wages	95 450
	Stationery and postage	3 000
	Bad debts	2 500
	Insurance	6 000
	Sundry expenses	16 000
	Auditor's remuneration	6 500
	Director's remuneration	15 000
	Loss on sales of equipment	2 000
	Depreciation	16 000
	Profit from operations (273 000 – 178 450)	94 550
	Investment income	5 000
	Listed investments	2 000
	Unlisted investments	3 000
	Finance costs	(14 300)
	Interest on bank overdraft	(2 000)
	Interest on mortgage loan	(4 800)
	Interest on debentures	(7 500)
	Profit before tax	83 450
	Income tax (29%)	24 200,50
	Net profit for the year	59 249,50

4.8 CALCULATING THE BREAK-EVEN POINT

For any business, the gross sales volume level needed to reach the break-even point must be calculated. (Also see Chapter 15 for more information on the break-even point.)

Break-even is the volume where all fixed expenses are covered.

To begin the break-even analysis, first estimate the business's fixed expenses (also known as overheads) which mostly consist of monthly expenses but also expenses like insurance and taxes which are paid annually or quarterly. It is important to make the most accurate predictions of semi-variable expenses such as electricity and internet and communication costs even though their amounts will differ every month.

For the purpose of a model break-even calculation, let's assume that the fixed expenses for Happy Traders are as follows:

Administrative salaries	R1 500
Rent	R800
Utilities	R300
Insurance	R150
Taxes	R210
Telephone	R240
Car expenses	R400
Supplies	R100
Sales and marketing	R300
Interest	R100
Miscellaneous	R400
Total fixed expenses	**R4 500**

The business's gross profit must be able to cover all these expenses. What must the total sales volume be if the gross profit margin is 30%? **Answer:** R15 000 total sales volume because 30% of that is R4 500.

If the gross profit margin of a business is 40% and your fixed expenses are R20 000, the break-even figure should be R50 000. **Answer:** R20 000 x 100 / 40 = R50 000.

Some expenses can be moved between being categorised as direct or indirect expenses which is why the profit and loss statements and break-even target number must be reevaluated at least once every six months.

Ways to lower break-even

There are three ways to lower your break-even volume; only two of them involve cost controls (which should always be your goal).

1. **Lower direct costs, which will raise the gross margin:** Be more diligent about purchasing material, controlling inventory or increasing the productivity of your labour by more cost-effective scheduling or adding more efficient technology.

2. **Exercise cost controls on your fixed expenses:** Be careful when cutting expenses that you do so with an overall plan in mind. You can cut too deeply as well as too little and cause distress among workers, or you may pull back marketing efforts at the wrong time, which will send out the wrong signal to the market.

3. **Raise prices:** Most entrepreneurs are reluctant to raise prices because they think that business will drop in sales. More often than not that does not happen unless you are in a very price-sensitive market, and if you are, you have probably already become volume driven.

If you are in the typical niche-type small business, you can raise your prices 4–5% without your customers noticing. The effect can be startling.

eg

For example, the first model we looked at was:

Volume	R15 000	
Direct cost	R10 500	(70%)
Gross profit	R4 500	

Raising the price by 5% would result in this change:

Volume	R15 750	
Direct cost	R10 500	(67%)
Gross profit	R5 250	

You will have increased your margin by 3% and by so doing lowered the total volume you need to reach break-even.

The goal is profit

You are in business to make a profit, not just to reach break-even. However, by knowing your break-even point, you can manage your business more effectively.

- Distribute your marketing efforts in order to reach your target; for instance, spend more resources on promotional activities if you want to increase sales.
- You can control costs if you predict a 'slow' month. This happens in most companies, for example the retail industry straight after Christmas. However, losses can be minimised if you plan accordingly. Remember that a few bad months can quickly wipe out accumulated profits.
- You can maximise profits by knowing and understanding the elements of your break-even figure.

4.9 CASH PLANNING: THE CASH BUDGET (CASH FORECAST)

Up to this point, we have stressed the importance of being able to sustain profits over time.

Do not attempt any business venture if you cannot sustain profits over time.

Unfortunately, making a profit is not enough. While you must be able to sustain profits over a period of time, it is equally important to have enough cash available to manage the business on a day-to-day basis. You may be making a net profit but lack sufficient ready cash (money) to meet expenses as they occur. If this happens, you cannot continue trading and you will go bankrupt and have to close your business.

When you do not have money to meet expenses as they occur, you are in a situation known as technical bankruptcy. So to continue in business, you must have an adequate cash flow to meet your expenses as they happen.

To overcome this problem, it is extremely important that you pay close attention to the planning of actual money flowing into your business and actual money flowing out. It must be a first priority to know how much actual money you are going to receive and on what dates. You must also know when you have to pay expenses and what amounts are involved. A tool you can use to help with this cash planning is the cash budget.

The cash budget is a formal plan for forecasting future receipts and payments of cash.

Just as you would not purchase a new car without enough cash or at least a solid plan to cover a personal loan from your bank, your business needs the same careful handling of its expenditures. All businesses, no matter what type or size, need to develop a plan for their expected cash intake and spending. This is the cash budget.

4.9.1 The purpose of cash budgeting

The cash budget allows you to establish exactly how much cash is flowing into and out of your business. The budget can:

- be used to plan your short-term credit needs
- be presented to your bank or other financial institution to show proper financial planning

- help you predict months when there may be a cash shortfall
- highlight problem areas in your payment schedule – for example, payments to creditors may be lumped together on one date – more careful planning could spread this evenly throughout the entire year.

4.9.2 Consistent budgets

Consistency and accuracy is very important when engaging in the continuous process of cash budgeting. The process involves comparing budgeted amounts with amounts that can be expected from using typical ratios or financial statement relationships. For instance, your assessment will include all estimations of the payments made to your suppliers, payments for wages and salaries as well as all the other payments that you must make. In order to take advantage of special reduced rates or discounts or to make sure that you do not miss payments, the payments can be scheduled by date. Also, cash collections from customers and other expected cash receipts can also be accurately planned and scheduled by date. Maintaining a healthy cash balance without holding excessive balances of non-productive cash will become easier when enough time and effort is put into planning.

eg

Example of a cash budget

The following is an example of a cash budget for the ABC Company.

Cash budget for 90 days	
Beginning cash balance	R450 000
Add:	
Estimated collections on accounts receivable	R900 000
Estimated cash balances	R300 000
	R1 650 000
Deduct:	
Estimated payments on accounts payable	R 1 000 000
Estimated cash expenses	R200 000
Contractual payments on long-term debt	R200 000
Quarterly dividend	R75 000
	R1 475 000
Estimated ending cash balance	**R175 000**

4.9.3 Analysis of the example cash budget

Analysis of the financial statements of the ABC Company shows the accounts receivable remain at about R500 000 throughout the year. This means there is no seasonal fluctuation in sales.

- The accounts receivable turns over six times a year, or once every 60 days.
- The inventory throughout the year remains at about R800 000 and turns over every 90 days.
- The accounts payable remains at about R400 000 and turns over eight times a year; about once every 45 days.
- There is an accounts receivable collection period of 60 days and an average balance outstanding of R500 000. It appears that R750 000 is the amount that should be collected on the receivables in 90 days.
- Cash sales should amount to about R250 000 if the inventory of R800 000 valued at cost turns over once in 90 days and if the average markup is about R200 000. Therefore, if an inventory of R1 000 000 at retail turns over once every 90 days and R750 000 flows through accounts receivable, then approximately R250 000 must be sold on a cash basis.
- Cash payments for expenses are estimated to be R150 000 in the next 90 days. This figure can be roughly checked by referring to the expenses of the income statement. A rough measure of the cash expenses can usually be obtained by using the operating expenses less any non-cash expenses such as depreciation. For example, if there is no seasonal factor, the total amount divided by four should be an approximate check on the amount budgeted for the next 90 days.

4.10 SUMMARY

In this chapter we discussed the first stage in the planning process, namely performing a viability study. We discussed the reason for carrying out such a study and explained the various steps in the process.

When conducting the viability study, it is important to conduct market research to establish exactly who your customers will be, whether there is a real need for the product or service behind your idea, and who your competitors will be. It is also necessary to calculate what your income will be; to do this you need to be able to calculate the cost price of your product or service, calculate the selling price and from those figures establish what your profit will be. You must be able to draw up a cash budget and calculate the break-even point of the business.

The reason behind the viability study was stressed; to be viable, your business idea must be profitable and sustainable over a period of time.

Self-evaluation questions

1. Explain what a viable business idea is.
2. How will you know whether you have a product or service the customer wants?
3. What kind of information will be found in a customer profile?
4. How do you define a market?
5. Name and discuss the questions that need to be asked in order to see whether there is a need for a particular product and service.
6. What is the purpose of a mission statement?
7. What are the questions that need to be answered when formulating a mission statement?
8. Name the characteristics of objectives.
9. Why is it important to calculate the expected market share?
10. What do you need to calculate the expected market share?
11. How can one establish a target market?
12. Define indirect costs.
13. Describe what are manufacturing costs.
14. What is the formula to determine cost per unit for a manufacturing enterprise?
15. What is the formula to determine the total costs of a product for a service enterprise?
16. What is the formula to determine the total costs of a product for a commercial enterprise?
17. Define the break-even point.
18. What is a cash budget?
19. What is the purpose of a cash budget?

Chapter 5

The business plan

5.1 LEARNING OUTCOMES

After you have studied this chapter, you should be able to:

- understand the purpose of a business plan
- identify and describe the potential users of a business plan
- explain the character of a business plan
- understand the preparation phase in writing a business plan
- comprehend the different structures of a business plan
- draft a basic business plan.

5.2 INTRODUCTION

In Chapter 4 we discussed the first half of our business planning process: namely, how to do the viability study to determine whether one should proceed in starting a new business. If you have decided that your business idea is indeed viable, then you can move on to the next step – the business plan. This plan is a critical element in every phase of the entrepreneurial route to success as it provides with the initial foundation for growth and success.

The business plan plays a pivotal role in the entrepreneurial process. If you, as an entrepreneur, apply for start-up capital, a government grant or if you tender for a government contract, one of the first questions you will be asked is if you have a business plan. Also, private equity providers, like venture capitalists, require a comprehensive plan with the core purpose to indicate how their investment will return high yields. This suggests that a business plan is the only platform for judging your business, although on paper. Remember that the business opportunity is the core focus of entrepreneurial venturing and the business plan an essential supporting element. A business plan is a picture and blueprint of how the entrepreneur will participate in the entrepreneurial process.

Let us assess two entrepreneurial cases.

Refilwe Ngobeni, a third year business management student at a local university, invented an app that links the Johannesburg Securities Exchange (JSE) with cell phone and tablet end-users. This program enabled the customer to obtain information on any real time changes on share prices (both inclines and declines). At that time, the concept was unique and promised high income potential for the entrepreneur. Refilwe finished her formal studies and started the business formally. She spent hours refining the service but failed to develop a pricing strategy or even think about a marketing strategy. All her advisors said: 'Just do it'; 'The money will come by itself'; 'These apps will go viral and make millions in a short time frame' and, 'This is a million dollar opportunity.'

The reality was that not a single customer was interested because of the vast number of competitive/comparable apps that were developed within a very short time. Refilwe fell in love with her idea and neglected all the basic business principles. The total income of the business amounted to zero! The expense account exceeded the zero mark by far!

Peter opened a small outlet near his home to sell basic consumer goods like maize, milk and cooldrinks and even offered a public phone. As the sales increased, he realised that an opportunity existed for making yoghurt out of the milk that had not been sold and had date-expired; also a farmer close to Peter offered all his surplus milk not sold in the open market. He decided to expand and opened a small yoghurt factory. Peter was then also able to expand his sales area with the new product with specific reference to the large number of Spaza shops in his region. Because the business was doing well, Peter could again expand and build a cheese-making unit.

All these decisions were based on well-researched opportunities in the marketplace and on sound financial planning. Because of this planning, and given the vigorous growth of the business, Peter is investigating the possibility of buying the dairy farm currently supplying him.

These are typical scenarios drawn from the lives of emerging entrepreneurs. Because of a lack of planning, the first case ends in failure, whereas the second shows entrepreneurial performance and success. One of the cornerstones of success is in-depth planning and a formal written plan; the business plan is an integral part of this planning process.

5.3 THE PURPOSE AND PRINCIPLES OF THE BUSINESS PLAN

The primary objective of the business plan is to develop a blueprint to define your business. The plan is:

- a meticulous route map to entrepreneurial success
- a detailed written document stipulating how you will address all the business activities to exploit the identified business opportunity

- a planning document that explores and indicates the route to follow into the future
- a document that you, the entrepreneur, should formulate by yourself.

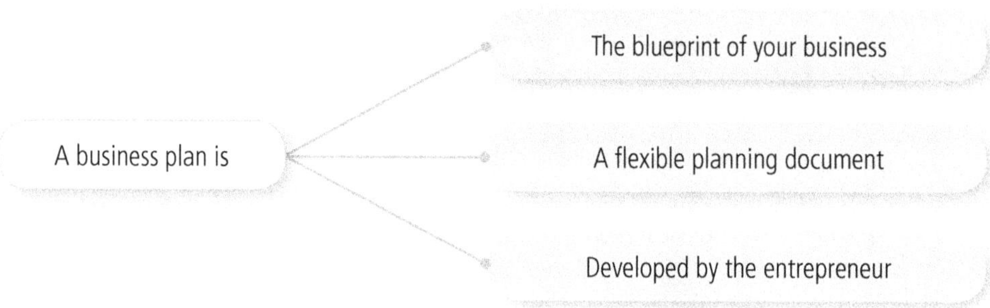

Figure 5.1: The business plan

5.3.1 A blueprint for the business

The business plan serves exactly the same purpose as an architect's plan, which includes a detailed building schedule with quantities and costs of all the items necessary to complete the work, such as bricks, mortar, wood, steel and labour. In the same way, the business plan lists all the facets of the proposed business. It consequently guides the entrepreneur to implement its planned strategies for establishment and growth.

5.3.2 A flexible document

The business plan is not a static or fixed document; it is a dynamic planning instrument that should be updated regularly to take account of changes in the business environment. For instance, customer buying patterns may shift towards healthier eating (for example, a trend towards low fat yoghurt); new competitors may enter the market with new, comparable products (for example, soya milk yoghurt). Your suppliers may also change their approach (for example, no more credit offerings, which could have a negative impact on cash flow). Timely adaptation to these changes is the only way for your business to survive.

5.3.3 A plan developed by the entrepreneur

The only way to understand your business properly is to develop your own business plan. This is the best way to end up with a unique plan that suits you and your business and coupled with that offers you the opportunity to strategically and operationally think of all the elements of your business. While it is possible to use the services of an external consultant, this may not be as effective and you may end up with an 'off-the-shelf', generic product. There may be areas or gaps in your business plan that are not part of your skills set that require the input of a specialist (eg financial projections or technical designs of the product).

5.4 OTHER USERS OF THE BUSINESS PLAN

A secondary objective of the business plan is to acquire start-up capital from a financier (eg a commercial bank or financial agency). It can also serve as a communication document to present to potential investors or venture capitalists. The larger suppliers of raw material may similarly ask to see the plan to evaluate your reputation, substance and financial position.

Some entrepreneurs use the business plan to motivate their employees; by communicating the long-term planning and goals, they hope to give their staff a greater sense of 'ownership'. However, there is a certain danger in making your plans known because the core competencies and intellectual capital may become known to your competitors if and when employees leave your service. A business plan is a confidential document and anyone who reads it should sign a non-disclosure agreement which states that they will maintain confidentiality.

Figure 5.2 summarises the other users of a business plan.

Figure 5.2: Potential users of the business plan

5.5 THE BUSINESS MODEL

A key component of any sound business plan is the design and formulation of an effective business model. All the elements of the business model are eventually translated into the business plan. Why then a business model?

The model is a clear indication of how you and your business will first create value for customers (in the modern world with its unique market dynamics, people want more value than ever before), and second what contributes to the efficiency of the business venture to create value for customers. The following elements should be included in your business model (and it is advised to formulate these before you commence with the business plan).

5.5.1 Value creation

(a) **The Value proposition:** This section indicates clearly what you sell or render of value to the customer. The unique selling proposition (usp) is also included, meaning how you will differentiate your offering from your competitors'. It is also critical to ask and address the following three questions:

- What are we selling? (product description)
- What problem do we solve for customers by selling this product?
- Who are our direct and indirect competitors?
- What value do we create with the offering?

(b) **Target customers:** Many entrepreneurs think that their product will be used by 'everyone'. That is one of the most popular mistakes we make. One has to focus on a specific group of customers with more or less the same needs to be satisfied. This is called the target market. A target market analysis includes detailed information on your potential market's demographics and geographics (location) as well as psychographics (eg buying behaviour).

(c) **Channels:** How do you get the product to the target customer? At first you have to make the selected target market aware of your existence. Your advertising or communication strategy should be formulated here. After that, the distribution channels should be outlined (eg in retail, the customer will walk into your store, thus a very short chain; but if you have a business-to-business proposition, a logistical process should be designed). This component also includes your social media strategy and exactly the benefits of each option (eg a Facebook page, and why it will reach your target audience).

(d) **Customer service:** How do you first attract new customers; second create loyalty and third get them to tell others (word-of-mouth) – an essential element for any small business as it could differentiate you from bigger businesses competing with you.

(e) **Income model:** How will your business make money? A brief description of your income streams (eg by selling goods, rental or an annuity model).

5.5.2 Efficiency

(a) **External parties:** In this section you analyse all the external entities that could potentially contribute to the efficiency of your business. The first starting point is your suppliers of input goods (eg raw material or packaging material); government agencies (eg SEDA or SEFA); organisational bodies (eg your chamber of commerce), etc.

(b) **Operational activities:** The operational process in your business should be well described because it will contribute eventually to effective cost analysis and cutting.

Here we describe all the primary activities (eg customer orders – deposit payment – design – manufacturing – packaging – distribution and delivery); as well as all the support activities (eg human resource management and IT support).

(c) **Resources:** Any business is driven by factors of production or input resources. It certainly depends on the nature of your business, but the following core resources are normally present in a generic small business venture:

- human resources (eg sales people)
- capital (eg starting and working capital)
- technology and or equipment (eg a software or hardware system)
- raw material, if applicable (eg milk for milkshake)
- intellectual property (eg a patent).

(d) **Costing:** The costing structure of any small business is critical in many ways, it not only assists in determining the viability of the start-up but also supports you in determining the pricing of your product to be offered to customers. Two fundamental cost types should be described here, fixed costs (eg staying the same over one year, like salaries and rental) as well as variable costs (eg it changes the more you produce, like raw material or labelling).

Your business model then prepares you to complete the entire business plan as discussed in the class.

The business plan, compiled after the model, is a planning instrument that shows the entrepreneurial process and describes how the entrepreneur will implement the process. However, it is not the nucleus of success. Many potential entrepreneurs may think that if a business plan is on paper, success will follow. Business success and entrepreneurial performance are dependent on much more. Initially, you would have identified a feasible opportunity in the market environment. As discussed, and explained in Chapter 4, you would then have undertaken a viability study. A viable opportunity therefore pre-empts the written business plan. The viability study creates a platform for writing the business plan.

Table 5.1 distinguishes between the opportunity and the business plan.

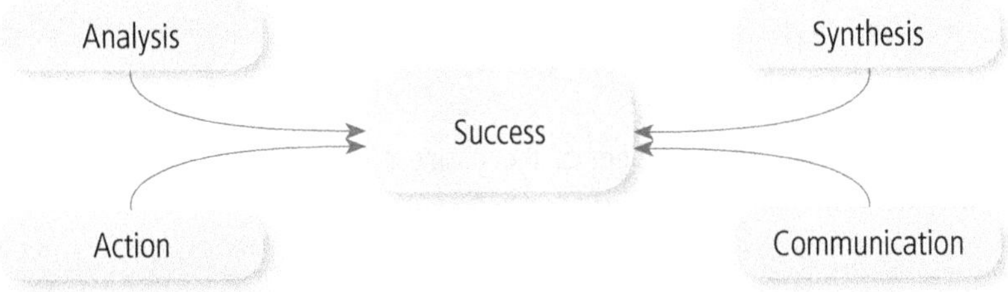

Figure 5.3: The mechanisms of a business plan in supporting business success
Adapted from Wickham (2006:197)

Table 5.1: From the opportunity to the business plan

Identify and evaluate the opportunity	• Creation and length of opportunity • Real and perceived value of opportunity • Risk and returns of opportunity • Opportunity versus personal skills and goals • Competitive situation
Develop the business plan	• Title page • Table of contents • Executive summary • Description of business • Description of industry • Marketing plan • Financial plan • Production/Operations plan • Organisation plan • Summary
Determine the resources required	• Existing resources available • Resource gaps and available supplies • Access to needed resources
Manage the enterprise	• Management style • Key variables for success • Identification of problems and potential problems • Implementation of control systems

Remember that the viability study pre-empts the business plan and contains valuable information to assist with drafting the plan.

5.6 THE STRUCTURE OF THE BUSINESS PLAN

The structure of a business plan is extremely important. It is advisable to structure your plan so that it meets the needs of your industry and the needs of the potential reader or user. A service-rendering business, for instance, will simply not have a production plan.

Adapt the structure and style to the needs of the reader, and remember that you will be the first reader and user. The following three basic structures are widely used.

Table 5.2: Structure 1 – The comprehensive structure

1. Cover page	
• Name and address of business	• Name of entrepreneur
• Nature of business	• Statement of finance needed (optional)
• Statement of confidentiality of report	
2. Executive summary	
3. Industry analysis	
• Current and potential trends	• Competitive anlaysis
• Market segmentation	
4. Business description	
• Background of entrepreneur or team of entrepreneurs	• Core product/s and or services
• Unique selling point/s	
5. Production plan	
• Operational process	• Physical outlay of manufacturing facility
• Machinery and equipment	• List of suppliers and their core competencies
6. Marketing plan	
• Pricing	• Distribution
• Promotion	• Sales forecasts
7. Organisational plan	
• Legal form of ownership	• Description of shareholders or members
• Management structure and role description	• Background of managers or project leaders (if applicable) ➠

8. **Assessment of risks**	
• Assessment of internal weaknesses	• Market risks
• Business risks	
9. **Financial plan**	
• Projected income statement	• Projected balance sheet
• Projected cash flow statements	• Break-even analysis
• Sources of finance and the application thereof	
10. **Addendum**	
• Marketing research information	• Contracts and patents/copyright (if applicable)
• Letters related to the business	

Table 5.3: Structure 2 – The general structure

1. **Cover page**	
2. **Executive summary**	
3. **Business description**	
• General description of business	• Industry background
• Primary goals of the business	• Uniqueness of the product/service
• List of suppliers and their core competencies	
4. **Marketing plan**	
• Marketing research and analysis	• Target market
• Market size	• Competition
• Potential market share	• Marketing strategy
• Pricing	• Advertising and promotions
5. **Location**	
• Advantages	• Zoning
• Taxes	• Closeness to suppliers
• Transportation issues	

6. **Management**	
• Management team – key personnel	• Legal structure – shareholding/ membership agreements; employment agreements; ownership
• Board of directors, advisors, consultants	
7. **Financial plan**	
• Financial forecasting	• Profit and loss
• Cash flow	• Break-even analysis
• Cost controls	• Budgets
8. **Critical risks**	
• Potential problems	• Obstacles and risks
• Alternative courses of action	
9. **Milestone schedule**	
• Timing and objectives	• Deadlines
• Relationship of events	
10. **Appendices**	

Table 5.4: Structure 3 – An alternative structure

1. **Cover page**
2. **Executive summary**
3. **Background and purpose of business**
4. **Marketing**
5. **Competition**
6. **Development, production and location**
7. **Management**
➠

8. Financials
9. Risk factors
10. Harvest or exit
11. Scheduling and milestones
12. Appendices

It must be re-emphasised that the structure of your business plan should adjust to the reader. Structure 1 is an all-inclusive plan and suitable to be used as the blueprint of the business.

In the case of financing institutions, you will have to adapt to their requirements and proposed structure.

5.7 GUIDELINES FOR WRITING THE BUSINESS PLAN

The structure and the content of your business plan will be unique to your business. Here are some guidelines to help with writing the actual plan.

- **Keep the plan respectably short:** Stick to a concise but clear plan (do not exceed 50 pages).
- **Organise and package the plan appropriately:** Follow a logical structure with a professional presentation (for instance, a cover page with the company name, logo and contact details, presented in such a way that the reader is interested in what is to follow).
- **Orient the plan toward the future:** You should clearly indicate what you intend to do in the future and also include a trend analysis and forecast.
- **Avoid exaggeration:** Do not inflate the potential of the business (for example, be realistic about sales and revenue estimates).
- **Highlight critical risks:** This part shows the reader that you are aware of potential problems and gives you the opportunity to explain ways to manage them.
- **Give evidence of an effective entrepreneurial team:** The management part of the plan is of critical importance as it should convey the skills and contribution of each member of your team to the overall objectives of the business.

- **Do not over diversify:** The plan should focus only on that segment of the market you identified during your market research (see page 74).
- **Identify the target market:** Give particulars of your target market and explain how you carried out your market research.
- **Keep the plan written in the third person:** rather use 'he', 'they' or 'them' than 'I', 'we' or 'us'.
- **Capture the reader's interest:** Financial institutions receive many requests for funds. Concentrate on clearly defining the uniqueness of your proposed business.

5.8 WRITING THE BUSINESS PLAN

You are now ready to start writing your plan. As an example, we are going to use Peter's business referred to earlier in this chapter. The full plan forms Appendix A at the back of this book, but a summary of the information that should appear in your plan is covered on the following pages.

5.8.1 The cover page

The cover page should contain the proposed name of the business, its address and relevant contact details. It should also be dated with a date relevant to the content and existence of the plan.

5.8.2 The confidentiality agreement

A business plan contains confidential information on the business make-up, core competencies, competitive advantages and financial condition of the business venture and the entrepreneur. It is therefore critical to safeguard the content by asking the reader/s to sign a confidentiality agreement.

5.8.3 The table of contents

The table of contents guides the reader to the information and should be accurately linked to the content of the plan (insert all the main and sub-headings accompanied by the relevant page number/s).

5.8.4 Executive summary

This summarises the entire plan in two to three pages. It provides the reader with an overview of the status of the business, the basic description of the business and owner/s, potential and current (if relevant) customers, and a brief summary of the financials.

It also indicates the purpose of the business plan (for example, financial requirements or investment potential in terms of shareholding). It is advisable to complete the executive summary after the entire business plan has been finalised.

5.8.5 Business description

This section explains in detail exactly what the business intends to do in the market place, in what industry it will operate, the trends and characteristics of the industry and what the business sells or intends to sell to its customers (the unique characteristics of the product/s). It furthermore points out the objectives to be achieved in the short, medium and long term.

5.8.6 Marketing plan

The marketing plan illustrates exactly how the product/s will reach the customer. This section highlights the intended target market, what type of media will be used to attract these customers and what pricing strategy will be applied. It also explains the proposed distribution strategy as well as the competition in the selected market. The best way to compile a marketing plan is to base it on proper marketing research findings.

5.8.7 Location

This section of the plan explains why specific decisions were made with regards to the establishment of the business. Such things as the proximity to suppliers and customers, the zoning of the property as well as transport factors should form part of this section. Another relevant aspect is the availability of skilled labour as a source to the business. The information contained in this section should be based on the findings of the feasibility study.

5.8.8 Management

This section must show how management will achieve the objectives that have been set for the business. It should illustrate the human competence of the business and include details of the management team and organisational structure (if applicable), the legal structure and available professional support.

5.8.9 Financial plan

The financial plan is to a certain extent the most critical component of the business plan. This section directly specifies what resources are required and how these will be financed and managed. The historical financial performance of the business should be included (in the case of an established entity), or the pro forma or projected financial forecasting in terms of the future expectations.

The nature and purpose of the business plan will depict the time frame of forecasting (for instance, three years or five years ahead). The main body of the financial plan should contain the projected cash flow and income statements as well as balance sheets.

A break-even analysis must also support the plan. The example (Peter's business) has a projection of one year only for the cash flow statements because of lack of space. It is advisable, however, to do realistic projections over a much longer time frame (for example, three years).

5.8.10 Critical risks

The risk assessment section must explain all the potential risks that could influence the normal and future operations of the business. These risk factors may be incurred by variables in the macro environment (such as legislation), market environment (such as competition) and micro environment (such as managerial issues). The reader has to understand how the management team will react and manage all the potential threats or risks upon its occurrence. It therefore explores all the 'what if' issues.

5.8.11 Appendices

These should include all the additional detailed documentation as mentioned in the body of the plan, such as:

- market research
- curricula vitae
- product specifications and photos.

5.9 SUMMARY

Every entrepreneur should remember the saying that 'if one fails to plan, one plans to fail'. A business plan is primarily a planning instrument and blueprint of the business venture, whether new or old. The structure of the plan should be adjusted to the nature of the business and its purpose (for instance, attracting finance). Always keep the reader in mind with specific reference to his or her level of knowledge. The length of the plan is less important than the quality of the content. All the components of the plan should communicate with each other and be strengthened by a well-structured executive summary. Remember, this business tool is flexible and needs continuous adaptation and improvement!

Self-evaluation questions

1. Explain the reason/s for drawing-up a business plan.
2. List three users of the business plan.
3. What is the executive summary?
4. List the critical risks associated with your own business idea.
5. Draft a business plan for your own business idea.

REFERENCES AND FURTHER READING

Longenecker, J.G., Moore, C.W. & Petty, J.W. 2003. *Small Business Management: An Entrrerpreneurial Emphasis.* Mason, Ohio: Thomson South Western.

Nieman, G. & Nieuwenhuizen, C. 2014. *Entrepreneurship: A South African Perspective.* Pretoria: Van Schaik Publishers.

Osterwalder, A., Pigneur, Y. & Smith, A. 2010. *Business Model Generation: A Handbook for Visionaries, Game Changers, and Challengers*. Hoboken, NJ: John Wiley and Sons.

Timmons, J.A. & Spinelli, S. 2009. *New Venture Creation: Entrepreneurship for the 21st Century*. Boston: McGraw-Hill.

Wickham, P.A. 2006. *Strategic Entrepreneurship: A Decision Making Approach to New Venture Creation and Management*. (3rd edition). Harlow, England: Financial Times – Prentice Hall.

Chapter 6

Product decisions

6.1 LEARNING OUTCOMES

After you have studied this chapter, you should be able to:

- explain what a product is and what it entails
- discuss what is meant by the product mix, and how the entrepreneur should decide on the product mix for his or her business
- describe the different product strategies
- select a suitable brand name for a product
- explain the function of packaging and design a good package for your product
- describe the implications of warranties.

6.2 INTRODUCTION

Deciding which product selection to offer customers is one of the most important decisions the entrepreneur can make, as the wrong choice will almost certainly mean the failure of the business. Proper research and planning is required to do this as failure to do so can and will eventually lead to the failure of the business. If the market does not like what you offer or does not buy into the offering, this will be the end of the business. If the correct product is selected this will imply that the business:

- meets the needs of the target market and that these needs are satisfied
- meets the business's own objectives (eg profitability).

Many entrepreneurs neglect this process of ensuring that the correct product offering is selected and make these decisions hastily – which can result in scarce resources being invested in a product for which there is no demand and no market. The result is that there are no sales, or insufficient sales, to justify the money invested, thereby leading to the business going bankrupt. By carefully selecting the product to offer, the small business has a better chance of success.

6.3 CLASSIFICATION OF PRODUCTS

Entrepreneurs must understand the various types or classification of products as the type of product will also determine the method of marketing and the approach to the market. It is therefore the responsibility of the small business owner to decide on the type of product to offer, and then to focus on the successful marketing of the product.

Products can be classified into three major types (Cant, Strydom, Jooste & Du Plessis, 2013:200).

6.3.1 Durable products

As the name implies durable products refer to those products that have a long lifespan and are not consumed quickly. These products are normally more complex and expensive. Examples are items such as appliances (Airfryer, stove, fridge), furniture (beds, lounge suites) and garden items such as lawnmowers. Since they last for some time they do not need to be replaced very often.

6.3.2 Non-durable products

Non-durable products, as the name implies, are products that are consumed over a short period. They include products such as groceries, soap and paper. They are bought frequently and should be easily available to the customer. The prices of these products are normally not very expensive and there is a fair amount of competition.

6.3.3 Services

Whereas durable and non-durable products are generally tangible products, services are usually intangible. Services are products that offer instant benefits as opposed to products that involve using, buying or owning. A service, being intangible, poses a challenge for the small business to convince customers of the value they add by means of these services. Examples of services include a dentist's service, laundry services, hair salon services and tutoring. Table 6.1 shows some services and service providers on offer.

Table 6.1: Examples of services and service providers

Accommodation	renting of hotel rooms, flats, guesthouses, eg Sun International Resorts
Household services	repair services for household appliances, cleaning of houses, gardening services, eg Hibiscus Gardening Services and Pool n Pond Specialists
Recreation	cinemas, holiday resorts, video game arcades, sports clubs, eg Virgin Active and Golfer's Village

Personal services	barbers, beauticians, florists, dry cleaners, eg Sorbet: Professional Beauty Therapy
Medical services	physiotherapists, dentists, optometrists, eg Smile Care Dental Studio
Educational services	typing courses, computer courses, small business management courses, eg Boston City Campus and Inscape Design College
Professional services	attorneys, accountants, consultants, eg Adams & Adams Attorneys and Deloitte
Insurance and financial	insurance brokers, real estate agents, banks, eg Pam Golding and OUTsurance
Transport services	taxis, delivery services, transport contractors, eg Gautrain
Communication services	paging services, cell phone companies, eg Cell C and 8ta

Another way of classifying products is by means of the target market group. These groups are based on the type of client and each needs to be approached differently from a marketing perspective. These include:

- consumer products (offered to individual customers)
- industrial or business products (offered to other businesses).

6.3.4 Consumer products

Consumer products are those products purchased by individuals for their own personal use. These products are usually divided into three groups: convenience, shopping and speciality products. Where a product is placed is determined by looking at overall customer behaviour when buying the product – ie how it is purchased by the majority of customers rather than selective customers. Let us look at each of these types of classifications.

(a) Convenience products

Convenience products are products that the customer wants to buy with the least effort, ie with convenience. These products are bought frequently and in small quantities. Their prices are usually low and the number of outlets offering these products is large. Think about a customer who wants to buy chips or butter. He or she does not want to go to too much trouble to buy the item but would rather buy it conveniently nearby. Think of all the 'convenience' stores at garages selling the items the customer wants. Examples of convenience products are bread, milk, ice cream and chips. Many of these products are bought on the spur of the moment, for example sweets, magazines and chewing gum, which you often find at the checkout till of supermarkets or cafés. Consumers know all they need to know about convenience products and not much effort is put into the purchases. Consumers will not hesitate to select a different brand if their preferred brand is not available at a convenient location.

(b) Shopping products

A shopping product is something a customer will put some effort into before he or she buys it. Mainly because customers do not have enough information on the product, they compare prices where brand preference is not so strong. Customers tend to shop around before buying the product. They compare all the alternatives in terms of price, quality, design and the like. Examples of shopping products are things like a fridge, lounge suite, stove and shoes. The small business that offers these types of products will have to know what things are important to their customers and use these to differentiate their offering from that of competitors. The number of outlets is limited, and they are normally located close to competitors because customers tend to compare prices and quality, among others.

(c) Speciality products

In the case of speciality products the customer usually has a good knowledge of the product and has a strong brand preference. He or she is prepared to go far to buy the product and will make a special effort to obtain the product. Examples of speciality products are exclusive leather handbags and shoes, watches such as Rolex, TAG, brand name apparel, and coffee machines. These products are usually available only at selected outlets. It might be that only one outlet offers the product in a specific area, which will give the customer a sense of exclusivity. This in itself is a differentiating factor. An important aspect of this type of consumer product is that it requires the customer to know what makes the product or the place selling the product so 'special'.

Consumer products are generally bought by individuals or households for their own personal use.

6.3.5 Industrial products

Industrial or business products are bought by a business for use in making other products or providing other services. The following are examples of different types of industrial products.

(a) Capital equipment

Capital equipment can be defined as equipment/machinery used in the process of producing other products or services. Examples of this type of equipment are office equipment, sewing machines and agricultural machines. These products tend to be expensive and last a long time. They usually require fairly high levels of technical knowledge and servicing/maintenance that extend past the time of purchase of the product.

(b) Materials and components

Materials and components are products used to make or deliver the final product. They might be raw materials (eg wood for paper milling) or processed materials (eg switches for use in assembling reading lamps). Materials – whether raw or processed – usually become part of the product (in other words, they change their form). Components also become part of the product but they do not change their form. Examples of components are spark plugs, buttons, and nuts and bolts. These products are usually bought on a contract basis and require some negotiation and assurances of stock and quality.

(c) Operating supplies

Operating supplies are products that are used by a business but not in the manufacturing of the products themselves. Examples of operating supplies are petrol or diesel, cleaning materials, pens and notepads. They are relatively inexpensive, have a fairly short lifespan, and are bought without much effort. This type of product must be readily available to those who want it and must be competitively priced.

(d) Industrial services

Industrial services are those services used by a business to support the production process but are not actually part of the production process itself. Examples are training, cleaning services, research and auditing, and food and catering services. The important thing about this type of service is that your customers need to be made aware of how the service you offer can help them to perform their tasks better and reach their objectives.

Industrial products are bought by a business for use in making other products or services. The above discussion gives an overview of the types of products. It is the small businessperson's responsibility to decide on the offering to the market, ie what the product–service mix should be.

6.4 THE PRODUCT–SERVICE MIX

There are no set rules as to what the product–service mix should be. This mix can be only one item that the entrepreneur offers, or it may be a range of similar products or a limited range of diverse products and/or services. These products and services may all have some sort of common bond such as fishing and camping gear or there may be no or a limited bond, such as offering camping gear as well as selling golf clubs. You, as an entrepreneur, will have to decide exactly what it is that you will offer your customers.

6.4.1 The product mix

An organisation with a variety of product lines has a product mix. A product mix consists of all the product lines and product items that you offer. Let us look in more detail at these terms (Cant et al, 2013:210).

Product line

A product line is a group of products within the product mix that contains similar product items. For example, in the case of a clothing store the product lines might include babygrows, sleepwear, socks and shoes, clothing for premature babies, toys, gifts and accessories.

Product item

A product item is a specific item within a product line. For example, in the evening gown line for a women's clothing store each individual dress has a specific style and brand name. Each of these individual dresses is a product item.

You should be able to see that all decisions that the small business entrepreneur makes about products will always relate to and affect the product items, product lines and product mix.

- The more product lines that your business has, the broader your product mix
- The more product items that you have within a product line, the deeper your product line.

The product mix is the total range of products that your business makes or sells. As the small business usually (or often) has limited funds, care must be taken to 'not be everything to everybody'. This means that it may be wise to focus on a limited number of product lines and a limited number of items per product line. This will reduce your investment in inventory as well as other costs such as storage fees, insurance and the threat of obsolescence.

6.4.2 The service mix

Businesses can offer products and services, ranging from a pure tangible product to a pure intangible service product.

It is possible to classify services in terms of the service component of the product. Some businesses offer only a pure service product (eg attorneys) and others sell only a tangible product (eg butchery). There are many small businesses, however, that offer a combination of products and services (eg a garden landscaping company that offers both the landscaping and designing service as well as the plants and accessories it uses).

Below are four possible categories where service levels differ.

(a) Pure tangible product

In the case of a pure tangible product, the business has a minor or no supporting service component. Examples of businesses with a pure tangible product are grocery stores, direct mail businesses and party decoration stores.

(b) Tangible products with supporting services

In the case of a product with supporting services, it is not only the product being sold but also the warranties, the after-sales service, installation and money-back guarantee. This whole package makes the product valuable to the customer. Many of these products are complex and need the help of good salespeople to sell them. Examples of these products are office equipment, expensive clothing, computer equipment, stereo equipment and home appliances. The supporting services often take the form of after-sales services such as repair and alterations. The combination of the product and the supporting services will help customers to decide whether to deal with the company or its competitor!

(c) Service with supporting products

This type of product/service package is also known as a hybrid product. Here the product will not be purchased without the accompanying service, for example buying a new car with a service plan. The product will not be purchased without the assistance of the manufacturer to ensure that it is correctly used and maintained.

(d) Pure service

In the case of a pure service, hardly any supporting products are needed. Examples are hairdressers and barbers and beauty therapists, who provide only a service.

A product–service mix is the sum of all the products and services offered by a business. Based on the needs and buying patterns of the target market it is important that the entrepreneur makes the correct decision regarding the product–service mix.

6.4.3 Factors affecting the optimal product mix

The entrepreneur should be aware of the factors that have an impact on their product mix as these can have a definitive influence on the success of the product mix. These factors include:

(a) The overall business objectives

Often the objectives set in terms of profits and market share will affect how broad the product mix is. If the business wants to be seen as the market and product leader in imported wines, for example, this will imply that they will need a broad and deep product mix.

(b) Changes in the marketplace

The world economy has been in a state of flux and even chaos over the past decade and it is expected to continue on this rollercoaster ride, especially in light of the trade war between the United States and China that began in 2019. Issues such as these and many others influence all businesses and their offerings. The effects of this turmoil in the business environment have been widescale unemployment and rampant inflation in some cases, which also affect what people spend their money on. This may lead to consumers looking for cheaper, lower-quality products or even different types of products. You must be aware of the changing needs of your customers in order to know what changes you may need to make to your product mix. For example, many companies who used to sell only the top brands of clothes, electronic equipment, and so forth, have added cheaper, lesser-known brands to their range in order to cater for the new tastes and circumstances of their customer base. Similarly, retailers who traditionally did not carry certain products will start offering these products due to the changing needs and buying patterns of customers. Think of Woolworths over the past few years. Traditionally, Woolworths carried only their own brands but due to market forces started adding well-known brands such as Kellogg's, Mrs Ball's Chutney and Coca-Cola to their range of products.

(c) Competitors' actions

You may decide to make your product offering different from that of your competitors. You may also offer products for which the competition is not so strong. Some furniture companies, for example, have added free delivery to their product offering, and a clothing store might include free alterations. In this way customers perceive them as offering more value.

(d) Production considerations

You may be able to make more efficient use of your production facilities by adjusting your product mix, especially if you have finances and spare production resources to allow you to do so. For example, a manufacturer of leather briefcases might expand his or her product mix by making leather belts on the machinery during the times when demand for briefcases is low.

6.5 PRODUCT DECISIONS

The small business owner needs to make serious decisions regarding product mix. These decisions are sometimes complex but none the less must still be made. Some of these decisions include the following:

6.5.1 Product diversification

Product diversification is the process of expanding the product mix by adding new product items or product lines to the existing mix. These products may or may not be related to the existing range. For example, a textile designer who designs fabric might diversify into upholstery and curtain making.

6.5.2 Product specialisation

Product specialisation is the process of eliminating some product items or product lines from the product mix. For example, there are pool shops which specialise only in the offering of pool and spa products and services. In this way the expectation of a customer is that when visiting such a store his or her specific need regarding their pool or spa will be addressed. You also get stores that may specialise in only one product such as balloons. A wide and deep range is offered in such a store.

6.5.3 Product simplification

Product simplification is the process of limiting the shape, sizes or appearance of certain products. For example, a manufacturer of umbrellas may decide to make only three sizes, five colours and four styles of umbrellas. This is usually done to reduce costs and to concentrate on the fast-moving items.

6.5.4 Product differentiation

Product differentiation is the process of persuading your customers that your product, which is essentially the same product as your competitor's, is unique. For example, marketers of oven cleaners or surface cleaners may decide to differentiate their product from that of competitors by using a slightly larger holder with the words '33% more for the same price'. Similarly, a plumber could differentiate his service by stating that the call-out fee includes the first hour of labour. Thus differentiation makes it difficult for the customer to compare offerings as they are not directly comparable.

6.5.5 Product obsolescence

Product obsolescence is the process of developing new products to last a specific time – physically or psychologically. Physical obsolescence means that the product will wear out, for example a briefcase designed to last for five years. Psychological obsolescence means that the product does not actually wear out but a new model or style makes it old or outdated. For example, when a new version of a cell phone is released, the outdated technology is still useful but the cell phone is perceived as being outdated. The manufacturer does this to gain repeat sales.

6.6 BRANDING AND TRADEMARKS

Branding and trademarks are used to identify products in the marketplace. According to Cant et al (2013:213), a brand is a 'name, term, design, symbol or any other feature that identifies your product as different from those of the competitors'.

A brand is a name, sign, symbol, design or combination of these which identifies a product or service.

Why are brands so important and why do companies like to 'build their brand'? Brands are used to differentiate the products or services of a business from those of its competitors. When we talk about Mercedes Benz we tend to have a specific image of the company and what it stands for, while the image for BMW will conjure up a different impression. In other words, you use branding to identify your product or services for your customer. Second, when you build a good reputation for a brand, it makes it easier for you to introduce a new product or service to the market by using the same name. This is called brand extension.

Brand extension is using an existing brand name to help with the introduction of new products.

A trademark is a brand or part of a brand that has been granted legal protection – it protects the seller's exclusive rights to use the brand. The business that registered the trademark gets exclusive use of that trademark and no competitor is legally allowed to use it. Examples of trademarks are KFC, OMO, Super Sun, and Kaizer Chiefs. There are legal implications for the small business entrepreneur registering a trademark, but if they want to build their brand and make sure no one else grabs it, it needs to be protected and that means that it is imperative that it be registered.

A trademark is a brand that has been granted legal protection.

6.6.1 Types of brands

There are many types of brands that the small business entrepreneur can decide to use. First, there is a choice between a manufacturer (national) brand and a private brand.

Manufacturer (national) brand

A manufacturer brand is owned and used by a manufacturer of a product and is usually sold nationally (in other words, across South Africa, in different kinds of outlets). Examples of manufacturer brands are BMW, OMO and Coca-Cola.

Private brand

In the case of a private brand, products are sold under a brand name created by a retailer or a wholesaler. Many South African supermarket chains offer popular products in their own private brands (for example, PnP Housebrands such as milk, sugar and washing powder). Private brands are generally not promoted to the extent that national brands are and are therefore not as widely recognisable.

Second, there is a choice between a family, individual or company name within a brand.

Family brand

For the family brand, the seller uses the same brand on an entire line or mix of product items. For example, Kelvinator sells all its products, such as washing machines, stoves, fridges and microwave ovens under the Kelvinator name.

Individual brand

For the individual brand, the product is known by its own name instead of the name of the company making the product. For example, Procter & Gamble sells multiple brands, like Dove and Pampers.

Company name with a brand

Some manufacturers choose to use their company name together with an individual product brand name. The individual name differentiates the product from others, while the company name adds a firm's reputation to the product, for example Cadbury Dairy Milk and Cadbury Flake.

6.6.2 Importance of brands

Brands are important for both customers and manufacturers. Manufacturers' brands provide the following advantages:

- Brands are the central point around which the advertising and merchandising of the product revolve, as you can make customers aware of the brand and also get them to recognise it.
- They create loyalty. Manufacturers should aim to build a brand to such an extent where brand loyalty and trust of the brand is more important than price sensitivity. Price premiums can be charged for a strong brand, which will prevent frequent brand switching.
- They create a differential advantage. Strong branding can help a manufacturer to compete across the whole market and creates a competitive advantage.
- They create price premiums. An established brand can demand higher prices.
- They protect the marketer from other sellers substituting similar products for their product.
- They allow the marketer to expand or diversify the product mix.

For customers, brands provide the following advantages:

- They identify and locate the product more easily at the point of sale.
- They imply a reliable level of quality since all products with the same brand name should have the same quality level.
- They offer protection to customers, because they usually identify the manufacturer of the brand.
- They can serve as a warning to customers if the product has previously not met their expectations!
- They create interest and character for the product image. A brand personality makes it easier for customers to form attitudes and feelings about the product.

6.6.3 Guidelines for selecting a brand name

There are a few general guidelines that the small business entrepreneur should keep in mind when selecting a brand name.

- The name must be easy for the target market to pronounce and remember.
- Try to select a name that is suggestive of the major benefits of the product.
- It must ideally be a name which can be legally protected.
- Try to select a name that can be used on several product lines.
- The name should be original.
- Choose a name that can be associated with quality.

6.7 PACKAGING

The importance and value of packaging must not be underestimated, so once a brand name has been decided on, the packaging needs serious attention. Traditionally, the main function of packaging was to protect the product, but this role has changed over the years. Packaging is now a marketing tool and in many cases customers buy the package and not the product.

Packaging is extremely important, as many products rely only on their packaging (size, shape, colour, etc) to attract attention on the shelf. In the case of many products, you think of the packaging more than the product itself. When seeing a box of washing detergent on the shelf the focus is on the holder and not the liquid inside: the appearance of the holder may influence your decision to buy the product.

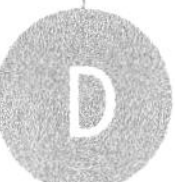

Packaging is the design and production of the container of the product item so that it can be protected, stored, handled, transported, identified and marketed successfully.

Enclosure and protection

- Protects the product, facilitates storage and handling of product.

Reusability

- Packaging can be reused for other purposes.

Communication

- Details about product and product images is communicated through the packaging's covering.

Market segmentation

- Product packaging is designed to suit market segment, for examples baby bottles that do not shatter when they fall.

Distribution

- Packaging facilitates dispatching of product and storage in warehouses or storage areas.

Product development

- Packaging can be considered as a part of the product development.

Differentiation

- Allows the product to be different from that of the competitors.

Figure 6.1: The roles of packaging

6.7.1 Types of packaging

The small business entrepreneur must decide what type of packaging to use for his or her products. Several choices are available.

(a) Family packaging

In the case of family packaging, all the products in the product mix have more or less the same packaging, for example ranges of shower gel/soap and body lotion.

(b) Special packaging

This type of packaging is used to give a product an exclusive image. Limited edition perfumes use unique bottles and they are especially popular as gifts. Speciality packaging can be successfully used to stimulate demand for a product.

(c) Individual packaging

In the case of individual packaging, each product gets its own special design. This helps to give the product an air of exclusivity. For example, a winemaker may choose a separate bottle and label design for each of his or her wine products.

(d) Reusable packaging

In the case of reusable packaging, the packaging is deliberately designed to be used for another purpose once the contents have been used up. For example, an ice cream manufacturer may package its ice cream in reusable plastic containers with lids that can be sealed.

(e) Multiple packaging

Multiple packaging is the practice of placing several units of a product (chocolate bars, soups, eggs, etc) in one **container** when offering them for sale in order to increase total sales. For example, a retail egg supplier may package six eggs in a carton. Multiple packaging can also help the small businessperson to introduce a new product or it can be used to give customers a special deal if they buy in quantity.

(f) Kaleidoscopic packaging

This type of packaging is done when certain elements in the packaging are changed regularly (for example, Rugby World Cup players on soft drink tins). The intention is to create a demand for the product by creating a demand for the packaging.

6.8 WARRANTIES

A warranty offers peace of mind to the customer. It is the business's promise to the customer that if he or she buys the product, it will meet the need that he or she is trying to satisfy. If this promise is then not met, the customer can use the 'warranty' to either replace the product or get his or her money back. A warranty can be written or verbal, or may be implied.

When will you use a written warranty? Some businesspeople think a written warranty is not always needed and that it may confuse customers or make them suspicious that the product is not as good as it seems! However, warranties are important for certain types of products:

- For innovative products a warranty will reduce the risk of buying a totally new product.
- For a relatively expensive product a warranty will reduce the economic risk of the product not performing.
- For a product that is complex to repair, a warranty will serve to assure the customer that he or she will not be left with a product that cannot be fixed.
- For a product positioned as being of high quality a warranty will serve to underline the impression of quality, the warranty being part of the total product that the customer buys.

In deciding whether to have a warranty, or what the extent of the warranty should be, the small businessperson needs to consider the following factors:

- the costs of offering the warranty
- the actual ability to provide the service that is guaranteed
- the competitors' warranties
- the expectations of the target market.

Care needs to be taken because when warranties are expressly stated there are legal implications. A warranty is a promise that a product will do certain things or meet certain standards.

6.9 CASE STUDY: CLOVER DANAO – A NEW APPROACH

Since Clover Danao's launch in September 2004 into the diverse South African consumer market, Danao has experience strong return on investment in terms of volumes, achieving sales of over 700 tons in the best months.

However, after extensive research of Clover Danone, the concept had shown its limitations. Therefore, a new strategy and marketing mix was developed for Danao:

- **Product:** Danao fruit juice and yoghurt blend in three flavours: orange, pineapple/peach and apricot/tropical fruit.
- **Packaging layout:** A carton pack on which the newest Spanish layout had been adapted to suit the pack, featuring strong use of the 'smiling rising sun' to communicate health and happiness, and to emphasise the morning as the ideal time to consume Daone.

- **Target market:** The whole family, but the core market would be women and mothers aged between 25 and 49 years, Living Standards Measure (LSM) 7–10.

Various companies and brands have had huge success internationally with dairy–fruit mix products whose position is based on the inherent goodness (functionality) of milk (dairy) and juice. The opportunity therefore existed to relaunch a 'new' dairy–fruit mix that would exploit the above-mentioned positioning, using the strength of the Clover mother brand to lend the product credibility and a sense of natural goodness and quality.

6.9.1 Selecting the target market

The Danao brand was ideal for the above-mentioned segment as it was already positioned as a healthy product. This new product would appeal to a new segment of the market to create new usage occasions and moments of consumption. Therefore, Danao's new marketing mix and target markets consist of the following:

- **Demographics:** LSM 7–10, aged 25–34, skewed towards urban black families with children.
- **Consumer profile specifics:** Health-conscious adults, family oriented, mums.
- **Unique selling point:** The goodness of dairy and fruit juice in one product.
- **Brand name:** Clover Danao Smooth: 'Double the Happiness'.
- **Product description:** A new blend of fruit juice and dairy (with yoghurt power) fortified with vitamins to match the current product.
- **Product performance:** Healthy, natural flavours and colours.
- **Comparable products:** Jog-juice, Yogi Sip and Tropika.

6.9.2 Product development

For the relaunch of Danao Smooth, product developers established that the key components of any 'healthy' product are the vitamin and/or mineral content, reduced sugar, and natural ingredients. The new dairy–fruit mix could be consumed at any time of the day to fill that hungry spot and provide an energy boost from a healthy natural product. Hence it was proposed to relaunch the Danao dairy–fruit mix, combining the inherent goodness of juice and milk (dairy). The reason Clover had to change the yoghurt content to milk was simply because of the agreement that it had with Danone, not to produce fermented/yoghurt products.

Clover Danao Smooth would therefore contain real fruit juice and dairy and would satisfy the following needs:

- nutritional
- appeal to the whole family

- value for money
- ideal to be consumed with meals
- pleasant fruity and tart taste
- smooth texture.

6.9.3 Branding and packaging

Management understands that the key to a successful product is developing a strong, visible brand name and appropriate packaging. Therefore, Clover did extensive research before changing the packaging and ingredients of the Danao product. In terms of consumer research, the new bottle design received a menu score of 9.12 out of 10. Consumers liked the happy, smiling fruit faces that appealed to kids and adults; they also liked the juice and dairy-pour shot and the real fruit pictures. The new formulation was preferred among consumers in terms of three out of the five flavours and there was no significant indication that the old formulation was preferred.

The new Danao Smooth was launched in September 2012 and the new packaging and formulation, ingredients and processes (using existing machines) meant that Danao would be even more profitable.

Answer the following questions:

1. What was the basic need that Clover Danao Smooth product met for its target customers?
2. What factors affected the choice of packaging for Clover Danao Smooth?
3. Suggest a possible promotional strategy that Clover Danao Smooth can employ at Pick n Pay retail outlets.

6.10 SUMMARY

It is important to have a thorough understanding of product decisions and be able to apply the elements that encompass them, as it will ensure that an organisation's offerings will meet the needs and wants of the market. This chapter focused on defining what a product is, the product mix and how to select the right combination as well as the different product strategies. Branding, a key product decision, was then discussed, followed by the function of product packaging and design. Finally, the importance and implications of warranties were explained.

Self-evaluation questions

1. Identify what type of product is involved in each of the following:

Example	Type of product
Providing dental services for families	
Demonstrating and selling recliner chairs	
Selling baby clothes online	
Designing a building for office use	
Offering French speaking classes	
Providing a home meal delivery service	
Manufacturing custom-made shoes	

2. Match the following examples with the appropriate category of the product–service mix.

Example	Product–service mix
Hair salon services	
Electrical contractor services	
Dietician at health clinic	
Interior designer	
Massage parlour	
Car clinic repair shop	

3. How will a small businessperson's objectives for market share and profit affect his or her product mix?
4. Why is it important for a small businessperson to be aware of the changing needs of customers?
5. Explain the difference between a brand, a brand extension and a trademark by completing the following:
   a. Explain what a private brand is. Give an example.
   b. When would you use an individual brand name for a product?
6. Imagine you have decided to open a butchery offering special made-to-order cuts of meat and other products. Think of examples of ways you can use each of the different types of packaging you learnt about in this chapter.

REFERENCES AND FURTHER READING

Cant, M.C., Van Heerden, C.H. & Ngambi, H.C. 2013. *Marketing Management: A South African Perspective*. (2nd edition). Cape Town: Juta Publishers.

Chapter 7

Price decisions

7.1 LEARNING OUTCOMES

After you have studied this chapter, you should be able to:

- Explain what is meant by price
- identify and discuss the factors affecting price
- explain the objectives of pricing
- describe the three basic pricing strategies
- discuss the various pricing adjustments.

7.2 INTRODUCTION

One of the most difficult tasks of a businessperson is to decide how to price a product or service. The reason for this is that it is not simply a matter of determining the cost, adding a mark up and arriving at your selling price. There are a number of issues to consider which include own supplier costs, transport, additional services such as delivery, installation, competitors prices and rental cost. It is clear that many factors impact on the decision of to what to charge and one element can mean the difference between success and failure. The effect of factors such as consumer demand, suppliers, government regulations, competitor prices, cost of capital and location of the business will influence the final price of a product or service. Pricing affects the chances of long-term success for a small business, because of its implications for profit. The significance of pricing lies in the fact that price is the only element in the marketing mix that brings in revenue, while the other three elements (product, promotion, distribution) are costs.

In a simple way, price can be defined as that which the consumer is prepared to pay for a product or service. This amount is in direct relation to the perceived value that the product or service has for the customer.

- Price plays two major roles: firstly it influences how much of a product customers purchase; secondly, it influences whether selling the product will be profitable.

Price is usually stated in monetary terms but can also be in the form of an exchange of goods or services – that is bartering. In such an instance the entrepreneur offers to pay for a product or service with some of his or her own products or services instead of money. For example, a small building contractor may get his or her bookkeeper to do his or her books in exchange for some improvements to the bookkeeper's home.

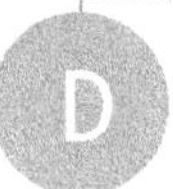

Bartering is the exchange of goods or services for other goods or services.

Table 7.1 lists the many different forms of price.

Table 7.1: Different forms of price

Term	What is given in return
price	product or service
tuition fee	education
rent	place to live
interest	use of money
fee	professional services
fare	transport
toll	use of roads
rate	hotel rooms
dues	membership
commission	salesperson's services
salary	work (monthly)
wage	work (hourly)
bribe	illegal actions

7.3 FACTORS AFFECTING PRICE

As stated previously the establishing of a price necessitates that a number of factors are considered. The primary task of a price is to cover costs and thereafter to make a contribution to profit.

Let us look at some of the factors that influence price:

- costs, which include the cost of the goods purchased as well as overheads such as salaries, rent and insurance
- prices charged by competitors
- type of product or service, ie its scarcity and complexity
- image that you want to attach to the product or business such as a discounter, or high-end supplier
- supply and demand
- profit expectations
- environmental factors such as politics, climate, laws.

7.3.1 Costs

The cost of raw materials is often beyond your control, yet it is a factor that affects all businesses. If your costs are increasing you have several options:

- pass increases on to customers
- pass some of the increases on and absorb others
- stop selling the product.

For example, when the petrol price goes up, transport costs go up which are then usually passed on to the consumers.

What happens when costs decline? Here you have two choices:

- reduce your selling price and keep profits the same
- keep your price the same and make higher profits.

For example, when sugar prices drop, a chocolate maker can choose to increase the size of his or her chocolates and earn the same profit, or leave the price as is and earn more profit.

7.3.2 Competition

In many instances the entrepreneur only looks at his or her own cost structure, establishes the price and markets the product without considering what competitors charge. This can be the death knell for the business as customer generally will compare prices and unless the product or service can be effectively differentiated customers will buy competitors' products. Therefore in order to survive, the prices of competitors need to be taken into consideration. If your prices are too high, you may price yourself out of the market. If your prices are too low, your product may be regarded with suspicion.

The actions of competitors also have a great influence on the price you set. You need to consider the reactions of competitors to your pricing decisions. This is not an easy exercise but you must monitor both your competitors' price levels and their reactions to your pricing moves. For example, a competitor might respond to your actions by either cutting prices (price competition) or launching a new product (non-price competition).

You can also use competitors' prices as a guide to where you can set your prices.

How can you collect information on your competitors' prices? There are a number of possible methods that can be used:

- the sales force can obtain the information during visits
- checks in stores where your products are stocked
- customer surveys
- marketing research, such as focus group discussions
- buying competitors' products and estimating what their costs are
- calling competitors directly and asking for prices (like any customer can do).

However you decide to do it, competitive price checks must become a periodic aspect of your research activities.

7.3.3 The type of product or service

Price changes affect the sales of some products more than others. For example, if you open a bakery and the price of butter rises, it will probably affect your cake sales. If the price drops, the chances are that your cake sales will increase. If you have a grocery store, however, and the price of milk rises or drops, it will probably not have much effect on the amount of milk that you sell. To try to find out whether a price rise or fall will affect the sales of your product or service, answer the following questions:

- What volumes are purchased by customers?
- What are the reasons that they buy?
- Is the product or service a luxury or a necessity?

The customer profile can help you to get some of these answers.

7.3.4 Image

The image you decide on for your business is, to a large extent, affected by your price levels. If you want to have the image of a low-cost supplier, you will price low, keep expenses at a minimum and have a low-cost location. On the other hand, if you want to project an image of quality, you will price high, have good service support and a 'good' location.

7.3.5 Supply and demand

Two of the most important factors affecting your price are supply and demand.

Supply is the amount of a product or service that businesses provide at a given time and a given price.

Demand is the amount of a product or service customers are willing and able to buy at a given time at a given price.

When the demand for a product increases, the price of that product usually goes up. For example, let us assume you open up an exclusive clothing boutique which stocks locally produced leather handbags. When the handbags become fashionable internationally, the demand for them rises, and so your price for them will also probably rise because the supply is fairly limited.

A change in supply also affects price, however: when the supply of leather handbags from suppliers and producers increases, the price of handbags drops.

Always consider the effects of supply and demand on new products.

7.3.6 Profit expectations

The profit the small business expects to make will have an impact on the final price of a product. If the small businessperson wants to make at least 60% markup, this will affect the price as well as the demand for the product. The other factors mentioned previously will obviously play a role in the final price, but it may be that the small businessperson is the only supplier of the product, in which case he or she can charge a higher price.

7.3.7 Environmental factors

These factors generally refer to factors outside the control of the businessperson.

Weather conditions may lead, for example, to a decline in demand for swimwear, flip flops and light clothes if the winter is cold, resulting in prices having to be adjusted to generate sales. Similarly, a drought may lead to a farmer increasing prices as the demand for his product will outstrip the supply.

Other examples are government legislation, taxes and exchange rates. A good example of environmental factors can be seen in the changes to VAT that have taken place over time. The most recent increase to 15% in 2019 has led to some resistance in the market. It is important for a small business entrepreneur to be aware of these factors and their possible effects on the demand for the product. This awareness can be achieved through contacts with your bankers, by reading business magazines and newspapers and by asking your customers and suppliers.

Step 1 in setting prices: consider the factors affecting price

7.4 OBJECTIVES OF PRICING

The aim or ultimate objective of pricing is to ensure that the small business generates the sales needed to achieve its overall aims. This requires you to identify three broad areas related to objectives:

- increasing or maximising profits
- increasing market share
- increasing sales volume.

In trying to increase or maximise profits, the focus is on trying to make the most profit possible in the long term. This may be achieved by trying to obtain an average percentage of profit or trying to make the most profit you can on each sale. For example, a business may try to average 20% profit on every rand sold.

Some businesses focus on maintaining or increasing their market share. This means getting a bigger percentage of the business than your competitors. The idea is to strengthen your position relative to that of the competitors (getting a bigger slice of the pie). For example, the objective might be to increase market share from 8% to 12% over the next 12 months.

Other businesses set their prices so as to maintain or increase the sales volume that they have achieved. The idea here is to increase the overall sales figure.

In many instances a new start-up business will focus on survival over the initial period. Once the business is established the other types of objectives can become more viable. Survival is, in fact, the basic objective of any business.

There are seven major types of objectives when it comes to pricing and you can focus on one or more, and per category of product or service offered.

7.4.1 Survival

Some organisations focus on survival as one of their objectives simply because they want to stay in the game. These organisations will try to increase their sales by adjusting the price levels of their products in order to remain commensurate with the organisations' expenses. An example would be an organisation pricing below cost just to cover all expenses (fixed and variable) in order to stay in the market.

7.4.2 Profit

In trying to increase or maximise profits the focus is on trying to make the most profit possible in the long term. This might be achieved by trying to obtain an average percentage of profit or trying to make the most profit you can on each sale. For example, a business may try to average 25% profit on every rand sold. Some organisations aim for satisfactory profits or return on investment (ROI).

7.4.3 Sales and market share

Some businesses set their prices so as to maintain or increase the sales volume that they have achieved. The idea here is to increase the overall sales figure. An example of this objective would be to increase sales from R700 000 per annum to R950 000 per annum. Be careful, though. You can easily increase sales by decreasing your price, but you may not make any money doing so. Some businesses also focus on maintaining or increasing their market share. This means getting a bigger percentage of the business than your competitors. The idea is to strengthen your position relative to that of the competitors (getting a bigger slice of the pie). For example, the objective might be to increase your share of the market from 10% to 13%.

7.4.4 Competition

The objective here is to meet and keep in line with competitors' pricing. This emphasises the importance of understanding your competitors, what they are offering and at what prices. Organisations also need to focus on differentiation to attain a better competitive advantage and achieve success. For example, if Samsung decides on a price increase, an objective for LG would be to follow that increase in order to stay in line with its competitor (Samsung).

7.4.5 Product-quality leadership

It would be a profitable objective for organisations to implement themselves as product-quality leaders. If customers perceive an organisation as having higher quality products, then this gives an organisation the advantage of charging higher prices for their products or services. An example would be to compare Lexus with Mercedes Benz: most people believe Mercedes is a high-quality brand and that is why the company are able to price high.

7.4.6 Social responsibility

The aim here is to price products to the advantage of the community by making prices more affordable to them. It includes products that there is a great need for, for example the anti-retroviral drug to treat HIV. Many will not be able to afford this medication and that is why the firm who supplied this drug offered it to the South African government for free for a period of five years.

7.4.7 Non-profit and other public organisations

The objective of these organisations is simply not to make a profit, but rather to enhance and increase the value of the organisation. They rely on gifts, donations and financial support of others to cover their costs.

Step 2 in setting prices: decide what you are aiming to achieve

7.5 DECIDING ON YOUR BASIC PRICE LEVEL

Once you have analysed the factors affecting price and established what you want to achieve through pricing, you need to set the basic price level for your product or service.

In order to set a basic price, entrepreneurs need to consider at least the following options:

- cost-oriented pricing
- customer-oriented pricing
- pricing relative to competition.

7.5.1 Cost-oriented pricing

Many small businesses determine their basic price according to their costs. The idea is to set your price high enough to cover your costs and still make a profit. Before we look at using costs as a basis for prices, we need to understand certain types of costs (Cant et al, 2013:340).

Table 7.2: Fixed costs vs variable costs

Fixed costs	Variable costs
equipment costs	cost of materials
rentals	cost of components

Fixed costs are those costs that stay the same no matter how many products are produced. Examples of these are salaries and wages, equipment costs or rental. All of these are incurred and stay the same whether the business is going full steam ahead or not making anything.

Variable costs are those costs that increase proportionately with the amount of products produced. Examples of these are costs of materials and components. The more products you make, the more raw materials are used up.

Let us look at three of the cost-oriented methods for setting a basic price:

- cost–plus pricing
- rate of return pricing
- break-even analysis.

Cost–plus pricing

Many small businesspeople use this method. Here you determine the cost of the product and then add a set percentage to the cost for the profit margin. This method is popular and easy to use.

eg

Assume you are a manufacturer of garden shade nets. After some financial analysis, you find the following:

Variable cost	R60
Fixed cost	R15 000
Expected sales	5 000 shades

The unit cost for each shade is: unit cost = variable cost + (fixed cost ÷ expected sales)

$$= R60 + \frac{15\,000}{5\,000}$$

$$= R63$$

Assume you want a profit margin of 40% (also called the markup):

$$\text{Cost–plus price} = \frac{\text{unit cost}}{(1 - \text{profit margin})}$$

$$= \frac{63}{1 - 40/100} = \frac{63}{1 - 0.4} = \frac{63}{0.6} = 105$$

You will charge customers R105 for each shade and make a profit of R42 per unit (R105 – R63 = R42).

Using the cost–plus method, and using the information in the example above, calculate what the price will have to be to make a:

(i) 50% markup

(ii) 60% markup

(Answers: (i) R126; (ii) R157,50)

Rate of return pricing

This method is similar to the previous one but brings another aspect into the calculation: namely the cost of investing your money in the business. The idea is to set a price that gives you a certain rate of return on your total investment. This differs from the cost–plus method, which gives you a certain profit margin per item sold.

To use this method you need four figures:

- an estimate of the units you will sell
- what each unit costs: variable costs + $\frac{\text{fixed cost}}{\text{estimated unit sales}}$
- the total amount of money invested in making and selling the product
- the target rate of return you want on your money.

Assume you invested R30 000 to produce and sell garden umbrellas. You want to make 30% return on your money and you think you will be able to sell 5 000 garden umbrellas. The variable cost is R60 per unit and the fixed costs are R15 000. The price you will set to achieve this rate of return is:

target return price = unit cost + (target rate of return × total money invested ÷ estimated sales)

$$60 + \frac{15\,000}{5\,000} + \frac{(0{,}30 \times 30\,000)}{5\,000}$$

$= 63 + (0{,}30 \text{ x } 6)$

$= 63 + 1{,}80$

= R64,80

Using the information supplied in the example above, calculate what the price will have to be if you want a:

(i) 35% rate of return

(ii) 40% rate of return

(Answers: (i) R65,10; (ii) R65,40)

Break-even analysis

Break-even analysis is useful because it shows you how many units you will have to sell in order to cover your costs at a certain price. At the break-even point, the money brought in (price × unit sales) exactly equals the total costs to make that many units.

(Also see Chapter 15 for more information on break-even calculations.)

Anything sold over that amount at that price means that the business makes money. Any sales in units less than that amount at that price mean that your business is losing money!

Assume you make and market garden umbrellas. You want to price your garden umbrella at R70. Fixed costs are R15 000. Variable costs are R60 per unit.

$$\text{Break-even point in units} = \frac{\text{total fixed costs}}{\text{selling price} - \text{variable cost per unit}}$$

$$= \frac{R15\ 000}{R70 - R60}$$

$$= 1\ 500 \text{ units}$$

If your business sells 1 500 units at R70 each, it will cover all its costs. If it sells more than 1 500 units at R70 each, it will make a profit of R10 a unit.

Using the information supplied in the example above, calculate the break-even point for a price of:

(i) R80

(ii) R65

(Answers: (i) 750 units; (ii) 3 000 units)

All of the cost-oriented approaches to determining your product's basic price have one common flaw – they do not take into account that the price can affect the number of products that customers want.

7.5.2 Customer-oriented pricing

In this approach, pricing is not simply an issue of calculating a formula, but rather setting a price that is perceived by customers to be of value relative to what they get for the price.

Methods for customer-oriented pricing include :

- backward pricing
- prestige pricing
- odd-number pricing

- price lines
- skimming pricing
- penetration pricing
- bundle pricing.

Backward pricing

With this method you estimate the price that customers will be willing to pay for a product. You can find this out through market research, using surveys or focus groups. This process will also help you to determine what the cost of making the product and the cost of components should be, in order for you to be able to give the customers the product at the price they expect. Once you have this estimate, you work backwards to see at what price you will sell to your distributors, so that the price plus the distributors' margin equals the price customers expect to pay.

Prestige pricing

A business that follows this method uses price to try to show the quality or prestige of its product or service. You set a high price, assuming that customers think a high price means high quality. This method is often used when your target market is the high-income/high-status type of customer. For example, you may start a carpet cleaning business and price yourself high because your target market is the upper-income neighbourhood in your town.

Odd-number pricing

This refers to the method of using prices ending in odd numbers or less than a round figure (for example, R3,99 instead of R4,00). Why would you do this? Two possible reasons are:

- Customers may think that R3,99 is much lower than R4,00 because it seems closer to R3,00 than R4,00.
- Many small retail businesses use odd-number pricing to force sales people to ring up the sale on the cash register and give customers change.

Price lines

This method involves the use of only a few prices for each of your product lines. For example, you may use the price to indicate the levels of quality within your product line (for example economy line, value line, high-quality line). One advantage of this approach is that your customer may have more choice. For example, you may open a store selling paint and stock three lines: an economy paint priced at R39,99 for six litres, a medium-priced line at R59,99 for six litres and a high-quality/high-priced paint line at R79,99 for six litres.

Sometimes you may decide to price a line at a level that just covers costs in order to help the sales of other more profitable lines. Such a line is called a loss leader. The idea is to attract customers to the business with the loss leader, as they are likely to buy more expensive items as well. For example, a hardware store may price its Ryobi drills low as a loss leader, hoping at the same time to get sales of its regular-priced drills and related products.

Skimming pricing

When introducing a new product to a market, there are two different pricing options:

- the skimming approach
- the penetration approach.

When you follow the skimming approach, you price your product or service fairly high. The aim of the skimming approach is to maximise profits. You will follow this approach if:

- you do not have too many potential competitors
- customers do not know much about the product
- you do not need to recover your investment quickly.

Penetration pricing

A penetration pricing approach means that you price your product relatively low. The aim of penetration pricing is to penetrate or break into new markets, in other words, to gain market share. You will follow this approach if:

- you have many potential competitors
- customers do not easily accept high prices.

Most of the time, the actual price chosen is between the two levels (the high level of skimming pricing and the low level of penetration pricing).

Bundle pricing

In this approach you combine two or more products or services in a single price. For example, if you own a bottle store you might sell a bottle of red wine and a bottle of white wine at a set price for both. You might also sell a bottle of red wine with a wine glass and a copy of a wine guide for a set price. The idea is to provide the customer with a higher-value product at a better price than if he or she were to buy each of the items individually. Many businesses introduce new products through bundle pricing, and also use bundle pricing for special occasions such as Easter. For example, you may be a chocolate manufacturer and offer a carton of six chocolate eggs, a large chocolate Easter bunny and a woven basket for a better price than if a customer were to buy each item individually.

7.5.3 Pricing relative to competition

We have looked at using costs to determine your basic price. We have also looked at customer-oriented pricing.

Levels of pricing

Another approach to setting your basic price level is to establish the level compared with competing products and services. There are three options here:

i. **Pricing above the market.** Pricing above the market means pricing your product or service higher than similar products or services sold by competitors. You need to justify the higher price in the customer's mind through better quality, up-market image or better location.

ii. **Pricing below the market.** Pricing below the market means pricing below similar products or services offered by competitors in order to make up for the lower profit through higher sales volume. The idea is to sell more than your competitors do.

iii. **Pricing at the market.** Pricing at the market means pricing to match your competitors' prices. You will take this approach if you do not have a substantial competitive edge enabling you to price higher than competitors.

A further approach to setting your basic price level is to establish the level compared with competing products and services. There are five basic methods that can be used:

i. **Follow the leader pricing.** A company using this approach will follow any price changes made by the leaders within the industry.

ii. **Adaptive pricing.** This approach involves small companies that will react to price changes made by competitors who obtain a larger share of the market.

iii. **Opportunistic pricing.** The aim of this method is to price lower than the competitors or to avoid following price increases made by the competitors in order to attract and draw in customers.

iv. **Predatory pricing.** This approach involves setting extremely low prices in order to damage or hurt the organisation's competitors.

v. **Competitive bidding.** This is a process whereby the buyer will ask the seller to indicate a price at which a certain product should be sold.

Yet another approach for setting your basic price level is to establish the level compared with competing products and services. There are six basic methods that can be used:

i. **Going rate pricing (same level as the competitor).** If companies decide to use going rate pricing, they price products that match the competitors' prices. You will take this approach if you do not have a substantial competitive edge enabling you to price higher than competitors.

ii. **Above-market pricing.** Pricing above the market means pricing your product or service higher than similar products or services sold by competitors. You need to justify the higher price in the customer's mind through better quality, up-market image or better location.

iii. **Below-market pricing.** Pricing below the market means pricing below similar products or services offered by competitors in order to make up for the lower profit through higher sales volume. The idea is to sell more than your competitors do.

iv. **Customary pricing.** When using customary pricing, the prices of products or services must be based on tradition. This will result in all competitors' pricing being the same. An example would be products in a vending machine.

v. **Loss-leader pricing.** The aim of this method is to attract customers by pricing products lower than the competitor or even below cost.

vi. **Sealed-bid pricing.** This is when companies price products based on how they believe their competitors will price.

NB

The trick with the basic price level is to price the product or service at the level at which it will sell, not at the level at which you want it to sell.

Step 3 in setting price: establish the basic price level

7.5.4 Case study: KFC – Finger Lickin' Good

KFC – Finger Lickin' Good

KFC is seen to be affordable. However, in comparison to other fast food retailers of chicken such as Chicken Licken and Hungry Lion, KFC is often at a premium. In fact, KFC has always taken a hard line by never discounting or positioning on price, which is a tough stance to take in a category filled with price fighters.

In fact, many of KFC's competitors are all-out fighters and seasoned discounters. Think of Roman Pizza's blatant discount positioning, McDonald's small change campaigns and Steers 2 for 1 Wacky Wednesday specials.

Yet, KFC consumers are not concerned about price as confirmed by a TNS price elasticity study. In a survey of 1698 respondents, the KFC brand has the lowest absolute price elasticity of any brand for which TNS Research Surveys had calculated price elasticity in South Africa. This demonstrates that consumers are loyal to KFC despite pricing.

Any competitor thinking of competing against KFC will have to consider the above achievements carefully.

1. How does KFC price itself relative to the competition?
2. What factors have affected the pricing followed by KFC?
3. What pricing objective do you think KFC has adopted?

7.6 SUMMARY

Being able to determine the value of a product or service can be considered as the fine line between an organisation's success or failure and therefore, this chapter looked at factors that will affect the price that is charged for an organisation's products and services. Grasping the elements and objectives of pricing as well as being able to apply the three basic price strategies is essential in determining long-term success. Finally, price adjustments and the process of evaluating credit concluded the chapter.

Self-evaluation questions

1. Look at the examples below and identify the type of factor each represents:
   a. a drop in the value of the rand
   b. your product seen as being hip and trendy
   c. competitors entering the market with 'specials'
   d. focusing on an alternative market such as low to middle income.
2. Which customer-oriented method for setting a price is used in the following situations?
   a. You price a line so that costs are just covered, in the hope that customers will buy more profitable lines.
   b. You price a product so that customers think they are paying a much lower price for the product/service.
   c. You price a product so that customers think the high price means high quality.
   d. You price a product to give customers a product/service at a price they will be willing to pay.
   e. You price a product to offer customers a pen, pencil and notepad at a better price than that of each of the items individually.
   f. You price a product that the customers know little about.

REFERENCES AND FURTHER READING

Cant, M.C., Van Heerden, C.H. & Ngambi, H.C. 2013. *Marketing Management: A South African Perspective.* (2nd edition). Cape Town: Juta Publishers.

Chapter 8 Distribution: getting the product to the customer

8.1 LEARNING OUTCOMES

After you have studied this chapter, you should be able to:

- define what is meant by distribution
- identify the choices of distribution intensity
- distinguish between different types of middlemen
- describe the different types of distribution channels.

8.2 INTRODUCTION

What product do you think has made it the easiest for its customers to get the product when and where they want to get it? Some of you may think of a sweet product (like a Kit Kat), or even a beverage product (such as a Coca-Cola). One product that you may not have thought of is airtime – the cellular services providers have done a fantastic job of making that product available almost anywhere, from almost any outlet, whether in the city, in a rural area, from a retailer, online, your cell phone itself, or even from a hawker! The decisions made to get the product available to the customers are called distribution decisions.

Distribution focuses on the process of getting the product to the customer. It is not only about the physical outlet where customers can buy the product but, also the process of getting it to the outlet or to the customer. Furthermore, it focuses on the process of keeping these outlets supplied with stock in order to prevent out-of-stock situations. The fact is that at some point the small business will need a distribution strategy to ensure that its products arrive safely at the right place at the right time, thus helping to ensure maximum customer satisfaction. In starting a business today, many emerging business people use intermediaries to get their products to the customer, such as fulfilment specialists, who have physical stock but do not have ownership of the stock. These intermediaries help facilitate getting the product through to the final customer.

Distribution can be defined as the establishment of a system that gets your product to where the customer wants to buy it. In order to do this, a decision has to be taken on the distribution channel to be used.

The system that is used to get products and services from the producer to the final consumer is defined as a distribution channel (Cant & Van Heerden, 2017:294). This system consists of people and organisations.

A simple way of looking at a distribution channel is as a pipeline through which products flow from the producer to the customer. Within this pipeline are businesses that help in getting the product to the final customer; examples of such businesses are wholesalers and retailers. These businesses are termed middlemen or intermediaries.

A middleman or intermediary is a business that helps move the product or service from the producer to the customer through the distribution channel.

For example, a farmer sells his maize to the cooperative, which processes it and sells it to wholesalers who, in turn, package it into smaller packages and sell them to retailers who then sell them to the end-user. Customers will be able to purchase the maize in small quantities at various shops. The maize wholesaler (eg Ruto Mills) and the retailers (eg Pick n Pay) can then be termed middlemen or intermediaries in the distribution channel of the maize producer to the consumer.

Although we tend to always think about the distribution channel going from producer to final consumer, it can also work the other way – from final consumer to producer. This is called a reverse distribution channel (Cant & Van Heerden, 2017:316). An example of this type of distribution channel is when empty Coca-Cola bottles are returned – the empty bottles eventually end up at the bottler for Coca-Cola for reuse or for recycling. Many beer manufacturers will reimburse their customers for returning beer bottles (especially quart (750 ml) bottles) to the retailer when the customer wants to repurchase.

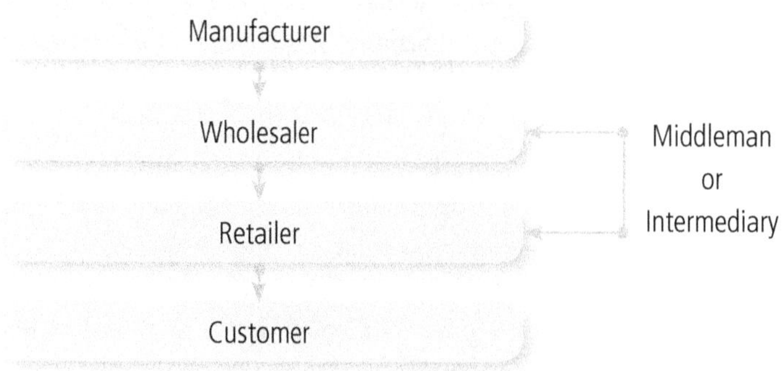

Figure 8.1: The basic stages of a distribution channel

8.3 CHOOSING THE INTENSITY OF DISTRIBUTION

The intensity of distribution is a very important decision for the small business and it revolves around the decision to decide how many outlets will carry or stock the product. This is called the intensity of distribution. This intensity will depend on:

- where the marketer is (location)
- the characteristics of the product
- the behaviour of the final consumers, and what they expect.

There are three options for the intensity of distribution:

8.3.1 Intensive distribution

With intensive distribution, you try to make your product available at all possible outlets. This means you will use all possible middlemen. Branding is important here because you need to ensure that the stock moves well. Examples of products that follow this route are milk, cigarettes and newspapers. An entrepreneur choosing to launch a new cola drink might consider this intensity, but it will imply the capacity to produce enough exists. A company like Coca-Cola wants its products available at every possible outlet and location, such as stores, street-corners through vendors, and even in office buildings through vending machines on each floor.

8.3.2 Selective distribution

With selective distribution, you select fewer outlets than you would with intensive distribution but take care in choosing which to use. Shopping products, such as furniture and clothes, are examples of products that are suited to this type of intensity. If an entrepreneur does not have that much capacity then this might be a good choice. For example, the new cola drink manufacturer may consider selling to a few retailers initially, such as Woolworths or even Liquor City.

8.3.3 Exclusive distribution

With exclusive distribution, you purposely limit the number of people who carry your product. Examples of this are jewellery products. Franchises also use exclusive distribution. For example, a chocolate manufacturer may decide to supply only sweet shops in upmarket shopping centres in big cities. The cola manufacturer may sign an exclusivity agreement with Woolworths, for example, or use only a high-end specialist retailer such as Norman Goodfellas to stock its product.

The choice of the intensity of distribution depends on the following product characteristics:

Price of the product

The more expensive the product, the more exclusive or selective (limited) the intensity. The lower the price, the greater the tendency for intensive distribution. Milk and newspapers can be bought on just about every street corner, while Rolex watches are found in one or two outlets in a town.

Technical complexity

The more complex the product, the more selective or exclusive the intensity should be. This is especially so if your product requires specialist training or knowledge. Think about aeroplanes and mining vehicles that are complex machinery and need demonstrations on how to operate them.

Selling requirements

If advice or sales assistance is needed, you should tend towards selective or exclusive distribution. If the product is suitable for self-service outlets, consider intensive distribution. Complicated statistical packages or other software normally need to be demonstrated and therefore will use exclusive or selective distribution. This is changing a bit, as the entrepreneur can use a direct online business model that provides support and information knowledge such as takealot.com or Amazon.

Service requirements

If there is a need for installing, maintaining or repairing the product, you should tend towards selective/exclusive distribution. (Source: Cant & Van Heerden, 2017:301-302)

Coca-Cola – Coke is an example of one of the products with very intense distribution. Think of the number of places in a normal day where you could purchase a Coke. You could buy one at the petrol station on the way to work. You could buy one at the street corner from a sidewalk vendor while waiting for the traffic light to change. You could buy one from a vending machine in the foyer of your workplace. You could buy one from a café or a restaurant at lunch. As you may notice, Coke is available almost anywhere.

Nike sport shoes – This is an example of a shopping product. The brand is available at most reputable sports shops, at most clothing stores and at many independent clothing retailers. It is also available at many of the markets frequented by street vendors – but you need to be careful that they are genuine and not counterfeit ones!

David Tlale designer dresses – David is a well-known South African fashion designer and his designs are available at only a few exclusive boutiques or at his own premises. This is an example of exclusive distribution.

Step 1 in distribution: decide on intensity

8.4 TYPES OF INTERMEDIARIES

It is important that the small businessperson is aware of the different types of intermediaries that exist. There are three types that can be identified:

- sales intermediaries
- wholesalers
- retailers.

What are the differences between them? Wholesalers and retailers are called resellers.

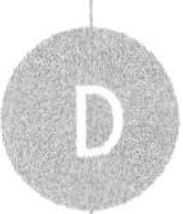

A reseller is an intermediary who actually owns the products he or she handles.

A sales intermediary brings producers and retailers into contact with one another, but does not actually own the product being handled. A sales intermediary's job is to be the link between the different people in the distribution channel.

8.4.1 Sales intermediaries

The two most common kinds of sales intermediaries are brokers and agents. A small business that has no salespeople usually uses agents to sell its products to wholesalers or retailers. Agents help a small business gain sales and usually charge a commission for their services. The agent usually gets a set percentage of the sales value as a fee for the service. For example, a manufacturer of women's dresses may use an agent to visit boutiques to sell his or her dresses to them. A broker usually just brings buyers and sellers together. The idea is to make negotiations possible between buyers and sellers. The person who asked for the service is the one who pays the broker. Insurance and real estate are two areas in which brokers are common. (Source: Cant & Van Heerden, 2017:295-296)

8.4.2 Wholesalers

A business that gets most of its sales income from selling to other businesses or organisations is termed a wholesaler. Makro, for example, is considered a wholesaler. This does not mean that it does not sell to private customers but that selling to resellers is the primary part of its business. A business that sells catering and cooking equipment and supplies, like cutlery and plates, to the catering and hospitality trade is an example of a wholesaler.

There are a number of different kinds of wholesalers:

- **Cash-and-carry wholesalers:** The cash-and-carry wholesaler is a business where a shopkeeper gets what he or she wants and pays cash for it. The shopkeeper has to transport his or her own goods.
- **Rack-jobber:** The rack-jobber is an intermediary who manages shelf space in retail stores. This kind of wholesaler usually specialises in certain areas (eg painting supplies) and ensures that the shelves in the shops are stocked with the product. The shopkeeper then gets a set margin on the products that are sold.
- **Truck-jobbers:** The truck-jobber is an intermediary who goes from shop to shop, delivering perishable products (products that do not last long), such as vegetables and fruit.
- **Mail order wholesalers:** The mail order wholesaler uses catalogues to inform customers of what is available and then sends out products that are ordered, usually on a cash-on-delivery (COD) basis. (Source: Kurtz, 2008:469–470) Many of these wholesalers now rely on their online and mobile marketing strategies rather than rely on mail order; Johnny's Liquor Hypermarket in Pretoria has used strong mobile marketing campaigns. Adendorff Machinery Mart still uses the postal system but also uses digital marketing to deliver its promotional specials to its customer base.

8.4.3 Retailers

A business that sells to the general public for private or home use is termed a retailer. There are many kinds of retailers:

- **General dealers:** General dealers have a very wide variety of products and are often found in rural areas.
- **Department stores:** Department stores are large establishments that have a fairly wide range of products in different departments, such as clothing, haberdashery, cosmetics, crockery and so on. Examples are Stuttafords and Edgars.
- **Speciality stores:** Speciality stores have only a few product lines but a great deal of variety in those lines. An example of these stores is a jewellery store.
- **Chain stores:** Chain stores are similar stores in various places that are controlled by one business. Examples of chain stores are Shoprite/Checkers and Pick n Pay.
- **Supermarkets:** Supermarkets are self-service stores offering a fairly wide variety of grocery and household products. Spar stores are a good example of supermarkets.
- **Hypermarkets:** Hypermarkets are large stores with a wide product range, low prices, sizable parking and a fairly large target market. Examples are the Pick n Pay Hypermarkets and Checkers Hyper.

- **Spaza shops:** Spaza shops are small shops in townships and informal areas that stock limited quantities of staples.
- **Internet retailers:** One of the newer developments in retailing is the explosion in retailers that are found on the Internet. These vary from retailers specialising in certain products like kitchen products (eg Yuppiechef) to those that offer a very broad range of products (such as takealot.com or Amazon).

Step 2 in distribution: decide on the types of intermediaries you will need

Deciding on the type of middleman the small businessperson wants is one thing, but getting them to actually stock the product may not be possible. Take for example a new manufacturer of a range of kitchen utensils. The small businessperson might have a beautiful range, but the outlets such as @home, Game and Woolworths may not be interested in stocking the product for whatever reason. The outlet that the businessperson wants is not always willing to stock the product and thus alternative options must be sourced.

1. What sort of intermediary (category) and specific type of intermediary would you need for the following situations?
   a. You own a real estate business and pay somebody to make negotiations possible between buyers and sellers.
   b. You own a hardware store and use the services of a paint supplier to keep your shelves stocked with painting supplies.
   c. You manufacture tracksuits and pay someone a commission to sell your range to wholesalers, retailers and the public.
   d. You are the owner of a café that also sells fruit and vegetables.
2. What three factors will influence your choice of the number of potential outlets that should distribute your product or service?

8.5 CHANNELS OF DISTRIBUTION

A distribution channel can be direct or indirect.

When one is talking about a direct channel it means that there is no middleman between the producer and the customer.

An indirect channel on the other hand is a distribution channel with one or more middlemen between the producer and the final customer.

A leather manufacturer who sells to customers from his or her factory is using a direct channel of distribution. If the manufacturer sells to leather goods stores, which then sell to customers, he or she is using an indirect channel. Of course, nothing stops the leather manufacturer from using both direct and indirect channels, and this is called a multi-channel distribution strategy. This would also apply to a manufacturer using retail outlets such as a leather store but also selling though the Internet. Verimark has its own retail outlets and digital site, but also markets its products through retailers such as Pick n Pay and Makro! The trend now is to follow a multichannel strategy as long as you can control the service delivery and the availability and fulfilment of orders through the channels.

Table 8.1: A multi-channel distribution strategy

Direct channel	Indirect channel
Leather manufacturer	Leather manufacturer
⇩	⇩
⇩	⇩
⇩	Leather goods stores
⇩	⇩
⇩	⇩
Customers	Customers

Let us look at possible channels for consumer and industrial products.

8.5.1 Marketing channels for consumer products

We have already said that consumer products are for use by individuals or families. Examples of this type of product are cakes and household appliances. What channels might be used by a small business producing consumer goods? Some of the possible options are shown and discussed below.

Table 8.2: Various distribution channels for consumer products

Consumer products: Various distribution channels				
Producer	Producer	Producer	Producer	Producer
⇩	⇩	⇩	⇩	⇩
⇩	⇩	⇩	Agent	Agent
⇩	⇩	Wholesaler	⇩	⇩

➠

↓	↓	↓	↓	Wholesaler
↓	Retailer	Retailer	Retailer	↓
↓	↓	↓	↓	Retailer
↓	↓	↓	↓	↓
Customer	Customer	Customer	Customer	Customer

Producer to customer

The producer to customer distribution channel is short because there is no middleman. The small business can use its own sales force, the Internet or mail catalogues. Examples of businesses that use such channels are Tupperware and the book and cosmetics and clothing clubs that sell through the mail. Most service businesses (for example, dry cleaners) use a direct channel such as this.

Producer to retailer to customer

There is a producer to retailer to customer distribution channel where the small business uses a retailer, such as a supermarket or spaza shop, to sell to customers. An example is where Nando's uses retailers such as Shoprite/Checkers to sell its sauces to the public.

Producer to wholesaler to retailer to customer

This kind of channel is used by many small businesses. For example, a manufacturer of paintbrushes might sell to a hardware wholesaler, who then sells to hardware stores all over the region.

Producer to agent to retailer to customer

This kind of distribution channel is commonly used by many medium to small businesses that cannot afford their own sales force and that rely on agents to sell for them. For example, a clothing manufacturer might hire an agent to sell their products to all the independent clothing stores. Likewise, a chemical manufacturer may use an agent to sell their cleaning products to both retailers and industrial buyers.

Producer to agent to wholesaler to retailer to customer

This kind of channel is often used when many small businesses sell to a large number of wholesalers around the country. For example, a hair product producer might use agents to sell to wholesalers, who then sell to retailers and hair salons.

8.5.2 Marketing channels for industrial products

Industrial products, which are used in the production of services or other products, generally follow four types of distribution channels.

Table 8.3: Common distribution channels for industrial products

Industrial products: Common distribution channels			
Producer	Producer	Producer	Producer
↓	↓	↓	↓
↓	↓	↓	Agent
↓	Agent	Industrial distributor	↓
↓	↓	↓	Industrial distributor
↓	↓	↓	↓
Industrial user	Industrial user	Industrial user	Industrial user

Producer to industrial user

Most industrial products are sold directly to the user. For example, a manufacturer of overalls might sell overalls direct to factories.

Producer to agent to industrial user

If a small business is not able to sell its own product it might use an agent to do it. Agents are also useful when you are introducing a new product or going into a new market because they can use their contacts and experience in the industry to get sales.

Producer to industrial distributor to industrial user

The industrial distributor acts like a wholesaler and usually handles products that are not highly priced, such as office equipment, office supplies and operating supplies. Industrial distributors usually carry sizable stock so as to be able to deliver promptly to customers.

Producer to agent to industrial distributor to industrial user

Here the small business entrepreneur who cannot afford his or her own sales force can use an agent to reach the important distributors of the product.

The question of whether or not to use a direct channel requires careful consideration. You have to consider many factors and weigh up which channel option will be best for your business. A number of the factors to consider are shown below.

Factors that may direct the business to use a direct distribution channel include:

- a product that needs a demonstration such as a software package for accountants
- a product that needs to be tested under supervision such as a new type of chemical in the medical field
- the need to go into long and complicated negotiations
- a product that needs specialised after-sales service

- not being able to convince existing channels to carry stock
- very high middlemen profit margins
- very concentrated industrial markets (with few buyers).

Factors which may justify a more indirect distribution channel:

- lack of financial resources to establish own channels
- a need to use resources elsewhere in a business
- lack of know-how in getting distribution
- not enough of a product mix to operate on your own
- a large number of potential buyers who are, however, widely scattered
- a lack of selling skills or selling knowledge.

These considerations are important and can be addressed through channel choice and/ or design of support and informational value through digital marketing sites for those businesses that haven't got their own salesforce.

Step 3 in distribution: decide which channel or channels you will use for your marketing distribution

What type of channel will the following use?

1. general dealer
2. bakery business
3. garden bulb dealer
4. insurance company
5. library
6. paintbrush company.

8.6 SUMMARY

Establishing a distribution strategy is vital for an organisation in order to be able to deliver products to geographically dispersed customers so that they can keep their outlets supplied with stock in order to prevent out-of-stock situations. This chapter has therefore focused on the distribution strategy by discussing distribution intensity, the different types of intermediaries, as well as the channels of distribution. In essence, this chapter allowed the reader to understand the basic principles of making strategic decisions in order to make the product available to the customer.

Self-evaluation questions

1. Explain each of the following terms that you have learnt:
   a. distribution
   b. retailer
   c. distribution channel
   d. wholesaler
   e. intermediary
   f. direct channel
   g. reseller
   h. indirect channel
   i. sales middleman.
2. Answer the following questions:
   a. With what is distribution concerned?
   b. What do middlemen do that is so important?
   c. For each of the different types of middlemen below list some examples:
      i. sales middlemen
      ii. wholesalers
      iii. retailers.
3. What is the difference between a direct and an indirect channel?
4. List the possible channels for marketing consumer and industrial products.
5. What are the factors affecting the selection of a distribution channel?

REFERENCES AND FURTHER READING

Cant, M.C. 2014. *Marketing: An introduction*. (2nd edition). Cape Town: Juta Publishers.

Cant, M.C. & Van Heerden, C.H. 2017. *Marketing Management: A South African Perspective*. (3rd edition). Cape Town: Juta Publishers.

Kurtz, D.L. 2008. *Principles of Contemporary Marketing*. International student edition. Thomson: South-Western.

Chapter 9 Marketing communication: communicating with your market

9.1 LEARNING OUTCOMES

After you have studied this chapter, you should be able to:

- explain the three main objectives of marketing communication
- define the various marketing communication mix elements
- identify the factors to consider when selecting a marketing communication mix
- discuss the steps in developing a marketing communication plan.

9.2 INTRODUCTION

It is no use having the best product or service and nobody is aware of it. Businesses need to make use of marketing communication to inform their market of the products and services they offer. In order to decide on the best combination of the marketing communication mix element it is, however, important that the small business knows who their market is and which media would be the best to reach them.

Promotion for an entrepreneurial business: Robyn Roberts Studio

Robyn Roberts Studio is a business that designs and manufactures fashion outfits for special occasions and specialises in bridal wear. It operates from a house in Cape Town and this location is in a residential neighbourhood and not in a retail area. For this reason, visibility and awareness of the business is a challenge because the business relies on referrals.

The business uses its website effectively to generate enquiries. Its Facebook page provides a method of keeping in touch with past and future clients, and by posting pictures of brides in their designer dresses they can generate awareness in their market. They also generate publicity through coverage of some of the weddings of their celebrity clients wearing their custom-design dresses. They are also active with the press and magazines in terms of the fashion editorial sections, and this has helped build awareness and created some leads to follow up. The Studio also participates in bridal expos and fashion shows because these activities bring them into contact with potential clients and provides access to them in a popular manner.

Source: Adapted from Van Heerden, 2013.

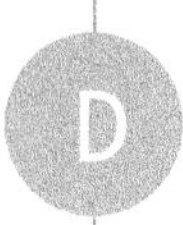

Marketing communication can be defined as a collection of activities and methods used by the business to communicate primarily with its customers but also with all other parties of importance including staff (Cant & Van Heerden, 2017).

When looking at this definition, current customers as well as potential future customers are included. These groups need to be informed of the company's products and services, as well as be made aware of the brand. Furthermore, employees who are generally in direct contact with these customers need to be aware of the products and services, as well as any specials that may be on offer.

From the discussion above we can summarise that there are three generally accepted communication objectives for marketing communication. These are:

- to inform the target customer or specific audiences about your product and services to generate awareness
- to persuade the customers or target audiences to take some specific action that will hopefully lead to sales for you
- to remind customers or target audiences about your products and services or their specific attributes.

Remember, however, that marketing communication is only one element in the marketing mix and that it is closely integrated with the other three elements. The maximum effect of the marketing mix is achieved only if all mix elements work together. This is highlighted in Figure 9.1, which shows that the marketing communication mix works together with the other elements of the marketing mix. The term generally used for this is integrated marketing communication (IMC), and reflects the attempt at alignment and synergy in designing how one communicates with one's markets and stakeholders.

Figure 9.1: The role of marketing communication in the marketing mix

Source: Adapted from Lamb et al., 2004:315; 2015:382.

The marketing communication mix consists of a number of methods that can be considered by the small business. There are eight main elements of the marketing communication mix which include advertising, sales promotion, publicity, personal selling, public relations, sponsorship, direct marketing and digital marketing (Cant & Van Heerden, 2017:364-365). These elements are briefly discussed below:

1. **Advertising:** Advertising is a paid form of non-personal communication about a product, service or idea directed at a large target audience. Examples of advertising media include radio, television, newspapers, magazines and the Internet. A business that manufactures and installs blinds could take out an advertisement in a home decoration magazine to advertise its services.

2. **Sales promotions:** Sales promotions are marketing activities designed to act as incentives and provide extra value to the customer. Such incentives include coupons, free samples, prizes, contests and sweepstakes. A business that produces artisanal cheeses could rent a stall at a market and give away small samples of its cheeses to taste to try to induce sales. There are three types of sales promotions. Consumer sales promotions are used to attract the consumer and get them to purchase. Examples of these include samples, contests, and price discounts. Trade promotions are aimed at your distribution channels to stock and promote the products to their customers. Some examples would be free-stock deals, trade shows, exhibitions, promotion giveaways such as a calendar, and special prizes such as a trip overseas. Sales-force promotions are aimed at your sales force to motivate them in their sales tasks, and could include competitions, bonuses and prizes.

3. **Publicity:** Publicity refers to the public information about a firm. It's a form of non-personal communication and is not directly paid for. In this way, organisations can achieve free and positive exposure for the organisation. A veterinary hospital could provide free care for injured owls and rehabilitate them. At the same time it can get coverage by communicating to drivers to be on the look-out for owls at night and also get coverage for its work in the press.

4. **Personal selling:** Personal selling involves interpersonal communications between the buyer and seller. The aim is to persuade the buyer to make a purchase. It involves direct contact with the customer either face to face or over the phone. A business advising companies on how to save on electrical costs will have to visit those companies and sell their services to the relevant departments.

5. **Public relations:** Public relations help an organisation to communicate better with its customers, stakeholders, employees, suppliers and the community in order to build good relationships with them. It is important that organisations create favourable attitudes and a positive image of themselves. A nutritionist could, for example, offer free nutrition seminars for schools and women's groups, and the ensuing improvements in relationships with his or her stakeholders could generate value for all.

6. **Sponsorship:** Sponsorship means that the organisation supports an event, activity or another organisation either financially or through the provision of the organisation's products and services. A retail business could sponsor a fund-raising event to benefit the Nelson Mandela Children's Fund, or even donate a percentage of its profits to the fund.

7. **Direct marketing:** Direct marketing involves communicating directly with the customer to encourage a response (such as an order, a visit to a store or website). Some of the methods include direct mail, telemarketing, direct-response advertising and online computer shopping services. A direct mail campaign by an educational toy manufacturer to new mothers emphasising the importance of stimulation in the development of their children is an example of this method.

8. **Digital marketing:** Digital marketing involves reaching the consumer by using new technology that will enable the organisation to reach the customer with greater impact and increasing frequency. It includes the Internet, cellular technology, inter- active TV, multimedia and touch-screen kiosks. Many businesses utilise tools like blogs, Facebook, Twitter and LinkedIn to supplement their web presence in promoting the business. Nomu, a well-known spices and condiments company based in Cape Town has a presence in many retail outlets but has a strong blogging and email- based campaign where recipes using its products are sent to its website subscribers (visit them at www.nomu.co.za).

9.3 FACTORS TO CONSIDER IN DECIDING ON A MARKETING COMMUNICATION MIX

The marketing communication mix to be used needs to take a number of factors into consideration. Some of the more important ones are listed below (Lamb et al, 2015:401-404):

9.3.1 Location of customers

The location of customers is crucial in the selection of media to be used. The more dispersed customers are, the less effective some methods of communication become. If customers are widely scattered over a broad geographical area, advertising may be the best option. If not, then a choice such as personal selling may be more appropriate. For example, a small business selling cakes will have to use marketing communication to let all its possible customers know what products and services it offers. However, if its customers are spread out all over the region, personal selling may be too expensive and time-consuming and the small business may have to rely on advertising in regional newspapers to communicate with customers, use social media like Facebook or Twitter, or use other agents such as *tuisnywerheid* (home industry) stores to sell on its behalf.

9.3.2 Characteristics of the target market

The most important decision that a small business marketer can make is to identify the target market for the business. A target market is the specific group of customers at whom the business aims its goods or services. The better you understand and define your target customer, the better chance you will have of success. Once identified, this target customer (or target market) will influence all aspects of the business. This includes the product, the look of the business, the pricing – everything. If it does not know the target market, a small business may try to reach everyone and end up appealing to no- one. Groups of people most likely to buy its products and the common characteristics among them should be identified. The idea is to build a customer profile of the people who have a common need and then try to satisfy that need. Some of the characteristics that are important include shopping patterns, transport used, disposable income, age, loyalty status, etc.

9.3.3 Nature of the product

Certain products, by their nature, suggest certain methods of marketing rather than others. For example, a mass-produced, low-tech, low-priced product will be more suited to advertising. A business selling low-priced radios, DVDs and consumables such as Johnny's Audio store will probably advertise in a local newspaper such as *The Pretoria News*. By contrast, a product which is expensive and fairly high-tech may require personal selling. An entrepreneur who designs a new financial services app for individuals to manage their finances would likely rely on personal selling to financial services institutions to get them to purchase and use the app.

9.3.4 Available budget

The selection of an advertising medium will in most instances be determined by available funds. Many small businesses look at what they can afford and then select some of the potential options. Although expensive marketing communication does not necessarily mean good marketing communication, the amount of money available for marketing communication will to a large extent determine the methods that the small business entrepreneur will use and the options that he or she will have. Innovative use of public relations and digital marketing (such as YouTube) can help get a new entrepreneur to make target customers aware of their product or services offered to customers.

9.3.5 Stage in the product life cycle

As the product goes through its stages in the life cycle, the marketing communication mix changes. During the introduction stage, the main aim is to make the customers aware of the product. Extensive advertising and public relations will inform the target audience and heighten awareness levels. The use of sales marketing communication in this stage encourages early trial of the product. Personal selling can also be used to persuade retailers to carry the product. During the growth stage, heavy advertising and public relations continue in order to build brand loyalty. However, it is no longer necessary to use sales marketing communication as customers at this stage need fewer incentives to make a purchase. When the product reaches maturity, competition increases. In this case, persuasive and reminder advertising as well as sales promotion marketing communication is extremely important in order to increase market share. As the product goes into decline, advertising and public relations are reduced but personal selling and sales promotion marketing communication may still be continued.

9.3.6 Type of buying decision

The type of decision has an influence on the choice of marketing communication tool. In routine customer decisions, the use of reminder advertising and sales promotions may be considered, such as when someone purchases a cool drink. If it is a new product then the use of publicity and public relations can also help get awareness, as well as digital and social media usage. If the decision is more complex and has more risk than customers may be more careful and more involved. They may look at options and compare with other products more, and so personal selling may be important here, as well as the use of the Internet, social media and print advertising for the collection of information to reduce their risk in the decision. Think of the difference between you purchasing a solar power water heating system for your home (complex) versus purchasing a cool drink on a hot day (simple).

The businessperson needs to consider all these factors to determine the choice of marketing communication promotion methods.

9.4 STEPS IN DEVELOPING THE MARKETING COMMUNICATION PLAN

The marketing communication plan consists of several distinct steps as shown in Figure 9.2. Each of these steps will be discussed briefly.

Figure 9.2: Steps in the marketing communication plan

Source: Adapted from Strydom, 2015:212-217

9.4.1 Perform a situation analysis

The first step is to analyse the organisation in terms of what marketing communication is currently being done, what the competitors are doing and what the industry trends are. This step enables the organisation to determine its strengths, weaknesses, opportunities and threats.

9.4.2 The objectives of marketing communication

Selecting the objectives of what you want to achieve with marketing communication is very important and means much more than achieving only an increase in sales. Although increased sales is the result that you hope to achieve, it is important to keep in mind that marketing communication deals with communication and you should think of setting a specific communication objective. Any marketing communication campaign has to start by stating clearly what you are trying to achieve. Generally communication objectives are to:

- Inform customers and potential customers of the product, service, location of the business, any specials and so forth. For example, if a new exercise studio opens, it wants to inform the market where it is, the times it will be open, fees charged, availability of parking, range of classes (Pilates, yoga, spinning, etc).
- Persuade customers to buy the product or try it. Whenever competition is high and loyalty is strong, it is more difficult to get customers to buy the product. The focus may then be on persuading customers to at least try the product and service before making a decision. For example, a motor repair business might say that BMW owners should try it because the owners have been trained in BMW maintenance and have worked with BMWs for over 20 years.
- Remind customers of the products and services. Coca-Cola is very strong in reminder advertising. Even though they are the best-known brand in the world they keep on reminding people of their product – to make sure people keep the product in mind when buying cooldrinks. It is also used to reassure customers who have already bought the product or to increase the loyalty of those who have bought before, making sure you have established the groundwork for possible future sales. For example, a nursery will use outdoor signs at the nursery keeping the market informed that for the past two years they have been rated the best nursery in the area.

A small business will have a number of different marketing communication objectives. Some examples of these are:

a) Inform

- Tell the market about a new product/service.
- Suggest a new use for your product/service.
- Tell customers about a price change.

- Explain how the product/service works.
- Describe available services.
- Correct wrong impressions about your business.
- Build up a good image.

b) Persuade

- Build up a preference for your brand.
- Try to get customers to switch to your brand.
- Get customers to buy now.
- Get customers to let you call on them to sell.
- Change the way customers think of your product/service.

c) Remind

- Remind customers that they may need your product/service.
- Remind customers where they can buy your product/service.
- Remind customers about your product/service during off-seasons.
- Keep customers aware of your product/service.

9.4.3 Decide on the target audience

Once you know what you want to achieve, you have to decide with which groups you are going to communicate. These groups are called the target audiences. The target audience are those individuals or businesses or groups who display similar characteristics to whom you want to communicate your message.

The target market would probably make up a target audience, but there could be other groups involved. For example, if you have just opened up a motor repair business and have chosen the drivers of vehicles in your immediate neighborhood as your target market, then your target audiences might be the small business owners in the area, the housewives in the homes around you and the drivers of automobiles. Note that you should treat each target audience separately, because their needs and information requirements are different. For example, the small business owners will be concerned with having their vehicles available for business, the housewives might be concerned with safety and reliability, and the automobile drivers in the area might be concerned with convenience.

It is important to find out what each target audience already knows about the business or product, so that you can work out what to do with your marketing communication effort. For example, it is no use telling the target audiences in the example above that you are better at servicing cars than the franchised automobile dealers, if the target audiences do not know that your business exists!

9.4.4 Decide on the message you want to convey

Once you know who the target audiences are, you will have to decide on your message, or what you want to tell them. This message will help you achieve your objectives. Your knowledge of your customer will be invaluable because it is important that you get and hold their attention and so influence them. Your customer profile, information obtained from research and continuous contact with customers, will help you to decide what to say to customers. It is critical to remember that you must decide on your message according to your target audience.

Figure 9.3 highlights the components of messages.

Figure 9.3: Two components to a message

The message content is the basic idea and information that you want to get through to the target audience. It is important that your audience understands the message the way you want them to.

The message form is the combination of verbal, visual and audio signals that present the message content to the target audience in the most suitable way. The longer the message and the more wording used, the less the chance in many instances that it will be read. A careful mix between words, colour, sound and visual display should be used. The selection of media will influence this as well.

The content of the message is important because you have to show:

- why your product is different
- the benefits that you offer to the customer
- why the customer should buy your product rather than that of your competitor.

The form of the message should attract attention and maintain interest long enough to get the message across. Sometimes an irritating radio advertisement will attract attention and get people to notice it. It has to stand out from all the other advertisements.

You need to be especially careful to avoid being ambiguous; or confusing the target audience. It is in this area of marketing that marketing consultants or advertising agencies are especially helpful.

If you are unsure of the message that you want to put across, you can always do research on your target audience to see if your message is clear and understandable, and has an impact on your audience. Rather make sure it is understood and does not upset anyone before incurring the costs of flighting the message in media and then finding out it is not understood or it upsets large portions of the target audiences.

9.4.5 Select the marketing communication mix elements

Once the message you want to convey to your target audience has been chosen, the organisation will have to decide on a marketing communication mix in order to deliver that message. As previously mentioned the marketing communication mix consists of eight elements: advertising, sales promotion, publicity, personal selling, public relations, sponsorship, direct marketing and digital marketing (Cant & Van Heerden, 2017:364). Each of these elements has its own strengths and weaknesses, so careful consideration must be taken when choosing the right method.

The AZ Trading promotion mix

AZ Trading is based in Gauteng and provides document presentation and document security solutions to its customers, focusing on office machines and office supplies. This is an intensely competitive industry, so the company has been careful in the selection of its promotional mix. It has managed to get listed in buying-group catalogues and on many dealer websites that feature the type of products it specialises in. It has also managed to get its products displayed in many retail outlets, and has been a participant and member of the industry association board. The company makes use of telesales to approach customers, both existing and new, in terms of selling its products and services. It also gets coverage of its products through print media, and has an active website to both support the effort and to provide information to clients on its products. It also participates in road shows and exhibitions to increase awareness of the company and its products and to generate leads.

Source: Adapted from Nieuwenhuizen, 2013

9.4.6 Determine the marketing communication budget

Marketing communication is a very expensive task and usually amounts to a large part of the organisation's total budget. It is important that the organisation sets the marketing communication budget at a level that maximises profitability and return on investment. The organisation should also ensure that the budget is allocated to the different marketing communication mix elements. There are many ways to determine the total amount allocated to the marketing communication mix. Some include:

- spending what you can afford
- spend what competitors are spending
- spend a percentage of last year's sales
- objective and task method.

As mentioned previously, many entrepreneurs do not have large budgets when they start up, so innovative and novel ways of using digital marketing, social media, and public relations can help the entrepreneur build awareness and achieve the marketing communication objectives.

9.4.7 Develop the marketing communication campaign

Developing the marketing communication campaign consists of three steps. The first step is to determine the specifics of the campaign including the media used, expenditure and time schedules. The second step is to ensure that these specifics are assigned to people for successful implementation. Third, checks must be done to ensure effective performance of the marketing communication activities. An entrepreneur often has to plan and implement the plan by themselves, so clear planning and measurement will help to improve the likelihood of the goals being met.

9.4.8 Evaluate the results

Finally, the campaign must be controlled and its performance evaluated. The aim of this step is to determine if the objectives have been met. Standards must be compared to the actual performance to determine if corrective actions are required. The reasons why the objectives have been or have not been met are therefore important to be able to guide the possible corrective actions to take.

9.5 SUMMARY

The use of marketing communication techniques by a small business requires the entrepreneur to think creatively and innovatively. This is because the communication campaign will require the use of scarce business resources. Thus the planning and controlling of communication efforts will be of the utmost importance. As an entrepreneur you must be able to identify what is successful and what is not, and to ensure that all resources used help to achieve the overall goals of the business.

Self-evaluation questions

1. Decide whether each of the following is trying to inform, persuade or remind.

   Tick your answer in the appropriate box.

	INFORM	PERSUADE	REMIND
new, improved catering service			
just opened – ladies' boutique			
still the best boerewors in town			
compare and decide – you will love our cakes			
easy to use – cleans and shines all floors			
just minutes away – call us for free delivery			
winter is coming soon – have you had your car checked?			

2. Explain each of the following:
   i. marketing communication
   ii. message content
   iii. marketing communication mix
   iv. message form
   v. target audience
   vi. marketing communication budget
   vii. sales promotion
   viii. consumer sales promotions
   ix. trade sales promotions
   x. publicity
   xi. personal selling.
3. What factors must be considered in determining a marketing communication mix?
4. List three possible objectives of marketing communication.

REFERENCES AND FURTHER READING

Cant, M.C. & Van Heerden, C.H. 2017. *Marketing Management: A South African Perspective*. Cape Town: Juta Publishers.

Lamb, C.W., Hair, J.F., McDaniel, C., Boshoff, C., Terblanche, N.S., Elliot, R. & Klopper, H.B. 2015. *Marketing*. Cape Town: Oxford University Press.

Nieuwenhuizen, C. 2013. *Business and Marketing Cases*. (5th edition). Cape Town: Juta Publishers.

Strydom, J.W. 2014. *Introduction to Marketing*. (5th edition). Cape Town: Juta Publishers.

Van Heerden, C.H. 2013. *Contemporary Retail and Marketing Case Studies*. Cape Town: Juta Publishers.

Chapter 10 Advertising your business

10.1 LEARNING OUTCOMES

After you have studied this chapter, you should be able to:

- understand how to approach the steps in the development of an advertising campaign
- understand the process of selecting, identifying and discussing the various advertising media that will be suitable for different small businesses
- understand the value (purpose/mechanics) of disruptive media solutions
- understand the value and application and use of the Internet as an advertising medium.

10.2 DEFINING ADVERTISING

The general expectation of a small business is that whatever advertising is done it must be fast, effective and affordable. The reason for this is that it is generally accepted that larger companies will take more time to build and establish their brand than a small business. Where a large company will focus mainly on a longer-term strategy of brand building and sales, a small business will focus more on generating sales over the short term and brand loyalty over a longer period. To a large extent this is because small businesses usually have limited resources and need to generate cash faster.

Unfortunately, small businesses have unrealistic expectations of the effectiveness of advertising. It must be remembered that advertising is only one component in the mix available to the business.

Advertising can be defined as: 'non-personal, one way, planned messages paid for by an identified sponsor and disseminated to a broader audience in order to influence their attitudes and behaviour' (Cant et al, 2013:444).

Good advertising will usually generate positive influences that should lead to more sales. However, if the advertiser gets it wrong, the money spent on advertising will be wasted. Advertising is costly but also necessary for a business. By not advertising, a business stands the chance of not surviving, but if the advertising is poorly executed the business can still fail.

A small business must plan very carefully how it aims to advertise the business in order to get the most value for advertising money spent. The factors that need attention in this regard are as follows:

10.2.1 Define the target audience

A business cannot advertise if it does not know who it is advertising to. So, in order to run a proper advertising campaign, the business must identify existing and potential customers of the business. The small business generally has limited funds available and needs to selectively target the market. It is not feasible for the small business to try to target the mass market because a lot of wastage will occur, which means money lost on non-customer prospects. While the market analysis will define the demographic characteristics, geographic concentration, product usage patterns and purchase habits of target markets, it is important to define the audience for the advertising message. There may be more than one target audience and so these too need to be defined. If done this way, the business can focus on selected audiences more specifically. A travel agency for instance may have a variety of target markets. For example, older people who are retired and looking for a scenic and relaxing cruise may be targeted for an Alaskan cruise, while young adults who want to party may be targeted for Caribbean singles cruises. As statistics are available on population figures, age groups, sex etc, it is possible for businesses to estimate the potential market size.

10.2.2 Determine the advertising message

Knowing who the target audience is, their characteristics and so on, makes it easier to decide on the message to convey to the market. This will obviously also depend on the objectives set for the campaign. It makes it possible to formulate the advertisements in such a way that the target audience will understand the message communicated to them and regard it as relevant to their needs. Various models, such as the hierarchy of effects, have been developed by advertising experts to describe the way advertising works and to set objectives of advertising. A popular model of the hierarchy of effects is AIDAS, which in layman's terms mean the following:

A: Attention: The advertisement must attract the attention of the selected target audience. This may be the use of a whale jumping out of the water for the Alaskan tour, or by using an irritating voice on the radio to attract attention.

I: Interest: Once the attention has been grabbed, interest in the product or service is needed. This may be the mention of a discount, or a 'buy one get one free' offer.

D: Desire: A desire to form part of the group, to own the product or to secure its benefits must be obtained. Seeing a person in an advertisement with a slim and healthy body can create a desire to use the product to look like that.

A: Action: The person must be enticed to act (buy). This can be facilitated by making it possible to pay online, or send an email to be contacted, or even to obtain credit terms, which can lead to action.

S: Satisfaction: This refers to the customer being satisfied with what was sold to him or her. If this is not achieved, the potential of return business or loyalty is not possible.

This suggests that the advertising strategy is designed to move the potential customer through the hierarchy of effects. An advertisement may, however, be designed to achieve only one of the effects in the hierarchy (for example, to attract attention or stimulate interest), while subsequent advertisements will build on the rest.

You will need to define a message strategy that will spell out the focus of the message. The message might focus on the benefits of the product/service or on developing/reinforcing an image; it could focus on developing associations that are value-laden; it also decides on the promise. Just as in war, strategy is half the battle. In other words, the message strategy is as important as advertising itself.

To translate the strategy into an advertisement, the small business can commission an advertising agency or handle the work 'in-house' (within your business). The role of the advertising agency is covered later in the chapter.

10.3 WHERE SHOULD THE ADVERTISEMENTS BE PLACED?

You may have the best designed advertisement, but if placed in the wrong media, it will be a waste of money and effort. Placing an advertisement in the right media is based on the identified target audience (showing once again why the selection of the target audience is so crucial to the campaign). The media selected is critical to the success of the total advertising campaign.

Media are the vehicles (or channels) through which advertising messages are transmitted to the target markets. It is important to select the right media that will reach the target audience, and to make sure that costs are kept as low as possible. Selecting the most appropriate advertising media presents a challenge, especially for small businesses with limited budgets. Many factors can and will influence the media to be used and it is the task of the small businessperson to be aware of these factors and to take them into consideration when deciding on the media.

10.3.1 Factors influencing the selection of media

The choice of media will depend on a variety of factors, which include the following:

(a) Geographic concentration of market

The greater the geographic spread of the target audience, the larger the range of media options available to the small business, and vice versa. For example, seniors targeted for an Alaskan cruise will be in each province and in the more affluent areas of each province. This may require the use of national newspapers or, if funds are limited, a focus on the province where the business is located. If the business is, however, for example an electrical and plumbing business, the entrepreneur may focus on the use of regional newspapers and radio aimed at his target market. These statistics are available for each medium, as most will have a profile of their readers or listeners.

(b) Demographic and psychographic characteristics of the target market

Each target market has unique characteristics and can be defined according to certain factors, such as age, gender, location and lifestyle. The selection of media should suit the market. Customers of an upmarket restaurant will probably appreciate publicity articles in newspapers and magazines, whereas patrons of a local pub and grill will be more effectively reached by means of outdoor signs. An important demographic factor to consider in South Africa is literacy. If the target audience is mostly illiterate, you will have to use radio rather than printed media. This will also affect the choice of words and phrases.

(c) Costs

One of the most restrictive factors for a small business is the amount of money available. Most small businesses have very limited funds and cannot afford long, drawn-out campaigns. They need a medium that is affordable and that will reach the target market at a reasonable cost. A major mistake many small businesses make is to select media solely on price. In many cases the cheapest medium may be the worst because the message will not reach the target audience. A small budget can, however, be used effectively with dramatic effect. This implies that the businessperson knows his or her market and the available media to reach the market.

(d) Varying advertising costs

There are marked differences in cost between and within types of media. For instance, there are different tariffs for advertising on radio and in print. Within a newspaper, there are different costs, depending on the colour, size and position of the advertisement. The potential reach of each medium must be taken into consideration when deciding which to use.

(e) Frequency of message

To have an effect, an advertisement will have to be broadcast more than once. For example, one slot on DStv will not have any effect, but four slots a day for two weeks will. Similarly, a once-off advertisement in a newspaper will be ineffective. Repetition is needed if any impact is to be achieved.

The small business entrepreneur (or owner) can make use of a variety of advertising media, each with its own advantages and disadvantages. In the following sections, we will look at each medium in terms of its potential for success for small businesses.

10.3.2 Radio advertising

Radio is a medium quite extensively used by small businesses due to the relative inexpensiveness, reach, targeted audiences and ease of use. Radio is a source of entertainment, information and companionship, and is available to advertisers on a community, regional and national basis. It is a very important medium in South Africa because of its wide penetration in the population.

Radio can be used effectively to build familiarity and involvement with a product or service. The human voice is a powerful selling aid and, when reinforced by local and topical content, is a very personal medium. Station personalities normally have great rapport with their listeners and are especially valuable for endorsing products. Think of Black Coffee, who has established himself as a DJ, and Riaan van Heerden, who has done the same as a peak time radio host. Many small businesses use them to read their messages, as the appeal is so much higher.

Programming is designed to target distinct audiences, and advertisements are normally quick and easy to produce and update. Radio airtime is usually purchased in packages and is relatively inexpensive compared to television advertising. Given the fact that radio advertisements are short and have no visual support, the script and jingle need to be short, catchy and memorable. How many times have you not found yourself singing along to the tune of an advertisement? Repetition is also necessary since there is no guarantee that your target audience will hear the advertisement when first broadcast.

It is important to know something about the listening patterns of potential customers. You can contact radio stations to obtain information on the type of programming, musical format, geographical reach, number of listeners and station ratings, for example. Many stations offer opportunities to sponsor various programmes.

Community radio has become an important addition to the medium. Advertising rates are lower than those of national radio, as it is strongly focused on one geographic area. Some stations offer attractive packages, often including the production of the advertisement.

10.3.3 Newspaper advertising, display advertisements and classifieds

A viable medium for many small businesses is the use of newspapers. Newspapers include national daily newspapers, national Sunday newspapers, regional daily newspapers and local community newspapers (known as 'free sheets').

National newspapers offer very high circulation and wide coverage, whereas local newspapers reach a more targeted audience. Most small businesses advertise in local newspapers or 'buy' specific delivery zones of newspapers instead of advertising in the full run of a national publication. So, for instance, *The Pretoria News* will focus on the Tshwane area, which is a large geographical area, while *The Record* is a small suburban newspaper distributed in a few suburbs of a town.

The following factors need to be considered when advertising in newspapers:

- Properly planned, newspaper advertising can be a relatively cost-effective method of advertising. Advertisements are sold by column and inch.
- Newspapers cover specific geographical areas, which allows for more 'focused' advertising.
- Newspapers are flexible about the positioning and type of advertisements that can be inserted. Advertisements can be designed, purchased and altered at short notice.
- Newspaper sales representatives might offer to help in designing the layout and copy of your advertisement and should keep you posted on upcoming special sections or promotions. It might be advisable to approach a graphic design or advertising agency if you want your advertisement to stand out, particularly if you want an integrated message across several promotional instruments.
- Newspapers generally have a very short lifespan (usually one day).
- Readership and circulation must be considered before you select a newspaper. For example, circulation drops on Saturdays and increases on Sundays, which is also the day that the newspaper is read most thoroughly. Although circulation figures might be high, there is no assurance of readership.
- Position or location of the advertisement is important. A smaller advertisement can get lost in a large page. If your advertisement includes a coupon, try to have it placed at the edge of the page to make it easier for the reader to cut out the coupon. The use of colour makes it stand out from other advertisements. It may be a little more expensive but if it is, for example, the only blue section in an otherwise black and white page, it will be noticed.
- The print quality of newspapers is often inferior.
- High information content is possible, since newspaper advertisements incorporate information about the product/service.

Classified sections are typically found towards the back of the newspaper, although there are also specialised papers that contain only classified advertisements. As the name suggests, classified advertisements are categorised into sections. Such advertisements are similar in appearance and packed together in narrow columns; they are generally not visually appealing. The difference here is that these advertisements are perused by readers and attract attention through the classifications under which they appear. You can be creative in the design of classified advertisements and it is very important to be consistent. Look at the advertisements in the services section, for example. There is a heading, 'Au Pairs', and the advertisement for an au pair that uses a bold font, slightly larger in print size and blocked stands out more than the advertisements of other au pairs. It is also eye-catching.

10.3.4 Direct mail advertising

Many small businesses make use of leaflets to market their products or services. These are distributed widely and their effectiveness can be linked to the structure of the content of such a brochure. An offer such as '20% off if you produce this advert with your order' is a means of measuring the effectiveness of the leaflet. Direct marketing is one of the most accountable forms of advertising tools, since both costs and results can be precisely measured. Furthermore, it allows a business to understand the needs and preferences of its customers and so move closer to the customer base. More intimate relationships with customers will almost certainly give smaller businesses the competitive edge over larger companies.

Direct mail is one of the oldest methods used by marketers to communicate with buyers.

Direct mail is defined as personally addressed communications sent through the postal service.

Direct mail may employ letters, catalogues, price lists, brochures, leaflets, circulars, newsletters, cards and samples. The one major drawback, however, is the fact that the postal service in South Africa is unreliable.

There are three aspects to a direct mail campaign:

- The mailing list, which includes existing and potential customers. The list may be developed by the business or purchased during start-up.
- The proposition, which should be designed to encourage recipients to respond. Accuracy of information and a simple response mechanism are important.
- Creativity in the mail shot (printed material mailed to people whose names appear on the mailing list) is more likely to be read and remembered and creative mail shots are less likely to be discarded as 'junk mail'.

While direct mail allows for focused targeting, highly personalised information content and the stimulation of direct response, great care must be taken to ensure that it is not perceived as junk mail. Responses need to be monitored to update a database for future use. It must be expected that the response rate will in most cases be between 2% and 5% only.

10.3.5 Signs and displays

Signage is a key component of developing and maintaining an identity for your business. Signs appear on business premises, letterheads, business cards, cars and trucks and employee uniforms, all of which present the opportunity to communicate a consistent message to the target market. Signs and displays are often considered as part of public relations, but they also serve an advertising purpose. It is your task as a small businessperson to ensure that the signage is easy to understand and effective in drawing attention.

10.3.6 Television advertising

Very few small businesses can afford TV advertising, but it is discussed here mainly to cover all the avenues available comprehensively. Television is sometimes referred to as the 'king' of media. This is because it reaches such a large audience. Comprehensive data on television audiences is available, enabling the advertiser to identify and target the desired audience profile. The cost of commercials is based on the number of viewers who watch the programme and the time of day when the programme is aired. However, the high costs of production and airtime normally make television advertisements too expensive for small businesses. A 30-second television commercial in prime time could cost between R800 000 and R1,5 m. Thirty-second slots in off-peak hours will be cheaper. (Certain variables, such as station, programme and average audience rating, time of year and target market, need to be considered.)

Television demands a high degree of creativity in production because commercials must compete with other commercials and elements in the viewer's environment. Fortunately, the medium allows for great creative flexibility and appeals to the senses using sight, sound, colour and movement. This invariably requires the input of an advertising agency. Small business advertisers who operate with limited budgets can contact local stations and ask for details on budget packages and rates for first-time users. Although this might mean that advertisements are flighted during off-peak hours, this may be appropriate for the business's target audience. Other factors to consider include long lead-times (for production and media scheduling) and information content constraints (duration of advertisements: 30 or 60 seconds).

Regional television advertising

There is also the option of advertising on regional television (for example, KZN Tonight). Given the fact that the target audience of a small business is normally quite small, this may be a realistic, cheaper and equally effective alternative.

10.3.7 Magazine advertising

More and more medium-sized businesses are making use of magazines to market their products. These are normally businesses who sell via other outlets or through mail order. Many of the principles that apply to newspapers also apply to magazine advertising. There are two categories of magazines: consumer magazines include general or specific-interest magazines; trade magazines are aimed at specific types of businesses. This categorisation allows for considerable selectivity. It is likely that customers who buy special-interest magazines will be interested in the type of products or services that are advertised in them (for example, *Ideas* readers will have an interest in DIY and crafts).

Magazines are usually weekly or monthly publications and have an extended life (readers usually keep them or pass them on to other people). While the quality of the print and paper and creative flexibility is superior to those of newspapers, the costs of space and production can be high. Advertising messages in magazines are normally more image-oriented and less price-oriented.

The advertising office of a publication can provide a 'media kit' containing information on demographics (age, sex, income level, etc), reach, readership and circulation, as well as a sample of the publication.

Specialist publications

These may provide more appropriate print options for small businesses. A magazine such as *Baba en Kleuter* or *Finweek* is aimed at a very specific readership and many small businesses use this to sell, for example, baby products or financial products or complimentary items. Such advertising is affordable and speaks directly to its target audience. Trade publications such as *Supermarket & Retailer*, for example, are viable media options because they are targeted at specific groups.

10.3.8 Outdoor advertising

Outdoor advertising, including posters and transit advertising, is normally positioned in areas of high-volume traffic to deliver a high opportunity to see (OTS) rating. The outdoor advertising industry offers excellent market coverage and frequency, while having an enormous impact. It remains one of the most cost-effective ways to reach audiences across all Living Standards Measure (LSM) groups – a categorisation of South Africans based on specific lifestyle measures. It is possible to share the cost of outdoor advertisements with suppliers, manufacturers or other businesses by featuring their product or service.

At the point of purchase (supermarket checkout till, petrol station, etc), poster advertising provides an excellent trigger. In the case of billboards or mobile advertising, however, people often catch only a fleeting glimpse, so the message must be short and simple. There are certain legal and environmental regulations as to where billboards can be placed. There are also businesses that specialise in outdoor advertising as a medium. They take full responsibility for messages, maintenance of billboards, etc.

Some of the more popular forms of this diverse medium are:

- billboard and poster advertising along roadsides, in shopping centres and on benches or bins

- station and on-board advertising, which includes posters appearing in bus shelters and on trains, buses and taxis
- mobile advertising on trailers, vehicle and truck fleets in the form of posters and messages; many small businesses use this option to market their services as it is durable and flexible.

10.3.9 Publicity and other low or no-cost advertising

The value of publicity for the small business is generally underrated by businesspeople. Appearing as a guest on a radio or television talk show or interview-type programme provides good publicity. Newspapers, especially, are always on the lookout for filler articles on some topic or other, so contacting them with a new idea, concept or even community project can lead to a write-up and exposure in the market. If you want to pursue this option, write a letter to the producers or editors of various programmes and newspapers and follow up with a personal visit or telephone call. Likewise, you can submit articles to related publications to increase the visibility of your company and establish your expertise in your field.

Posting advertising circulars on free bulletin boards – for example, in libraries, shopping centres, supermarkets and hair and beauty salons – can increase awareness of the business. You can hand out pamphlets at shopping centres or place them under windscreen wipers in parking lots. Office stationery can also be printed with advertising messages.

Seek out referrals from previous customers, as this is a good way to develop a 'satisfied client' list, which can then be used in advertisements.

10.3.10 Speciality advertising, including giveaways and promotional items

Speciality advertising are articles on which the company's name or logo appears. Examples are office stationery, flash drives, mouse pads, calendars and T-shirts. The value of these items has, however, diminished over the years as many companies are doing this now and the choices are limited.

One company, however, has succeeded in getting much mileage out of these types of items by being innovative and proactive. Ettienne and Co. Attorneys, located in Bloemfontein decided to hand out stainless steel coffee mugs to customers instead of a brochure. The coffee mug is designed for customers on the go, the company details and its services have been printed on the mugs, and it was sourced from China at a very low price. Also, when hot liquid is poured into the mug, the company logo becomes bright and noticeable on the side. The company hands out these mugs to selected customers only. The lifespan of the item is long and because the Ettienne and Co. Attorneys logo is on the mug, the lifespan of the advertising is pretty long and it will become a talking point among individuals.

10.3.11 Trade shows

There are numerous trade shows that can be used by small businesses. Trade shows make use of display booths set up by businesses to display their products or services to potential customers. Trade shows include computer, baby, crafts and DIY, wedding, building and garden design fairs and exhibitions.

10.3.12 Electronic media and social networks

The use of electronic media such as email has gained momentum over the past years and today is a major marketing tool for big and small businesses. More and more small businesses are using social media tools to get their brand and message across, but the overuse of these media has led to many complaints of spamming and actions from the service providers to block these messages. A coordinated plan is required to make social media effective. It will not bring instant fame but will gradually build up your brand if managed correctly.

10.3.13 *Yellow Pages* or directory advertising

As specific reference publications, directories allow for highly targeted advertising. Industrial and commercial directories are used almost exclusively by buyers in particular fields. Prospective customers can easily locate and contact your business if they know who you are and what classification to look for in the first place. The advantage of this for small and medium businesses is that a single advertisement works for a whole year. The disadvantage is that this implies long lead times. The cost of using this medium depends largely on what competitors are doing within the same industry. To stand out from the competition, a business might opt for a full-page colour advertisement. Advertisements should be large enough to incorporate vital information for the reader to make contact. Advertisements must be simple, unique and attention-grabbing.

NB

Remember that directory advertising is about providing information to a customer who is actively seeking the advertiser. Much of the 'sell copy' for a product or service is unnecessary since people have already looked the business up. Consequently, it serves as an excellent support medium.

10.4 DISRUPTIVE SOLUTIONS

Even though television is often out of reach, small and medium businesses have many alternative media options to choose from. There is a danger of being caught up in the glamour of advertising. It is not always a solution to the problem to direct your entire budget into expensive television campaigns which may not be the best way of building your brand.

Alternative or non-traditional media is proving highly effective in a world cluttered by marketing messages. When it comes to media outside the mainstream, there is an almost limitless choice. It seems you can put your marketing message on just about anything these days – from TVs in public transport like the Gautrain and garage car washes, to loyalty cards and even inside the lids of cereal boxes. And if a medium does not exist, you can usually find someone who would be happy to create it for you. With alternative media the options are boundless and, when properly used, so is the value.

Clearly, small businesses can employ a host of different, exciting, innovative and highly effective methods of advertising. These include:

- SMS competitions on cereal boxes and chocolates where entrants can win airtime and cash
- competitions and sweepstakes on social media like Facebook and Twitter
- advertisements on restaurant menus
- advertisments on the back of till slips – Pick n Pay, for eg, prints their Smart Shoppers special offers shared with other advertisers on till slips (the ability to advertise in small local areas maximises cost-effectiveness, reduces wastage and gets the message directly into the customer's hand)
- advertisements at the back of toilet stalls in shopping malls in cinemas, clubs and restaurants (A4 posters slid into frames mounted on doors are often used to great effect)
- queuing media, which include light boxes, display cabinets, interactive promotions, belt advertising (queuing belts in cinemas, banks, post offices, etc) and floor graphics in foyer and lobby areas.

It is the nature of marketing and entrepreneurs to constantly find new and innovative ways to market their products and services. Every now and then a new approach pops up and with technology this is becoming more frequent and innovative.

Creativity rules the advertising world, and this is evident in these disruptive solutions. For example, a commercial for Woof! dog food, which produces dog food, treats and accessories, shows a dog howling at five o'clock in the morning as he sits at the back door of a house. The dog owner looks out of his bedroom window and tells the dog to be quiet because he does not want to disturb the neighbours. After a few minutes, the neighbours turn on all the lights in their house and the dog owner knows he is in trouble. The dog continues to howl and does not quieten down until the owner throws one of the Woof! treats out of the window. The dog immediately runs and fetches the treat and peace is restored to the neighbourhood.

List other disruptive solutions that you can create for small and medium advertisers that will both have an impact on and reach many potential customers.

10.5 DIGITAL AND ELECTRONIC APPROACHES: THE INTERNET

The changes occurring in the business environment continually provide marketers and advertisers with new opportunities. Nowhere is this more evident than in the rise of the Internet, and particularly the World Wide Web (the Web). In this section, we will look at Internet advertising, email marketing and the use of text messaging such as SMS, and WhatsApp applications.

10.5.1 Web advertising

The advent of the Internet has changed the way we do business. For many small businesses, the Internet can be an economical and efficient way to market to customers. By fostering new and different forms of interaction, it ensures low-cost, real-time interactivity between vast numbers of people worldwide.

Advertising on the Internet can take a variety of forms. The multimedia capabilities of the Web allow advertisers to use colour, graphics, movement, video and even sound. Typically, businesses use their websites as vehicles to advertise themselves and their products or services.

Many small business owners are under the illusion that creating a website will automatically cause people to flock to it. Unfortunately, the opposite is true. It is getting harder and harder for smaller sites to cut through all the noise and clutter of the Web to get noticed.

You can obtain articles on website marketing from https://smesouthafrica.co.za/ and www.marketingtips.com. https://www.nichemarket.co.za/ is an example of a site where small and medium enterprises (SMEs) in South Africa can obtain a listing on a business index and have their own Web page. Sites such as these provide SMEs with effective, yet inexpensive, Internet advertising and online exposure.

How visitors browse or use websites is measured by indicators such as click-through rates (number of times users click on a feature, such as a banner advertisement) and page views (the number of times a particular page is requested from a computer server). It is important to remember that high click-through rates and page views do not necessarily mean that the site is successful. To measure success accurately, the small business entrepreneur needs to examine more meaningful data, such as visitor profiles and online behaviour.

Banner advertising on established sites that cater for desired target audiences is very common. Banner advertising is a type of advertisement that appears as a banner (horizontal band) across the whole or part of the width of a Web page. The costs of banner advertisements vary between agencies and developers. A banner exchange is available, where a banner advertisement can receive a specific number of exposures on other member websites. Banner advertisements are very important as they are considered the offline advertising which is part of an offline campaign, so banners that provide no incentive to 'click here', or that sport the wrong company logo, can actually damage the reputation of a business.

It is important to recognise the distinct advantages of using the Internet as an advertising medium.

10.5.2 Email marketing

Email marketing allows the marketer to benefit from powerful new capabilities – fast campaign testing and execution, the ability to customise messages and the capacity for immediate response analysis. Email is a tool that allows marketers to provide customers with compelling reasons to buy their product or service. By using new e-marketing tools, the small business can create a personalised dialogue with its customers and customise products or services according to customers' specific needs and wants. At the same time, the business can focus its efforts on its most valuable customers.

The first step in email marketing is to learn as much as possible about your customers (the target market) so that you can send them information at the right time that they will find relevant and respond to. This calls for a proper method of storing customer information and managing responses; this can be done by establishing a database. The database updates customer profiles and can include simple contact details or complex response and purchase histories.

Many small business owners market their products and services through newsgroups and mailing lists. These provide the benefit of reaching a highly targeted audience and the opportunity to network with other businesses, prospect for customers and increase the visibility of the company. Newsgroups are general discussion groups in which a person posts a message to the group and the message is distributed all over the world to different news servers. Mailing lists are groups of people who communicate by email about a particular subject. (Consumers can now sign up to receive commercial email messages about topics of interest.) The company can respond to queries and comments, thereby increasing exposure of its products and their benefits.

Electronic newsletters are a powerful weapon small businesses can use to market their products or services. Sending them is an effective way of building good relations with clients and is inexpensive.

10.5.3 Text message/SMS advertisements

A new form of advertising, which capitalises on the exponential growth in ownership of cellphones, is the use of text messaging, such as the Short Messaging Service (SMS), WhatsApp, Twitter and many more, to advertise. A small business entrepreneur could make use of these media to announce a special offer or a new product or service.

Compiling a database of customers' cellphone numbers. is critical to the use of these applications. A disadvantage might be offending customers by invading their privacy. Customer permission should be requested in advance.

eg

StudentNotes.co.za

When StudentNotes.co.za launched in 2010, its goal was simple: to provide quality study notes to university students created by other students. The company's objective was to develop, over the next three years, from an unknown brand into one that is readily recognisable at nearly all the universities in South Africa.

The company decided that the first step in the marketing process would be to distribute posters and flyers. This had worked for the founder when he initially sold his notes on campus, so surely it would work again? The founder took the designs to the University of Pretoria campus where he was studying and he printed 500 flyers and 20 posters. The initial marketing had some success: students were visiting the website and downloading some of the free notes. By using Google Analytics the founder could see that most of the visitors were from the Pretoria area where he had done his marketing. There were, however, no new uploads of notes, nor did anyone purchase the few premium notes.

After a few months, the company decided to find some free advertising space. The founder emailed the Department of Education, 62 newspapers and 14 radio stations across South Africa and provided them with a marketing release about the website. Weeks went by with no replies from any of the recipients. Finally, a journalist from *Die Matie* newspaper (the University of Stellenbosch newspaper) contacted the founder of Studentnotes.co.za. She explained that the newspaper was interested in the story and that it would do a small piece on it. The response from this piece was by no means spectacular, but it meant that free exposure for the website has been obtained at a university other than the University of Pretoria.

Parallel with this marketing, StudentNotes.co.za used social media platforms, including Facebook, to increase brand awareness. A fan page and friends page were created on Facebook. The fan page was used to create the real marketing platform on Facebook. The hits on the Studentnotes.co.za website that originated from Facebook were starting to grow.

10.6 SUMMARY

Generating positive, cost-effective communication with customers and potential customers is essential for any small business. The process involved in developing an advertising campaign for a small business is the first topic of discussion in this chapter followed by the various advertising media that can be used for different small businesses. Disruptive media solutions are also explained, and emphasis is placed on convincing small businesses to switch to using alternative and digital media. The chapter concludes with a discussion on the importance of using the Internet as an advertising medium.

Self-evaluation questions

1. If you were the founder of Studentnotes.co.za, which other inexpensive advertising media would you have used during the company's first few years of operation?
2. In your opinion, do you believe radio and television advertising would have been an effective advertising strategy to use?
3. Which advertising strategies do you think Studentnotes.co.za should employ in the future?

Chapter 11

Operations management

11.1 LEARNING OUTCOMES

After you have studied this chapter, you should be able to:

- understand operations management (OM) in its widest context
- explain the dynamics of OM
- list the five basic functions of OM
- list the principles of OM that promote value, time and lean production
- describe the three areas of planning and control of the operations transformation process
- define process management and the lead-time elements of a process
- list the typical OM performance objectives
- distinguish between the elements and components of productivity and increased productivity
- distinguish between lean and agile supply
- distinguish between the three main categories of operations systems
- identify layout types
- do fixed capacity planning and adapt capacity
- do basic production scheduling
- understand the concepts of operations improvement, maintenance and SHE management.

11.2 INTRODUCTION

The historic industrial revolutions were all based on the inherent human need to improve, develop and to be creative. This technology capability leads to creative technology management for improvement, maintenance, and quality of operations. These operations are not all necessarily part of a dominant innovation network characterised by the developed countries but they still bring smaller niche innovations to the fore. New developments in technology are natural outcomes from creative mankind and today we see smart factories, a digital economy, new types of knowledge management and exponential organisations. Money sees the lure of crypto, computers become smaller, and normal buildings become intelligent building systems.

Entrepreneurs have a different mind-set and they should always be looking for new ideas, new opportunities, new designs, new solutions and innovation. Entrepreneurs are those who want to fill all sorts of gaps even if they are already running a successful business. They believe there is always room for improvement – the improvement can manifest by different means such as a new business idea coming to fruition, or a new business going to the next level or a weak business that is re-engineered to a success story.

Most successful entrepreneurs achieved results because of, and also in terms of, operations management. To copy what everyone else is doing or to simply buy a franchise is not real entrepreneurship. The global market needs dynamics in terms of agility, which is the ability to respond to market needs and opportunities. In this context, operations management refers to innovation, improved designs (of products, services and processes), time-to-market, customisation, creative distribution, servitisation and others. In the context of a settled business, the essence of operations management is to transform inputs, to add value, to be productive (efficient and effective) and to always seek ways to do things better.

Entrepreneurs usually have an interest in new developments: either to help them with their business idea, or to create and market their own technology. Technology is associated with new gadgets, devices, machines, or processing that make life easier. Technology involves all applicable operations, materials and knowledge in order to satisfy a need with a view to improve people's private or work environments. This includes discoveries and inventions, provided that they can be applied economically.

11.2.1 Inspiring inventors and inventions

The innovative economy will see how innovative capacity is spurred by technological externalities and more innovative supply chains. Organisational agility (eg mass customisation) will become the skill of the future. This will enable operations to respond with minimum disruption in terms of business process re-configurability. Service operations will increase and concepts related to service innovation, deployment of service innovations, productisation of services and servitisation of products will become more relevant.

There is a leader behind every success story and in the eyes of many sport lovers one of many Scottish creations that stands head and shoulders above the rest is golf. The royal game has its roots in 15th century Scotland. This game became one of the highest paid industries. The Scots have given many other gifts to the world – they invented the television, the fax machine, the telephone, the refrigerator, the steam engine locomotive, the speedometer, the MRI scanner and many others.

The Falkirk Wheel in Scotland

The world's first rotating boatlift is not only a unique massive steel construction but a symbol celebrating the dawn of Scotland's new canal age. The Falkirk Wheel is Scotland's most exciting example of 21st century engineering designed to raise and lower boats between two different-height canals. In combining creative art and operations design, they produced a dramatic moving sculpture that is far from conventional. The wheel weighs 1 200 tonnes and the boatlift is 35 metres high and 27 metres long. Boat journeys through the wheel take only 15 minutes overall.

The well-known entrepreneurs, such as Bill Gates, Richard Branson, Adrian Gore and Warren Buffet have a lot to teach us. They have different philosophies and 'lessons for greatness'. But all of them have one thing in common – creativity. Howard Schultz (Starbucks) focuses on investing in people who can be creative. Adrian Gore (Discovery Health) believes in pushing people to look for innovative solutions and to do things differently and create value for all involved. Richard Branson believes greatness moves past the conventional. All these leaders have a wide variety of good ideas and multiple operations (eg Virgin) to make things happen.

South African inventions

The following are a few examples of creative ideas that were transformed into top inventions by South Africans:

- The public hates to stand in queues, so the idea to buy tickets for entertainment, before the event, was germinated to solve the problem. Computicket was invented – the first computerised ticket-sales system in the world.
- The popular idea to get a device (process technology) that will clean the pool for you. Operations skills made the idea a reality. KreepyKrauly – an automatic pool-cleaning device was originally a South African invention (now owned by an American company). Other pool-cleaning devices that originated in South African include brand names, like Baracuda and Pool Ranger.
- The glue that really does the trick – Pratley's Putty – a two-part clay-like mixture which bonds into a very hard and strong compound. Operational skills made this idea an invention.
- The idea to increase the sales of pure fruit juice: Appletiser and Grapetiser – pure fruit juice recipes in a sparkling format.

Source: SA 2005-2006, *South Africa at a Glance*

11.3 BASIC CONCEPTS OF OPERATIONS MANAGEMENT

This chapter focuses on general OM terms, core concepts, principles and functions. This chapter will help any student in entrepreneurship who is unfamiliar with OM to establish a learning foundation for what is also called 'POM' (production and operations management). The emphasis is on the basic OM body of knowledge in terms of the needs of entrepreneurs who usually start small. The content focuses more on important OM principles and typical small business operations than on large, complex systems, large projects or mechanised continuous operations.

11.3.1 Perspectives and definitions of Operations management

Everything we see around us, sit on, eat, read, wear, buy and enjoy comes to us courtesy of operations managers who planned and controlled the operations systems involved.

- Operations management (OM) is very challenging and satisfying because it creates all valuable, therefore sellable things, and everyone lives by selling something. OM is, therefore, for those who like to be creative and make things happen (not for those who only dream, watch things happen and wonder what happened).
- Creating good ideas, making products and providing services is the ultimate purpose of any business and all managers are, in fact, operations managers. Operations management is the business function that is concerned with making products and providing services. Production management was the term used in the past for the manufacturing of products. Today, we use the term OM to cover both manufacturing and service delivery organisations.
- OM gets as close as we can in business life to the act of creation. It is concerned with creating the products and services upon which we all depend. OM is about change, creativity, productivity and adding value. Since this is the very reason for any organisation's existence, operations management should be at the heart of its affairs.
- No factory produces goods for the sake of staying busy, or transforms or assembles resources just for fun. All OM managers are value-driven, a pursuit during which the worth of all inputs is increased by each transformation process in the eyes of the next customer in the process. Hence, the focus of this chapter is on value and, more specifically, on its main dimension, time and the processes linked by people as value chains.
- The essence of any transformation process (be it micro, macro or any manufacturing system) is to add value and eliminate waste. This brings us to the familiar age-old concepts of productivity, effectiveness and efficiency. All OM concepts relate to optimising resources, which implies value. Most of these OM principles relate to the well-known JIT (just-in-time) philosophy. JIT systems eliminate waste, promote value-adding activities, quality and focus on lead-time reduction.

It is clear that OM is a dynamic and creative discipline. Business life is primarily concerned with creating goods and services, putting operations management at the heart of its existence. Whether micro- or macro-processes are concerned, students will realise that all managers directly and indirectly transform resources and create products and/or services for internal and external customers.

11.3.2 Operations management functions

Operations management involves the following primary functions:

1. product and service design (demand creativity)
2. demand and capacity planning
3. operations system design (demand creativity)
4. production planning and control
5. improvement, problem-solving and maintenance (demand creativity).

All entrepreneurs and managers, irrespective of their job title, create products and services for customers. In this sense, all managers are operations managers. Slack et al (2004:xi) states how challenging OM is becoming. Managers have to find solutions to technological and environmental challenges, the pressures to be socially responsible, the increasing globalisation of markets and knowledge management. All these challenges signal a positive message to potential entrepreneurs. They do not need to or have to, but they can get involved if they want to.

11.3.3 Operations management demands creativity

Many people have good ideas which they find difficult to operationalise. Brainstorming sessions in general are fun, interesting and they usually produce several good ideas, which are never realised in practice. Unfortunately, it is due to a lack of technical and operational skills. Creativity should, therefore, go beyond good product, market and advertising ideas: it must especially focus on operations.

Creative ideas can have a large impact on operations – on the processes (optimising, simplification, streamlining), product packages, systems, technology, infrastructure, layout, resources and combinations thereof. If simple techniques, like learning to think and innovate can generate ideas causing significant savings or improvements, then one can understand why OM is associated with the excitement experienced by innovative organisations. It can have an enormous financial impact on a business. Researchers, therefore, need to live in an environment in which ideas spawn new concepts that, in turn, lead to new products and new technology or system designs, which may lead to improved or new business operations.

11.3.4 Operations management and process management

Stevenson (2012) refers to process management as a central role of all management. The processes associated within the different functional areas are the following three process categories:

- Upper management processes refer to governing, visioning, designing, strategising, and so forth.
- Operational processes are the core functional processes (such as purchasing, production and marketing) that make up the value stream.
- Supporting processes such as information technology, accounting and human resources management.

All operations have certain 'creative' process technologies, which assist the transformation process and make production easier. Here, we refer to all sorts of machines, alarms, gadgets and gauges to support the primary process. Trolleys, scales, racks, cleaning tools, mechanical tools, calibration of filters and machinery set-up are a few examples.

It is therefore important to understand that the transformation process is not confined to the factory. A process view of the business is important because an organisation is only as effective as its processes. Processes cut across departmental boundaries and this view goes beyond the main manufacturing process.

This 'nested-process' concept reinforces the need to understand the interconnectivity of all processes and operations in the business. This also helps people to understand how their small contribution adds value to the whole operating value chain, which is the cumulative work of all processes in the business. Value to the customer at a loss or expense for the business is not productive, sustainable or profitable. The people in any operation are the catalyst that makes the whole operation come alive (Slack et al, 2004:121).

The processing time as such is not the only factor that determines how long it takes to complete a particular job. OM always attempts to reduce or eliminate lead-time elements in a process. The primary lead-time elements are as follows:

- **Queue time:** the period during which a job stays in the queue at a work centre
- **Processing time:** the actual time needed to process the job
- **Set-up time:** the time needed to prepare equipment for processing a new job
- **Waiting time:** the idle time between the processing of a job and its passage to the next work centre
- **Inspection time:** the time needed to check whether the job complies with quality standards
- **Transportation time:** the time needed to transport the job from one work centre to the next.

11.3.5 Creative designs inherent in operations

Everything that exists started as a design. Good products come from good designs and good OM. Conversely, bad products usually originate from bad designs. A good construction business can hardly build a good house if the design is not good. It is difficult – or even impossible – to improve faulty designs of products or systems. If the re-engineering of a design is not necessary, the original design was not too bad. OM, therefore, includes the science of design. In general, one must design for cost-effectiveness. The durability of an acrylic product (such as a custom-made hearing protector) makes it much less costly than a disposable foam ear-plug over a short period of time.

11.3.6 Principles of Operations management

A value chain is the ideal series of transformational processes whereby each step increases the value of an item. OM promotes a systematic approach (eg value analysis) to reducing the cost of a product without impairing its quality, value or function. OM also teaches the theory of constraints so as to maximise flow rate through bottlenecks and constraints.

The following OM principles promote value, saving time and resources:

- Know and team up with the next and final customer. This principle implies breaking barriers and building relationships. It refers to the customer as the next process.
- The entire company must become dedicated to continual and rapid improvement in quality, cost, response time, flexibility, variability and service.
- The entire company must have a unified purpose via shared information and team involvement in the planning and implementation of change.
- Reduce the number of product or service components and operations (processes) and the number of suppliers to a few good ones.
- Operation design entails organising resources into multiple chains of customers, each focused on a product or service (or 'customer family'); create workflow teams, cells and 'plants in a plant'.
- Capacity involves utilising human resource potential and creativity by investing in human capital (as the internal customer); QWL ('quality of work-life') means investing in cross-training for mastery of multiple skills.
- Capacity entails maintaining and improving present equipment and human capital before considering new resources and automating incrementally when process variability cannot be reduced by other means.
- Process management entails aiming for streamlining and simplicity by making it easy to provide goods or services without error or any process variation.

- Cutting flow time (lead-time, waiting time etc), distance and inventory (sub-assemblies and idle work-in-process) along the chains of customers.
- Cutting set-up, changeover, get-ready and start-up lead-times.
- Just-in-time production, or at the customer's rate of use; decrease cycle intervals and lot size.
- Recording and processing one's own data at the workplace and ensuring that front-line improvement teams have the first chance at problem-solving before experts are brought in.
- Cutting administration and reporting; controlling causes, not symptoms.

11.3.7 Examples of transformation processes

NB

All operations should be value-adding processes in which inputs are transformed into outputs. The single most important input-transforming resource is the human component. Human beings act upon transformed resources and are present in all operations. Productivity depends directly on human capabilities – competence, qualification and motivation – to produce effectively and efficiently. These capabilities must be maintained and sustained. QWL (quality of work-life) is one strategy that directly affects operations.

OM also deals with the planning and control of operations. The following table illustrates the three areas of OM planning and control.

Table 11.1: OM planning and control of three areas of the transformation process

OM planning and control of	OM planning and control of	OM planning and control of
(1) Inputs: transforming resources (people, creativity, capital, R&D (research and development), technology, learning, market information and feedback) and transformed resources (energy, materials and clients)	(2) Transformation systems: • macro-processes • micro-processes • operations systems (eg service shops, work centres, assembly lines, job shops and process technologies)	(3) Outputs: value, goods and services, improvements, new designs, technology, delighted markets, competitive advantages, sustainability, etc

Look at the following examples in Table 11.2 for a better understanding of the transformation process.

Table 11.2: Examples of the transformation process

Business type	Inputs	Transformation	Outputs
Hospital	Patients, doctors, nurses, theatres, rooms, ambulances, equipment	Medical procedures, therapy, service delivery, professional handling and care of patients, application and administration of medicine	Improved quality of life, satisfied clients, recovered and healthy patients, extended life expectancies
Bakery	Flour, sugar (ingredients), equipment (such as ovens), trained people (bakers, knowledge of recipes)	Food preparation according to specifications, machine setup, mix, mould, bake and pack	Cakes, pies, bread ready for delivery
Custom-made ear plugs	Trained audiometrists, materials and equipment to take moulds, transport to visit factories, laboratory	Filters, calibrated, soft moulds transformed to acrylic ear plugs, filters and cords assembled, ear plugs packed, workers personally fitted and seal test done	Personalised hearing protectors, comfortable ear plugs worn with ease, noise-induced hearing loss is eliminated

11.3.8 Operations management performance objectives

Large companies, such as Mercedes, General Electric, McDonalds and Vodacom, are all known for service-delivery or other features, such as quality, speed or cost-effectiveness. These are referred to as performance objectives. The many dimensions of quality (such as reliability, consistency, low variability, responsiveness) can also be regarded as performance objectives.

What are the main performance objectives of OM? Besides the quality objective, operations managers also contribute to business strategy by other means. JIT is associated with advantages, such as low lead-times and inventory reductions. This objective is integrated with dependability, which can be regarded as a separate performance objective. Speediness is another performance objective. Flexibility, the ability to be agile (upscaling agility with agile teams), change and adapt, is another important performance objective. Although productivity and efficiency (and their measures) are primarily associated with operations management strategy, the strategic operations objective could be low cost and affordability.

The tenet that 'there is no such thing as a free lunch' can be taken as the bottom-line of the trade-off theory. Operations managers must consider trading off one aspect of performance against another. This trade-off model of performance has been challenged to give the best of both worlds to the market. The best example is the quality versus cost trade-off, which has been overcome by many operations even those in the agile supply market. The main job of operations managers is to change whatever in the operation is causing one performance objective to deteriorate as another improves and the trade-off is the mainstay of continuous improvement.

11.4 OPERATIONS MANAGEMENT IS CENTRAL TO PRODUCTIVITY

If a small business manufactures a table ineffectively and inefficiently, it has, nevertheless, been 'productive' in the sense that it actually produced something, although the output did not fully justify the input.

Hence, we need measures of productivity, since the operations manager's key challenge will always be to increase the value of output relative to the cost of input. More output with the same amount of input increases productivity, but the same level of output using less input also increases productivity.

There are many configurations, but the bottom-line is that sustainable profitability is impossible without productivity. This means the output value (usable outputs), after being exposed to a uniquely designed transformation process, must be higher than the value of the separate pieces of available inputs (resources).

11.4.1 Macro-productivity

Macro-productivity refers to the context of a nation's entire production. The Gross Domestic Product (GDP) per capita is the measure of the value of the total output of a country divided by its total population (seen as the inputs to produce the outputs).

A national economy is made up of individual businesses and the productivity of the country is the sum of the productivity of all its individual operations. A macro-perspective on productivity management refers to the country/economy as a whole and the governance of productivity growth.

The National Productivity Institute (NPI) offers many suggestions in this regard. Examples are infrastructural programmes and investments, a well-functioning legal and accounting framework, creating a market-friendly environment, research and technology support, promotion of small and medium enterprises, export trade stimulation, education and training policies and a healthy labour market.

11.4.2 Micro-productivity

Micro-productivity refers to an individual business's operations. It focuses on how well operations perform in terms of value, effectiveness, efficiency, utilisation, impact and quality. The first measure is the ability to achieve production. Second, productivity is measured by means of the following quotient: 'output divided by input'.

Productivity measurement defined

It is imperative to define productivity correctly. Merely saying it is 'output divided by input' is not the whole story. One can be 'productive' without really producing usable output. In other words, we can have high efficiency, but low effectiveness. Effectiveness is the 'how good' or 'how valuable' dimension as related to market needs. Productivity is, therefore, not only efficiency, but also the quality of inputs, resource utilisation and effectiveness.

These are terms associated with quality management, which is vital for productivity. These qualitative improvements in inputs are significant because they create sustainability, durability, stability and cause output to increase without any additional capital or human resource inputs. This brings us to a more accurate quotient for productivity:

$$\frac{\text{Output income (ie usable output quantity)}}{\text{Input expenses (ie available input quantity)}} = \text{Productivity (P)}$$

Productivity is a complex topic because of the different types, dimensions and measures of productivity. The ability to achieve production is simply not enough. For instance, one may produce things, without having a market to sell them to. An entrepreneur may manufacture hundreds of items, without selling many of them. Suddenly, the ability to produce has a nasty flavour.

If there is a market, then the ability to produce for that given market is also not enough. This is because the cost of manufacturing may not be viable (cost-effective).

Thus, a productive system must have the ability to be effective and efficient. Without these elements it would be difficult to make sense of productivity. This means output must be effective and efficient. The danger is to focus only on one (eg efficiency) at the cost of the other (eg effectiveness).

11.5 OPERATIONS STRATEGY AND OPERATIONS DESIGN

The new industrial revolution opens the door for more opportunities for entrepreneurs. Markets become more demanding and smart products and services demands smart factories with new operations designs. Strategy refers to actions or decisions that commit the business to moving in a certain direction or adopting a position in the market. Carefully made decisions that help the business to achieve its goals and those that have a high impact and particular significance can be regarded as strategies. This strategy is based on an operations strategy. Slack et al (1998:77) define operations strategy as the total pattern of decisions and actions that formulate the role, objectives and activities of each part of the operation so that they contribute to and support the organisation's business strategy.

11.5.1 Operations design

The operations strategy implies an operations system. Entrepreneurs need to take note that their idea, product and/or service range will demand a specific operations design. Is it a small factory, a service shop, a job shop, an assembly line or a combination of several other types? The product should fit the operations design (the specific market need will determine the appropriate operations design, eg lean or agile supply).

The basic differences between a lean and agile operation are summarised in Table 11.3.

Table 11.3: Lean vs agile supply

Distinguishing attributes	Lean supply	Agile supply
product variety and life cycle	low variety and long life cycles	high variety and short life cycle
forecasting mechanism	algorithmic	consultative, qualitative
profit margin	low	high
market	predictable	volatile
stock demand	stable long-term	immediate availability and volatile

The agile supply operation is market-sensitive and can respond nimbly to demand. It needs unconventional mechanisms to hear the daily voice of the market and have direct access to customer requirements data to create a virtual supply chain that is information-based rather than inventory-based. Electronic data interchange enables partners in the supply chain to react to the same data (real demand), rather than to the distorted picture when orders are transmitted from one to another in the chain. The route to sustainable advantage lies in being able to leverage the respective strengths of network partners to achieve greater market responsiveness.

The operations design for very high volume and very low variety is a continuous mode of operation. The layout will, therefore, suit a highly mechanised plant. The operations design for a unique functional need, low volume (one item) with high flexibility will suit a project mode of operation. The layout is temporary, with no clear flow lines and because the product position is fixed, the layout is referred to as a fixed-position layout. The same three dimensions (variety, volume and product scope) are used to come up with a job mode of operations design – batch-operation design or repetitive-operation design.

Product design will determine process type (intermittent or continuous), as well as layout and flow of work. The entire network of micro- and macro-processes will consist of the basic flow (and layout type), the technologies used (process technologies, equipment and machines) and job design. Process design is not merely an assembly line. It may also include network decisions pertaining to suppliers if the business is backwardly integrated into the supply chain and decisions relating to the capacity level of each operation in the supply network.

Each operation in the network will select a process type based on the variety–volume characteristics of the operation. Small variety and large quantities will dictate a specific process type. Process type, on the other hand, will dictate layout type, although process type and layout type are not always totally deterministic. In general, the OM function has three important strategic roles (Slack et al, 1998:45), namely:

- the operations function as implementer of business strategy
- the operations function as driver of business strategy
- the operations function as a support to business strategy.

11.5.2 Types of productive systems and their characteristics

All transformation systems convert inputs into outputs. All of these operations share the same operations management model, principles and performance objectives. These systems are also referred to as transforming resources that convert a combination of inputs – referred to as transformed resources (Slack et al, 1998). They are designed for the particular demand which will determine the system's dimensions, nature, scope and scale. This leads to different operations system designs, such as service shops, job shops, production lines, batch operations, mass services, projects and other combinations, as compared in Table 11.4.

11.5.3 Relationship between operation system type and layout type

Decisions concerning the layout type will not merely depend on choosing between the basic layout types, but also on understanding the advantages and disadvantages of the different types, or combinations, of layouts. The flow of transformed resources will be determined by both the feasibility and importance of the degree of regular flow. The opposite of this is high variety (when regular flow is difficult) and low volume (when regular flow is not feasible). The relationship between basic processes (or operations systems) and basic layout types are:

- projects and large jobs = Fixed-position layout
- jobs and batch processes = Process layout (layout according to similar processes)
- large batches and small continuous processes = Cell layout
- mass processes or pure continuous repetitive processes = Product layout (layout according to the product).

Table 11.4: Comparison of the characteristics of the three main categories of operations

	Continuous or repetitive operations system	Job/batch operations system	Project operations system
Product type	Standardised	Diversified	Unique
Product flow	Standardised	According to requirements of particular product	Virtually none
Materials handling	Materials flow determinable, systemised and automated	Handling depends on the product, therefore highly variable and expensive	Special equipment often necessary; high cost
Raw materials inventory	High turnover	Low turnover	Variable because of production time
Work-in-process	Small quantities	Large quantities	Single product
Production cost components	Relatively high fixed cost; low variable cost per unit	Relatively low fixed cost; high variable cost per unit	Relatively high fixed cost; high variable cost
Labour requirements	Highly specialised routine tasks at a specific rate	Highly skilled artisans working without supervision and with moderate adaptability	High degree of adaptability to various tasks commissioned

The layout of the productive unit, therefore, only governs the general configuration of facilities. Mode shifting is also possible after process re-engineering. This means the mode of operations system design (and layout type) may change from job to project or from batch to continuous (from custom to commodity). The purpose of effective layout is to streamline work flow by minimising handling distance and increasing facility utilisation.

11.6 OPERATIONS PLANNING AND CONTROL

Planning is about 'who', 'what', 'when', 'how' and 'where'.

Operations planning is governed by OM policy, defined as a set of guidelines for execution and control, as based on the operations strategy, which determines the prescribed, accepted actions within the operations function in order to achieve continuity, consistency and integration.

The result is that the operations manager's decisions are focused, thereby consistent with planning done by the business and that the operations function contributes to the creation of a competitive base.

Long-term planning involves factors such as fixed-capacity planning (eg deciding on the location and layout of a factory) and product planning (which incorporates product development and aggregate forecasting). These activities have a strategic element and decisions flowing from them would affect the operations system in the long term.

Medium- to short-term planning involves factors such as aggregate or variable capacity planning, item forecasting, master scheduling, operations scheduling and inventory management. The activities of medium-term planning are based on the decisions taken during long-term planning, since these – to some extent – determine the parameters within which the medium-term planning will be done. Furthermore, the operations manager organises the operations function by allocating responsibilities and creating structures (eg arranging departments and sections, as well as setting up chains of authority). This function also includes the creation of supplier networks.

Leadership involves motivating the workers within the operations function. A new development in the field of operations management is the focus on the human aspects of the transformation process.

Finally, the operations manager is responsible for control over the transformation process. This function includes all the steps taken to set standards and to evaluate the operations system against these standards. Some of the control functions exercised by the operations manager include quantity control (the measurement of productivity), quality control and cost control.

Aggregate planning refers to the anticipation of aggregate demand in broad terms and encompasses capacity planning. It is a broad view of the market and what an operation can handle in capacity terms. Master scheduling follows aggregate planning and results in a Master Production Schedule (MPS) statement as the main input to Materials Requirements Planning (MRP).

11.6.1 The specific objectives of demand management and demand management activities

- **Long-term objectives:** The long-term objective of demand management relates to fixed capacity planning.
- **Medium-term objectives:** In the medium term, demand management is used to determine aggregate demand. Normally, this is the demand for a group of products sharing the same capacity in the plant. Aggregate demand is utilised for adjustable capacity planning.

Forecasting can be defined as determining the demand for a product produced by the business, but with a view to accommodating future events.

Recording orders is another important component of demand management. The delivery promise can only be made once the order has been positioned in the master schedule, which in turn is dependent on the availability of finished product, assemblies and components.

11.6.2 Categories of forecasting

Broadly speaking, forecasting techniques are divided into three categories.

- First, there are qualitative techniques based mainly on judgement. Although data are used in these techniques, the forecast is done on the grounds of the forecaster's feelings about the data, rather than actual calculations.
- The second category is known as time–series analysis, which is quantitative. In this category, the data are manipulated mathematically in order to arrive at a forecast of the subsequent periods.
- The last category comprises the so-called 'causal methods'. The purpose of these forecasting techniques is to determine a cause-and-effect relationship. This is usually done by means of a mathematical expression or model.

Multi-period pattern projections

The time–series technique produces forecasts for more than one future period (be it a week, month or quarter). For example, the average of a number of monthly data points can be taken and used as a forecast for the next six months. The basic assumption is that no trend or seasonal component is present in the demand pattern.

Single-period patternless projections

This kind of forecasting technique also makes use of historical data, but the forecast is for the next (single) period only. The historical data usually reflect the most recent demand quantities. Capacity refers to the limited means of a productive unit to manufacture a certain quantity of products within a particular fixed period. OM may refer to capacity planning, as planning for adjustable (variable) resources, such as labour and aggregate inventory, over the medium term. It should also refer to fixed (non-adjustable) resources. Capacity control refers to the loading of resources and keeping work centres busy, but not overloaded.

Planning for future production capacity occurs in the following three stages:

- demand forecasting
- attuning the capacity of various machines/resources/facilities
- determining strategies for the full utilisation of capacity.

11.6.3 The 'Ms' of capacity

Business capacity is the greatest workload (or input) that a business can handle (transformation to output). The 'Ms' are used to describe the limits of any operation. These are methods, machines, money, material, manpower (including management).

Capacity is made up of combinations of the Ms and the optimisation of capacity is important to maximise production ability. Factors such as the learning curve have an impact on capacity. Trained and experienced manpower affects the rest of the capacity configuration in the sense that it determines how the other Ms are utilised.

11.6.4 Fixed-capacity planning

Fixed-capacity planning is the first long-term question facing OM. This planning must be done thoroughly in order to place the productive unit on a firm footing from the start. In this context, the term 'productive unit' means the factory, office, bank, shop, or similar institution in which goods and/or services are manufactured or provided. The elements of fixed-capacity planning are:

- occupational safety
- identifying a suitable location
- determining the size of the productive unit
- the layout of the productive unit
- the choice and design of, and specifications for, machinery and equipment.

11.6.5 Adapting capacity to a change in demand

The following strategies can be used to make full use of production capacity.

An operations unit consisting of a single experienced joiner can assemble 12 coffee tables per week. Demand increases to 20 tables. The business should, therefore, consider appointing another joiner. The productive unit can consider the following strategies if its capacity is too small to satisfy demand for the product:

- It could opt for differentiation of the product.
- It could also consider increasing capacity by acquiring additional fixed assets.
- The business could introduce overtime.
- An *additional shift* could be introduced. This, too, is a relatively cheap alternative, because the fixed costs have already been covered.
- *Temporary means of production* can be used. This phenomenon is often found in the case of seasonal productive units, such as hotels that employ additional staff during busy periods.
- Divisions experiencing a shortage of capacity could generate that capacity by a *transfer of surplus* capacity from other divisions.
- *Specialisation* of product can be considered if there are too many types of products and/or services.
- Additional machines could be obtained.

Assume a sub-assembly of the **TRAPSIX** golf cart needs to move through three machines in the production process, as in Table 11.5.

Table 11.5: Example of an assembly process

Work station	Machine	Capacity carts per day
Extrude	D	60
Weld	E	20
Paint	F	30

The machine with the smallest capacity (E) will limit the capacity of the entire process. Machine D has surplus capacity and more machines may be required (given that demand is higher than capacity). Calculate the smallest value into which each of the three capacity figures (60, 20 and 30) can be divided and determine how many additional machines are required (see Table 11.6).

Table 11.6: Additional processing capacity

Work station	Machine	Calculation	Additional machines needed
Extrude	D	120/60 = 2	1
Weld	E	120/20 = 6	5
Paint	F	120/30 = 4	3

The productive unit can consider the following strategies if capacity is greater than demand:

- Workers can be retrenched.
- The unit can work fewer shifts.
- Integration of product is an effective strategy at management's disposal.
- Management may decide to close a section of the factory and lay off some of the workers.
- The business can decide to phase out the temporary means of production.
- The business can move surplus capacity that was brought in from another department back to the original department.

Schedules are statements of volume and timing in different types of operations. Operations scheduling refers to the determination of the quantity of jobs and sequence in which jobs and activities are to be completed in the manufacturing plant. The scheduling activity is one of the most complex functions of OM because of the following variables: schedulers must deal with different types of capacity/resources simultaneously, machines and staff will have different capabilities and the number of possible schedules increases as the number of activities and processes increases.

11.6.6 The activities of operations scheduling

Scheduling is a very important skill inherent to OM and is regarded as an art. Schedules change frequently and need to match demand and capacity on a continuous basis.

The aggregate plan for a business indicates what final products the business plans to manufacture. **CARmats (Pty) Ltd**, for example, primarily produces 4 000 anti-rubber TPE mats per year, consisting of 2 500 small car trunks and 1 500 SUV liners. The MPS is a disaggregated plan and usually indicates the different product models and planned production per time interval (eg per month).

NB

The basic activity of scheduling is the pushing, pulling, routing, sizing and timing of work through work centres. Push and pull control refers to the system that triggers the work. MRP, for instance, pushes out the work without considering the exact time or use of the customer, while in a pull system, the pace is determined by the customer as the next process.

Operations scheduling comprises four distinct activities. First, the operations must be timed and routed. Timing involves making a decision about when a particular operation will take place and routing is done to establish the place where, or on which piece of equipment, the operation will be performed.

The second activity is known as dispatching. This involves issuing a shop order so that the operation can take place.

The third activity concerns control or establishing the status of the shop order. This is necessary, since the progress of the shop order must be known at all times. If necessary, a shop order may have to be expected so as not to delay the delivery of the final product, or to minimise the lateness on an order.

Expediting is the fourth activity of operations scheduling.

Effective scheduling

- provides a realistic schedule and allows for any essential changes
- allows enough time for all the operations (the time before, during and after operations)
- does not release all available jobs by means of shop orders
- does not schedule all the available capacity of the plant
- assigns responsibility for keeping to schedules to the workers or operators.

Apart from the fact that scheduling is much easier in continuous or repetitive manufacturing, the success of the so-called 'process operations' also depends on a number of other factors. These factors are:

- avoiding quality problems where possible and assuring reliability of suppliers
- monitoring the process and product design
- rigorous preventive maintenance
- optimal mixes and rapid changeover
- regular schedules and linear output.

Undercapacity scheduling means that less than the total available capacity is scheduled, for example 95% of available capacity for a particular shift. This means that the required output for the shift is only 95% of what could be produced at full capacity.

The nature of scheduling will depend on the type of operations system (eg make-to-stock, resource-to-order or make-to-order). The planning and control therefore differ for each product or operation. Low-volume operations have more speculation because of the different variables in the throughput process. For high volume make-to-stock operations, the demand time is very short compared to the total throughput cycle.

11.6.7 Forward and backward scheduling

The point of departure used in scheduling has a critical influence on the scheduling itself. The first approach is to begin at the present and to schedule forward, according to the times needed to complete all the operations necessary to complete the order. When all times have been added, the manufacturer can give the customer an indication of when the order will be ready. This approach is known as forward scheduling. On the other hand, in backward scheduling, the required time as prescribed by the customer can be used as a starting point so that the time for each activity is subtracted from the due date (see question 13 in the Self-evaluation questions section).

11.6.8 Gantt charts and other techniques

Gantt charts (time charts) are the most commonly used scheduling technique. They are simple to construct and easy to understand. Gantt charts give a visual impression of the progress made on the project or sub-project. The work packages of the job/project with its work package descriptors (tasks or activities) are on the left-hand side and the work duration at the bottom.

Another technique that can be applied to schedule any number of jobs on two or three machines is known as Johnson's algorithm. The algorithm ensures that the optimal sequence is found – that is, the sequence that will minimise the total processing time. Johnson's algorithm has as its point of departure the existence of a fixed sequence according to which the job moves through the work centres or machines.

The very simple **Johnson's algorithm** (also referred to as Johnson's rule) is a good example of how powerful an OM technique can be. This algorithm is widely used in small job shops, where volume is low and variety is high. Determining the optimal processing sequence (that is which job follows which), as opposed to scheduling work on a random 'thumb-suck' or first-come-first-served basis, can save operations managers a great deal of time and other resources.

In the following figure, jobs are extruded, then printed and finally cut.

Table 11.7: Plastic extrusion operation of five different jobs and three work centres

Trapsix (Pty) Ltd jobs	Processing time in the extrusion work centre	Processing time in the printing work centre	Processing time in the cutting work centre
P	6 hours	5 hours	5 hours
Q	8 hours	3 hours	7 hours
R	4 hours	2 hours	7 hours
S	3 hours	2 hours	10 hours
T	5 hours	5 hours	8 hours

Following the steps (not explained here) of the algorithm, the optimal sequence is:

S → R → P → Q → T with a total processing time (determined on a Gantt chart) of 41 hours. **TRAPSIX (Pty) Ltd** can, this way, optimise their time per job and gain additional capacity. If the sequence is randomly determined by 'thumb-suck', it will be found that there is an error margin of six to ten hours. A manager, therefore, who plans to do five jobs on this thumb-suck basis in a 42-hour week, will not succeed. In fact, the P → Q → R → S → T sequence will take 49 hours. Managers who do not use this technique will tend to lose up to 10 hours per week × 40 booked work weeks = 400 hours/eight-hour work days = ±50 days.

Applying this simple algorithm can, therefore, save a considerable amount of time, thus creating spare capacity.

11.6.9 Inventory management

Inventory management is the function of planning and controlling all types of inventory (raw materials, sub-assemblies, consumables, finished products etc). Inventory management is crucial, since capital must be tied up in other investments and not in idle stock. The inventory function has several interfaces with purchasing, warehousing, marketing and OM.

The essence of inventory management is to have just enough inventory at any given time. This implies two major dimensions, namely timing of inventory and quantity determination. Several techniques exist for timing and quantity determination.

The mode of operation will determine the type of timing and quantity planning and control. Resource-to-order (project operations) will keep no stock. Make-to-order (eg job shops) will hold the minimum inventory and will obtain inventory according to the custom order by the client. Make-to-stock (eg batch and repetitive operations) will do planning and control based on forecasting, safety stock levels and economic order quantities.

Control must be exercised over the financial investment in inventory, thereby saving on interest and cost. Keeping inventory goes hand in hand with certain cost factors, such as obsolescence, interest on capital investment, physical wear and tear, damages, transportation and insurance. If inventory control does not enjoy management's full attention, these cost factors can take on serious proportions.

The objectives of inventory management are as follows:

- A scientific, factual method to simplify purchases (by using mathematical models) needs to be created.
- There should be a reduction in possible losses as a result of obsolescence and incorrect or excessive purchases. Good inventory control turnover rates are necessary.
- Dead or slow-moving stock should be identified.

- Inventory control must serve as a source of information for management decisions.
- Losses should be prevented by controlling all incoming inventory as regards quality, quantity and the requirements as determined in the purchase order. This is important since it impacts directly on the quality of the finished product.
- Excessive variety should be avoided. The advantages of standardisation and simplification must be considered.
- Production should never be delayed because of a shortage of a certain inventory item. Such delays make an extremely bad impression on the customer.
- Ordering the most economical quantities through an effective control system is essential.
- All internal customers (the next process) and external customers should be given good service.

Carrying cost

Inventory ties up capital and is referred to as 'carrying cost'. There are several inventory carrying cost elements. Total carrying cost usually includes the following and may be direct or indirect.

- **Direct inventory carrying cost elements:** The two direct-cost components are capital cost (interest or opportunity cost) and holding cost. Holding cost refers to the cost involved in renting storage facilities, warehouse equipment, electricity, insurance, security, handling, bookkeeping, warehousing labour and damage.

Note in the example below, I = the annual carrying cost rate, which is based on the direct inventory carrying cost elements, namely capital cost and holding cost.

- **Indirect inventory carrying cost elements:** These are the costs attached to obsolescence, record-keeping, physical stocktaking, inventory planning and control by management. Other hidden cost elements are the cost of production floor space utilised for work in process, scrap and rework, as well as the cost involved in handling and containerisation.

The entrepreneurs of custom-made hearing protection devices in South Africa need to be flexible and adaptable to the high demand of quality ear plugs. Assume it would cost R2 750 to rearrange the Noise Clipper (Pty) Ltd laboratory facilities inside one of their work centres in order to eliminate R5 500 worth of inventory. If I = 0,25, will the rearrangement be worth it?

This is a saving of 0,25 x R5 500 per year (i.e. R1 375 per year), which means that the R2 750 will be recovered within two years. Hence, this would be worth considering.

Order cost

Order cost can be defined as the cost which must be incurred to place an order. An item may be ordered twice, three times or more per year – and even daily in JIT systems. If orders are placed only twice a year, such orders will, therefore make up 50% of the annual demand. If these orders are to be manufactured internally, the cost will consist mainly of machinery set-ups.

Inventory timing by means of the reorder point (ROP)

Inventory timing by means of the ROP can be regarded as the traditional model. This technique is as old as manufacturing itself. However, it is still a popular method and is found, for example in every household. A reorder point refers to a certain level of stocks at which the stock must be replenished or reordered.

There are variations of ROP. The periodic inventory system is used by restaurants, service stations and other retailers, where inventory is ordered daily or weekly. The two-bin system is also a continuous inventory system often used in small warehouses. As soon as one bin is empty, an order is placed. ROPs are calculated according to experience of consumer patterns, rule-of-thumb judgement, or by applying a formula. However, the formula also demands a degree of judgement, since it incorporates safety stock and demand patterns.

The ROP formula is:

ROP = D(LT) + SS

where ROP	=	reorder point
D	=	average demand per time period
LT	=	average lead-time
D(LT)	=	average demand during lead-time
SS	=	safety stock

Noise Clipper's laboratory's average monthly demand for Mr.cl-EAR cleaning spray for occupational hygiene is 105 litres. If the order lead-time is one week and a safety stock of five litres is applicable, what will the ROP be?

ROP	=	D(LT) + SS, in other words
ROP	=	105(7/30) + (105/30)5
	=	24.5 + 17.5
	=	42 litres of Mr.cl-EAR cleaning spray (this level signals a new order).

11.6.10 Material requirements planning

Material requirements planning (MRP) plans for various periods in the future and is also referred to as a 'push system'. An MRP computer run enables operations managers to answer questions, such as: a master schedule for three sizes of screwdriver indicates that all three screwdrivers (size 2 mm, size 7 mm and size 5 cm) use the same handle. The item master file shows the planning factors, such as batch order quantities of 20, a safety stock level of two handles, available inventory of 70 and the lead-time for orders of two weeks. In this way, MRP assists OM managers to establish when orders will be issued and what the planned orders will be. MRP can be complicated and is computer based.

11.6.11 Determining inventory quantities

The lot-for-lot approach

The easiest way is to make the batch size equal to net requirements. Only the quantity required for the parent item is bought or manufactured. There is no batching in larger batches. Orders must, therefore, be placed frequently, which results in high order costs or set-up costs.

The EOQ formula

The Economic Ordering Quantity (EOQ) model is one of the oldest models, having been developed by F.W. Harris in 1915. Although the assumptions are not always applicable in practice, they are still usually close enough to make the model useful.

11.6.12 Break-even analysis

This is a technique for determining the volume at which total revenues are equal to total cost or when the cost to make equals the total cost to buy. One can use this in a make-or-buy decision, or when two production methods are compared. It may also be used to determine the profit potential of a new product.

The Fairy Dale Hospital in Buffalo Bay, Knysna, considers a new procedure to be offered at R200 per patient. The fixed cost (portion of the total cost that remains constant regardless of changes in levels of output) is R100 000 per year. The variable cost (the portion of the total cost that varies directly with volume of output) is R100 per patient. What is the break-even quantity for this service?

Answer:

One can use the algebraic or graphic approaches. For the hospital to break even, the number of patients (Q) in Buffalo Bay must equal the fixed cost per year (F) divided by the unit profit margin (price (P) minus cost (C)).

This gives us the following formula for the break-even number of patients:

$$Q = \frac{F}{P - C} = \frac{100\ 000}{200 - 100} = 1\ 000 \text{ patients}$$

Consequently, if demand is less than 1 000 patients, the procedure should not be considered.

Break-even case study using the algebraic approach

CARmats (Pty) Ltd has developed and patented a new anti-rubber vehicle liner (trunk). Before trying to commercialise the mats and add it to their existing product line, they wish to get an idea of the possible success by determining the minimum break-even demand or volume.

The fixed cost is R56 000 per year, the variable cost per unit is R7 and the selling price is set at R25. Expected initial demand is ±415 units per month. Use the formula to calculate the break-even quantity (Q).

The answer is Q = 3 111 units per year. It will therefore be worthwhile to proceed with the device.

11.7 OPERATIONS IMPROVEMENT

Leadership is an important part of quality. True entrepreneurs have an innate passion for quality and they lead by their own example and influential power. However, they do need to take cognisance of a few important issues, namely:

- effective and constant communication
- creating the right attitude and motivation for employees to serve the customers to the best of their ability
- identifying and developing the abilities of employees so that they can contribute in the areas in which they are operationally active
- helping employees to understand the basics of sound management.

A good leader has the ability to see the big picture, strengthen the vision and then inspire employees to strive for its realisation. Leaders have a big impact on the culture of the organisation. Leadership hinges on vision, strategy and people empowerment. Management by fear is a sign of leadership inadequacy.

Leadership determines the components of the quality culture. These non-tangible components are:

- behaviour
- norms
- dominant values
- rules of the game for getting on
- climate.

11.7.1 Never-ending improvement through total quality management

The three main reasons why total quality management (TQM) should be adopted by OM managers is that it is intuitively attractive; second, the principles of TQM make sense unconventionally; and third, a TQM approach to management can dramatically increase operational effectiveness.

TQM is primarily concerned with the improvement of all aspects of operations performance; it is a holistic approach to quality. The TQM approach is far more than quality assurance (QA) or the detection mode of quality control. It is an approach to improving the 'smartness', competitiveness, flexibility and effectiveness of the entire organisation. It also removes the burden of wasted effort from people's lives by bringing everyone into the processes of improvement so that results are achieved in less time (Oakland, 2003:19).

Total quality management is a holistic approach to quality

Quality is a need of both the internal customer (the organisation and the operation) and the external customer. Quality matters to external customers because they want:

- to be respected and do not want any hassles
- a product and service that are value for money
- a product and service that are reliable and meet all their requirements
- a product and service that are available on time
- a product and service that improve their quality of life.

The main reason and justification for quality is the fact that it is absent in people's lives and we consequently seek measures to restore it. One way to obtain quality is by closing quality gaps and applying TQM. Quality management is, therefore, not only relevant in business, but also in the following seven areas:

1. quality of product
2. quality of service
3. quality of organisation
4. quality of processes
5. quality of work-life
6. quality of life
7. quality of being.

Quality of product can be defined as:

- conformance to the purchase order
- fitness for the intended function
- the degree to which the client or customer is satisfied
- a total composite of product and service dimensions that meets the customer's expectations.

Holistic quality refers to a product or service condition with multiple quality characteristics, one that is also managed, obtained or realised in a holistic way namely, by TQM.

Holistic quality:

- is not only a beautiful product
- does not only happen on the production floor
- is not merely inspection
- is not only about improvement techniques
- does not only prevent injuries/errors.

The word 'total' in the term 'total quality management' refers to quality's roots and its end. Quality cannot, therefore, be left to chance. It has to be managed and this becomes everybody's responsibility, not just that of the so-called 'quality department'.

Observe the following examples of definitions of TQM:

- TQM comprises actions needed to obtain world-class quality.
- TQM is the organisation-wide prevention of wastage, defects and injuries and its continuous improvement of quality.
- TQM is a comprehensive, uninterrupted programme to ensure quality throughout the organisation by placing the responsibility for it at source.

The overview of what quality is shows us that it is not easy to define and that it is often in the eye of the beholder. What do people look for when they consider the quality of a product or service? The best way is to use different quality dimensions.

Examples of quality dimensions pertaining to services are:

- Reliability means that one can depend on a service dimension as expected.
- Responsiveness is the willingness of the service provider to meet the customers' needs when these needs are expressed.
- Competence refers to the service providers' possession of skills and knowledge to perform the service.

The following attributes relate specifically to goods:

- Performance is the way that a product actually operates. Does it do what it promises to do?
- Features are the little extras that go with a product and make it unique.
- Reliability refers to the promise that it will perform and keep on performing as promised over a specific time span (eg the guarantee period).
- Conformance is the meeting of pre-set standards.
- Durability is the length of the useful life of the product – its life span.
- Aesthetics – the physical quality of the product, which makes it pleasant to look at.
- Perceived quality is the indirect evaluation of quality, for example the reputation of a specific brand.

11.7.2 Maintenance and replacement

Machinery and equipment are subject to a substantial degree of wear because their moving parts are in constant use. Machinery and equipment operating in dusty conditions are inclined to wear more quickly and require more maintenance.

The consequences of defective machinery and equipment are:

- Reduced production capacity. Machinery and equipment failures mean that no production can take place and this leads to a reduction in capacity.
- Increased production costs. Failures in machinery and equipment result in a higher hourly cost. Machine operators are idle while the machinery and equipment are being repaired. Moreover, the salaries and wages of the maintenance teams, as well as the cost of replacing the broken components, have to be discounted. Sometimes, back-up machinery must be hired or purchased, which also means extra cost.
- Lower-quality products and services.
- Threats to safety.
- Customer dissatisfaction.

Mixed maintenance strategies are adopted according to circumstances. Usually they are a combination of breakdown maintenance, condition-based and preventive maintenance. These types may also be categorised as follows:

- corrective maintenance
- preventive maintenance
- centralised maintenance
- decentralised maintenance
- sub-contracted maintenance.

11.7.2.1 Preventive maintenance

The following programme can be instituted to ensure effective preventive maintenance:

- **Training of maintenance teams.** The members of the maintenance teams must be properly trained so that any possible failure can be dealt with effectively.
- **Determining/predicting the possible time of failure.** The possible time of failure of the machinery and equipment should be scientifically determined. Proper records must be kept of the intervals between failures of the relevant components so that their average life span can be calculated.
- **Implementing Japanese principles.** The Japanese preventive maintenance programmes are based on the principle that workers accept responsibility for preventing possible failures.

The business must, at all times, try to minimise the maintenance cost. This can only be done by creating a proper balance between corrective maintenance and preventive maintenance.

Preventive maintenance becomes more expensive than corrective maintenance as the amount of maintenance increases. Preventive maintenance can, therefore, only be justified if either of the following two conditions occurs:

- when the possible machine failure can be predicted with a fair measure of accuracy, so that the machine can be repaired before it fails
- when the time spent on preventive maintenance is less than it would take to repair a machine which has already failed.

11.7.2.2 Total productive maintenance and improvement

Maintenance should never be seen as an isolated activity. It is part of a continuous improvement programme, since maintenance should lead to improvements. Maintenance strategy should be seen as part of TQM and total productive maintenance and as a mechanism to identify improvement opportunities.

This drive to maintain and sustain assets, equipment and resources has many hidden advantages. Besides improved operations, it cultivates pride and leads to other smaller initiatives (eg new methods and process technologies). Maintenance should never be only corrective or reactive. Improvements should be sought to minimise reactive and corrective maintenance. Preventive maintenance (as part of TPM) must always be improved and made part of all maintenance strategies within the organisation.

11.7.3 Safety, health and environmental management

OM is not only a quantitative subject, but also has a humanitarian side, since many operational solutions lie in employee motivation and well-being.

Unfortunately, many entrepreneurs are more concerned to get the business going initially than to worry about health and safety. This oversight can be detrimental; even large mining organisations tend to neglect health and safety.

Today, the role of OM is definitely moving increasingly towards safety, health and environment (SHE) management. A case in point is the new focus on the well-being of the 'internal customer'. Workplace health promotion is a strategic issue. The changing role of operations managers includes a new paradigm towards labour and work. Their challenge to create and sustain a workplace of health and safety excellence is increasing and there is a culture shift towards the philosophy of work and productivity within a SHE culture. Total quality management (TQM) is regarded as the vehicle to obtain organisational and business excellence.

Everyone should enjoy work and everyone can be a champion. A few quality principles can make a big difference, and a small positive change anywhere can have a positive effect everywhere.

11.7.3.1 Process technology improves health and safety

Any device that improves ergonomics or that can assist the value-adding process may be regarded as process technology. Besides robots, mobile phones and fax machines, a wide variety of technology is available to fulfil operational objectives.

Small things such as a scanner, machine tools and personal protective equipment can make a huge difference. The filtering of harmful amplitudes of noise by means of hearing protection devices not only protects hearing, but also improves localisation, comfort, speech discrimination and so forth.

The concern for health and safety should be informed by the conviction that safety is a matter of life and death. The sum total of all contributions (systems, strategies and behaviours) determines safety. This holistic view of safety is important and should come from an internal sense of moral obligation rooted in values and not only be driven by regulatory pressures. The majority (80%) of injuries at work are attributable to the unsafe acts of people, while unsafe conditions account for the rest of injuries.

11.7.3.2 Good housekeeping

Good housekeeping helps prevent incidents, just as cleanliness helps cut down on germs. A clean, orderly workplace will help workers in many instances. It helps to make workplaces more pleasant, makes workers feel better about their work, and prevents accidents. Treating a work area with respect will help avoid slips, trips, falls and bumps.

The following basic principles are part of good housekeeping:

- wipe up accidental spills without delay
- stack materials (and other means) neatly
- keep cabinet doors and drawers closed
- return equipment and tools to their proper place after use
- dispose of waste or trash promptly (including flammable liquids, oily and paint-covered rags and paper).

11.8 SUMMARY

This chapter has introduced the comprehensive OM body of knowledge. The dynamics of OM and the inherent importance of creativity were discussed first and the typical OM principles were listed. OM and process management were defined and the OM performance objectives discussed. It has been shown how productivity relates to OM. Section 11.5 dealt with operations strategy and design. This was followed by operations planning and control. Operations improvement covered the popular themes of quality, TQM and SHE management.

Self-evaluation questions

1. What are the five major functions of operations management?
2. Which alternative is correct? Production/operations management:
   a. Deals with the general management tasks of the activities within a business, whereby inputs, such as raw materials and labour, are transformed into physical products.
   b. Refers to the 'technical part' of the business where outputs are transformed into products and services.
   c. Primarily focuses on the transformation of outputs, like raw materials and capital.
   d. Is a new development in the business world which is of vital importance to finance new products.
3. Indicate the type of operations system and its associated layout type.
   a. flow production (continuous or repetitive operation)
   b. batch production
   c. job production.
4. Which of the following enterprises make use of a job system?
   a. a hairdresser
   b. a toy manufacturer
   c. an insurance broker
   d. a railway construction company
      i. a and b
      ii. b and c
      iii. a and c
      iv. c and d.
5. Which one of the following enterprises uses a product layout?
   a. a butcher
   b. a building contractor
   c. a TV repair workshop
   d. an electricity supplier.

6. Modern society is becoming more sophisticated. Indicate, by completing the table, the basic differences between the lean and agile operation for customers demanding low cost (lean supply) and customers demanding availability (agile supply) in the following table.

DISTINGUISHING ATTRIBUTES	LEAN SUPPLY	AGILE SUPPLY
Product variety and life cycle	low variety and long life cycles	
Forecasting mechanism		
Profit margin	low	
Market		volatile
Stock demand	Stable long-term	

7. Indicate the basic layout types associated with each of the following processes:
   a. Projects and large jobs =
   b. Jobs and batch processes =
   c. Large batches and small continuous processes =
   d. Mass processes or pure continuous repetitive processes =

8. Which one of the following service enterprises uses a fixed-position layout?
   a. a cinema
   b. a golf course
   c. a car-wash plant
   d. a pool repair company.

9. Planning for future production capacity is done in the following three stages:
   a. Demand forecasting ....
   b. Attuning the ....
   c. Determining strategies for ....

10. The monthly forecast and actual sales of Shoeshine Ltd are given in the table on the next page. What is the approximate sales forecast for October based on a three month moving average?

MONTH	SALES FORECAST (units)	ACTUAL SALES
January	211	200
February	183	195
March	156	140
April	175	135
May	157	185
June	153	190
July	170	220
August	198	235
September	215	200

11. The five elements of fixed capacity planning are:
    - identifying a suitable location ....
    - determining the size of the ....
    - the layout of the ....
    - the choice and design of ....

12. ROPs are calculated according to experience of consumer patterns, judgement or by means of a formula. The ROP formula is:

    ROP = D(LT) + SS

    Determine the ROP if the average monthly demand for Mr.cl-EAR cleaning spray is 105 litres. If the order lead-time is one week and a safety stock of five litres is applicable, what will the ROP be?

13. Litho have five jobs to be scheduled and processed by a particular work centre. The processing time, date received and due date for each job are given.Today is day 66 on the production calendar. By using some scheduling or priority rules, indicate the task (job number) to be completed first for the following situation:

Job number	Processing time	Date received	Due date
367	3	58	67
356	5	55	70
370	4	61	71
366	6	57	69
375	2	63	68

Indicate the task to be completed first when the following rules apply:

a. the earliest due date first

b. most difficult task

c. first-in, first-out

d. shortest processing time.

REFERENCES AND FURTHER READING

Adenforff, S.A. & De Wit, P.W.C. 2004. *Production and Operations Management. A South African Perspective*. (2nd edition). Cape Town: Oxford University Press.

Nicholas, J.M. 2001. *Project Management for Business and Technology – Principles and Practice*. Englewood Cliffs, N.J.: Prentice Hall.

Oakland, J.S. 2003. *Total Quality Management: Text with Cases*. Oxford: Butterworth-Heinemann Publishers.

Schonberger, R.J. & Knod, E.M. 2001. *Operations Management – Meeting Customers' Demands*. (7th edition). New York: McGraw-Hill.

Slack, N., Chambers, S., Harland, C., Harrison, A., & Johnston, R. 1998. *Operations Management*. (2nd edition). Johannesburg: Pitman.

Slack, N., Chambers, S. & Johnston, R. 2004. *Operations Management*. (4th edition). London: Prentice Hall.

Steenkamp, R.J. 2004. *A Guide to Passing Operations, Project and Quality Management*. Claremont: New Africa Education.

Steenkamp, R.J. & Van Schoor, W.A. 2002. *The Quest for Quality of Work Life. A TQM Approach*. Cape Town: Juta Publishers.

Stevenson, W.J. 2012. *Operations Management – Theory and Practice*. (11th edition). New York: McGraw-Hill Irwin.

Unisa. n.d. Centre for Business Management TQM programme and course in the basics of TQM. Study guide. Pretoria: Unisa.

Chapter 12 The human resource function

12.1 LEARNING OUTCOMES

After studying this chapter, you should be able to:

- draw up a job description for a post
- describe the process for employing staff
- compile an orientation programme for newcomers
- draw up a framework for a training programme
- explain the concept of human resource maintenance.

12.2 INTRODUCTION

The human resource – or personnel – function differs from the other functions of the business in the sense that the tasks and activities related to personnel also form part of all the other functions of the business. Each individual who has authority over other employees, from top management to supervisory level, is involved in personnel work to a certain degree.

Most businesses operate on a continuous basis. This means that they do not exist for a few months and then stop their business. They usually plan to be in business for a longer period of time. As time goes by, businesses grow and their employees get promoted, resign and some of them die. Those lost have to be replaced to enable the business to continue as before. Just as the heart supplies the body with blood to enable it to live, the human resource function supplies the business with people to enable it to do business continuously. One of the primary objectives of the human resource manager is to ensure that a business employs the right number and type of employees at the required time.

To achieve this, the human resource manager must carry out the following functions:

- Human resource planning (the process of ensuring that the business has the right skills at the right time).
- Recruitment (to seek and find potential employees).
- Selection (to choose the most suitable person for a specific post).
- Placement (when the employee is placed in the post).
- Orientation (whereby the new employee is introduced to the business, its procedures, the work environment and the other employees).

The human resource function is also a critical component of personnel well-being. The human resource manager is responsible for the best utilisation and maintenance of labour as a production factor in the business. This includes the training, development and maintenance of personnel (including remuneration, labour relations, personnel administration and working conditions).

Even though all businesses are not the same size, ranging from sole traders and small partnerships to large companies, there are always human resource activities to be carried out and managed. This does not mean, however, that each business has a separate human resource division. A small business (one with fewer than 50 employees) is, for example, unlikely to have a separate human resource division. In such a case, the entrepreneur or manager of the business will normally decide how the human resource function will be managed. There are many different options such as:

- one person may be appointed to handle all the human resource tasks
- one person may be appointed to handle all the human resource tasks in conjunction with another function, such as the financial function
- entrepreneurs could handle it themselves
- the entrepreneur could make use of temporary employees to handle the function
- the entrepreneur could outsource the human resource function (ie make use of an external business to manage it).

In larger businesses, it is not possible for the entrepreneur and line managers to handle all staff matters effectively themselves. They need expertise and assistance, and so a human resource division is usually established.

The head of the human resource function has various designations, including 'personnel director', 'personnel manager', 'manpower manager' or 'human resource manager'. The latter term is currently used by most businesses.

12.3 PROVISION OF HUMAN RESOURCES

12.3.1 Human resource planning

As mentioned, from time to time a business needs to employ new staff members. There are various reasons for employing new people. These could include replacing people who resign, or the business is expanding and people are needed to handle new technologies that are being introduced.

When a business expands or changes and a new position is created, a job analysis of the new position must first be done. The human resources manager, together with the relevant people associated with that section and position, must determine the following details of that position: duties, responsibilities, knowledge, skills, aptitudes and attitudes, outcomes and working environment. This can be done through observation, interviews and questionnaires.

Of course when existing positions are filled, this information should already be available. Based on the information in the job analysis, a job description and job specification are then compiled.

The job description is a written document that describes the title, purpose, duties, working conditions, relationships of authority and responsibilities relating to that specific job. The job specification contains the requirements needed by the person who will be doing the job. These include the employee characteristics and qualifications that such an employee needs.

The following is an example of an entrepreneur with a small clothing business, who cannot cope with the volume of work anymore. He decides to get assistance, but is not sure exactly what kinds of people are needed or how many.

The entrepreneur starts by doing a job analysis, ie collecting all the important data about the work, and makes a list of all the tasks that must be performed in the business (see list below). Then all the tasks that logically belong together and that can be done by one person are grouped, such as the tasks to do with money, income and expenditure. Such a combination of tasks can become one person's job.

List of tasks:

1. Conduct market research to determine what sizes, types and quantities of clothing are to be purchased.
2. Purchase stock.
3. Exhibit clothes.
4. Maintain stock at optimum levels.

5. Sell the clothes.
6. Keep records of accounts.
7. Keep the books up to date.
8. Calculate ordering and stock quantities.
9. Market the department.
10. Coordinate continually with the entrepreneur.

Grouping of tasks:

Person 1: Tasks 1, 2, 4, 9 and 10. This could be a head of department.

Person 2: Tasks 3, 5. This could be a salesperson.

Person 3: Tasks 6, 7, 8. This could be an accounting clerk.

Now, the entrepreneur has the option of appointing three people to do these tasks. If, however, the business is too small to warrant this number, some of the jobs could be combined, needing only two people to be appointed. An accounting clerk could also be appointed on a part-time basis, for example for one day a week.

Once the entrepreneur has decided on the number of possible new employees, job descriptions and job specifications should be drawn up for those positions. Job descriptions should be kept up to date so that the work poses a challenge and keeps an employee busy for an entire day. This process is explained in Table 12.1.

Table 12.1: Job analysis, job description and job specifications

Job analysis	
A process to collect all the important data about the job. This includes duties, responsibilities, skills needed, outcomes and working environment. From this, a job description and a job specification are drawn up.	
Job description	**Job specification**
This is about the job itself and includes the following:	This is about the qualifications required by the person who will be doing the job. It includes the following:
• Job status: permanent • Job title: accounting clerk • Location: administration section	• Qualification: B.Com with Accounting and Financial Management III • Experience: 2 years in similar position

- Job summary/outcome: manage and attend to all administrative and financial matters
- Duties: keep record of accounts, keep the books up to date and calculate ordering and stock quantities
- Equipment: computer
- Supervisor: UR Boss (owner of business)
- Job environment: private office with air conditioner
- Dangers: none
- Training: stock control
- Physical exertion: count stock on high shelves (use ladder)
- Responsibility: all administrative and financial matters
- Personality: friendly, confident, honest and hard-working

Of course you can also include in a job description any additional information you deem necessary.

You will probably use the job specification when advertising the position, so adapt it to your specific needs. Put in all the qualifications and attributes that you want the candidate to possess.

The job description and job specification are important aids for an entrepreneur. They are not only used for appointing new employees, but also for the following:

- control purposes where work done is measured against standards set
- performance evaluation to determine whether outcomes were reached
- promotions to see when employees are doing more than what is expected
- the identification of training needs where outcomes are not met
- the establishment of salary scales when looking at job content.

Now that you know exactly what type of person you need in the business (according to the job description and job specification), you have to look for the person to fill the vacant position. The process of finding suitable persons for the job is called recruitment.

12.3.2 Recruitment

If there are any people in the business that could fill the position, you could consider them for the job if it would be promotion for them. If there are no people who fit the requirements, you will have to look for suitable employees outside the business. So, the two sources available for recruitment are internal (existing employees) and external (the labour market outside the business).

A temporary shortage of staff, however, could be overcome by having the existing employees work overtime, training existing employees, subcontracting and outsourcing certain tasks.

Once the personnel need is determined, the entrepreneur, manager or human resource manager must find suitable workers and motivate them to apply for the available positions. Recruitment consists of those activities and efforts on behalf of the business to seek and find suitable potential employees and to persuade them to apply for the available positions in the business.

Remember that all the decisions and actions concerning recruitment (including the sources of, and general approach to recruitment) should fall within the framework of the recruitment policy of the business.

As an example, let us assume that there is a position in the business that has to be filled. As you have seen, the details of the position are set out in the job description and specification.

Recruitment can now be done internally or externally. Internal sources are usually tapped when suitable employees are available within the business. Of course, this depends on whether they have the potential to be trained and prepared for the available positions and groomed for more senior positions. Internal recruitment methods include job posting, self-selection, proficiency surveys and references.

- **Job posting** is one of the most popular methods of filling positions in a business. It includes: traditional noticeboards, email-based systems and iRecruitment systems. The positions are 'advertised' internally through any of these methods.
- **Self-selection** involves advertising the position within the business. Any employee who meets the requirements may apply.
- **Proficiency surveys** are done on employees within the business. Their training, experience and qualifications are updated and kept on file; when a post falls vacant, the job specification is compared with the surveys to identify a suitable candidate.
- **References** are used for recruiting both internally and externally. Current employees recommend their family and friends (often not allowed) for vacant positions.

If there are no suitable internal candidates, external sources have to be pursued. A combination of sources may also be exploited. Examples of external recruitment sources and methods are:

- **Training institutions** such as schools, colleges, and universities.
- **Self-presentation** where job-seekers present themselves at employment offices.
- **Advertisements** in newspapers, magazines and electronic media.

- **Employment agencies** who recruit on behalf of businesses. The following are examples of such agencies in South Africa: 'EmploySA', 'Careers24', 'Jobcrawler.co.za', and 'Affirmative Portfolios'. Of course, recruitment agencies are not free, and they will charge the business a fee. This fee could be calculated, for example, as a percentage of the salary of the appointed person. Some also negotiate a placement fee or recruitment commission.

- **Professional institutions** include specialised employment agencies, such as the South African Institute of Chartered Accountants and 'Executives on the web'.

Keep in mind that there is a cost involved in making use of employment agencies and professional institutions. However, this might be worthwhile if you take into account the internal costs, time and possible problems incurred by doing the recruitment and selection yourself.

The question that arises is which of these methods should one use. Lower-level posts, such as officials, artisans and junior sales staff, could be advertised in a local newspaper and on social media such as LinkedIn, Facebook and Twitter. Advertising on social media is free, you can post a targeted advertisement on a specific network, engage passive candidates and even build your brand in this way. If you are looking for a particular type of employee, you will have to advertise specifically. Specialised periodicals can be used. If you are looking for a human resource person, you could use human resource periodicals, magazines or professional associations. When middle- and higher-level positions are vacant, you may wish to advertise more widely, such as in the weekend newspapers or national periodicals.

To do this, you will need to compile an advertisement. The following information should be included:

- job title
- important features of the work
- requirements for the successful candidate
- salary/wage and fringe benefits
- location
- application procedure
- the person to whom applications should be addressed
- a brief background and description of the business.

Of course, you may omit some of the above information and add other details to suit your needs.

Look at current advertisements to give you more ideas. Look on the Internet, social media and in newspapers. Choose one advertisement for a position as a Human Resource Official. Compare the information in the advertisement with the information given above. Is it a good advertisement?

Figure 12.1 shows an example of a job advertisement from the Internet.

During the recruitment campaign, candidates apply for available posts. Once an advertisement has gone public, potential employees will start applying for the position and you will start receiving applications. Applications are accepted until a predetermined date on which applications close. The next step is the selection process.

12.3.3 Selection

Selection is the process by which the business chooses the most suitable person for the advertised position from the list of applicants.

Various selection methods may be used; it is advisable to use not only one but a combination. Each method has particular advantages and disadvantages. Whichever methods you use, they should give you the information you require. Cost-efficiency should also be taken into account. The following selection tools are available:

- application forms
- interviews
- psychometric tests
- physical tests and exams
- background investigations
- assessment centres
- medical examinations
- references.

Application forms consist of a list of general questions aimed at collecting applicants' biographical data and specific questions regarding the requirements of the vacant post. This enables you to obtain a general impression of how suitable an applicant is and to determine whether they meet the requirements for the post. You should familiarise yourself with the latest legislation regarding issues such as faith, age and gender.

HUMAN RESOURCES OFFICER – PORT ELIZABETH

Location: Port Elizabeth, Market Related
Job Type: Permanent
Sector: SMME sector – Clothing sales
Posted by: ESMF recruitment on March 29, 2019
Reference: ESMF-HR Officer (esmf@gmail.com)
Employer: ESMF Clothing Outlet

A small, successful clothing business in the city centre of Port Elizabeth is seeking to employ a bilingual, enthusiastic and friendly HR officer to expand the business. The successful candidate should have at least three years' experience as an HR Officer, and a degree or National Diploma in HR.

Job Specification

- Development and implementation of HR systems
- Provide counselling on policies and procedures
- Develop training and development programmes
- Assist in performance management processes
- Maintain employee records according to company policy and legal requirements
- Review employment and working conditions to ensure legal compliance
- Outstanding organisational and time-management abilities
- Excellent communication and interpersonal skills
- Problem-solving and decision-making aptitude
- Strong ethics

Requirements

- Effective organisational skills
- Interpersonal skills
- Meticulous attention to detail
- Proven experience as HR officer
- Proficient in MS Office
- Degree/National Diploma in Human Resources
- Min three years' experience in an HR Officer role

Apply before Wednesday April 11, 2019.

Please apply by sending your CV to esmfclothing@gmail.com before 11 April 2019. If you have not received a response within two weeks, please regard your application as having been unsuccessful.

Figure 12.1: Example of a job advertisement

Source: Adapted from Careers24 advert available: https://www.careers24.com/jobs/adverts/1386429-hr-officer-cape-town-northern-suburbs/?jobindex=3

The selection interview is a discussion between the applicant and the employer aimed at obtaining further information regarding the applicant. (The employer may also ask other managers and/or specialists to sit on the selection interview panel to assist with the process.) The interview gives the applicant the opportunity to obtain more information regarding the business and the job in question.

Psychometric testing is used to obtain information regarding the personality of the applicant or to make sure that the information obtained during the interview is correct. These tests must by law be performed by professionals in this field, and include personality and aptitude tests.

Physical tests are done to determine whether the candidate meets the physical requirements of the job. These tests can also identify possible hidden ailments.

Background investigations are done to check previous employment, credit records and even criminal records. The depth of such an investigation will be determined by the type of job applied for. Prospective employees who will be working with money will obviously be checked more thoroughly.

At *assessment centres* the job content is investigated and the aptitudes and behaviour required of the incumbent are identified. Exercises are designed for the applicant to do. The behaviour of the applicant is observed and recorded by trained assessors. This gives applicants the opportunity to show their specific skills, characteristics and behaviour. Examples of such exercises are the 'in-tray' exercises and case studies.

Medical examinations used to be quite popular as part of the selection process, but are now prohibited, unless:

- legislation permits or requires the testing
- it is justifiable in the light of medical facts, employment conditions, social policy, the fair distribution of employee benefits or the inherent requirements of a job (Employment Equity Act, chapter 2, section 7).

References provide information about the applicant's job history and are supplied by previous employers/managers/supervisors. This is done with the applicant's permission. The applicant would normally provide such references.

The selection procedure is not the same for all businesses and differs according to needs and preferences, but for most purposes the following steps can be followed:

Step 1: Conduct a preliminary selection interview

Determine whether the qualifications and interests of the applicant are suitable for the requirements of the position. The idea is to get an overall impression of the candidates and to provide them with general information about the business. Applicants who have not yet completed an application forms are asked to do so.

Step 2: Application form

Some businesses prefer to have the application form completed as the first step. They work through the forms received and then invite chosen candidates for a first interview. The application form is designed around the specific needs of the business. Personal information (such as qualifications, training and experience) is evaluated and compared with the job specifications. If you do not have such a form, look at other businesses' application forms and create your own according to your requirements.

Step 3: Selection tests

The type of work will determine the tests that need to be done. These are designed to obtain additional information, including intelligence, computer skills, personality traits and other special abilities that could not be obtained from the application form.

Various tests exist for the following: clerical aptitude, vision, interest and intellectual ability. These tests are done by specialists, and it is advisable to spend some money at this stage on having the tests done professionally rather than running the risk of appointing the wrong person and experiencing great frustration and possibly incurring expense at a later stage.

Step 4: Check references

Any information that is not yet known can be obtained from previous employers or referees. (A referee is a person whose name the applicant provides and from whom you can obtain more information on the applicant.) Such information can be obtained by phone, email or a personal visit.

This step is essential to determine the credibility of the applicant and should not be neglected. You can learn much from previous employers. Remember, however, to 'read between the lines' when you speak to previous employers, because they may gloss over important defects in the applicant's character.

Step 5: Final interview

During this interview, all the information gathered during the selection process is integrated, and you should aim to clarify uncertainties. In larger businesses a team/ panel is usually present at this interview; the panel would include the line manager, the human resource manager, a union representative and anyone else that this team considers necessary, such as a specialist in the field relating to the vacant post. This person could assist with specialist job knowledge. The candidate is also given an opportunity to ask questions and clarify any uncertainties. Of course in a smaller business the manager will decide on the members of the panel, if any.

The objectives of the final interview are to determine whether the candidate is suitable for the vacant position and whether they would be able to get along with the manager and the other employees in the section. Look at the applicant as a whole, the good and the bad points and remember that no one is perfect. Past performance is usually a good indication of what to expect in the future.

Prepare the questions that you want to ask. The following are examples of interview questions:

- Why are you applying for the post?
- How do you view your role in the business?
- How do you see yourself contributing towards making the business more productive?

Step 6: Medical examination

The candidate must be physically suitable for the job to be done. If there is any problem, it should be identified in good time. High medical claims and absentee figures will thereby be avoided.

Step 7: Final choice

The candidate who is finally selected is usually the one whose qualifications, experience and personality most closely match the job specification. Be objective, and remember that you need someone who can do the job.

Step 8: Final offer

Make an offer in writing to the chosen candidate. In the letter you should congratulate the person, give a starting date, salary scale and other benefits attached to the job. In larger organisations the administration and actual appointment are usually handled by the human resource section.

The applicant must now decide, within a stated time frame, whether or not to accept the offer. Changes to the offer may also be negotiated. Conclude a contract with the prospective employee/candidate. The contract usually contains the basic policy and conditions of service of the business; working hours, leave and overtime are also usually specified in this document.

If the offer is not accepted, the next most suitable candidate should be considered.

Step 9: Appointment

When the candidate accepts the offer, management authorises the appointment and the human resource section finalises all administrative matters. The selection process comes to an end here. In a smaller business the owner/manager will complete the appointment.

12.3.4 Employment and placement

Employment involves not only the process whereby the new employee reports to the workplace, but also the accompanying administrative tasks that have to be performed. The human resource manager ensures that the necessary forms, such as unemployment insurance, tax and medical aid (where applicable), are completed, and that any other outstanding information is obtained from the employee. Arrangements for the delivery of furniture and work items for the newcomer are also made (where applicable).

Placement, which is the penultimate step in the process of providing human resources, now follows. This is the process whereby the new employee is placed in the position applied for Placement also occurs when an employee is promoted, transferred or demoted. A good recruitment and selection process should automatically lead to effective placement.

12.3.5 Orientation

The orientation process should already be in progress at this stage. The orientation (also known as incorporation or induction) of newcomers is the process whereby new employees are firstly introduced to the business, its procedures, environment and work situation, and, secondly, to their co-workers, subordinates and superiors.

This is an opportunity that you should use to motivate new employees and put them at ease. There are many benefits for the business in the long term if new employees understand from the very outset how the business works and how to communicate effectively with their colleagues. This will also make a new employee happy and, hopefully, productive.

Proper orientation needs an orientation programme. List all the things you should do regarding the new employee:

- before the employee arrives at the business
- on the first day
- during the first two weeks
- during the first six months.

There are many things that you can do during these orientation stages. The following are some suggestions.

Before new employees arrive at the business

Congratulate the appointees. Send formal letters of welcome and information brochures about the business to the successful candidates. Information such as working hours, dress code, schools (for their children) and estate agents in the area and the general policy of the business is usually appreciated. Ensure that their office or workspace is in order and that the necessary furniture, equipment and stationery are in place before they arrive. Inform the other employees about the newcomers and explain what they will be doing.

On the first day

Be available to meet them and to introduce them to the other employees. Speak to them informally to put them at ease. Show them their office space or work areas. Finalise administrative matters, such as the completion of any necessary forms. Get them working as soon as possible. If necessary, appoint someone to orient the newcomers. Check with them about their transport and accommodation.

During the first two weeks

Newcomers should be introduced to the following systematically:

- the activities of their section and how it supports the business as a whole
- their duties and responsibilities (refer to the job description)
- how, when and where they will be paid
- working hours, leave policy, meal and tea breaks
- the use of the telephone and the Internet
- dress code
- recreational facilities.

During the first six months

To ensure that the maximum is gained from newcomers, orientation does not end after two weeks. New employees have to develop and become more productive. Identify any shortcomings and training needs and see that something is done about these.

An orientation programme can leave a positive and lasting impression on an employee. Management should take advantage of such an opportunity to motivate their employees and to inspire their loyalty. Understanding each other and communicating well from the start will have many beneficial results in the long run.

12.3.6 Human resource provision and the law

Since the implementation of the Labour Relations Act 66 of 1995 as amended by Act 12 of 2002, the Basic Conditions of Employment Act 75 of 1997 as amended by Act 11 of 2002, and the Employment Equity Act 55 of 1998 as amended by Act 47 of 2013, a number of important issues regarding the employment process have arisen. Human resource managers and entrepreneurs will have to adjust their policies and procedures and apply them fairly and consistently to all applicants. A failure to do so could have major implications for the business. The main issue here is that all forms of discrimination are forbidden by law. Details of Acts might change and business owners and managers must keep abreast of any such changes.

12.4 HUMAN RESOURCE TRAINING AND DEVELOPMENT

Most newcomers in a business are not always ready to perform their new tasks well. Someone who holds a technical or professional qualification still needs initial orientation regarding the policies, procedures and practices of the specific business. The training process, therefore, begins with the orientation programme.

12.4.1 The aims of training and development

The concepts of training and development are often taken to mean the same thing, yet they refer to two different activities within the business.

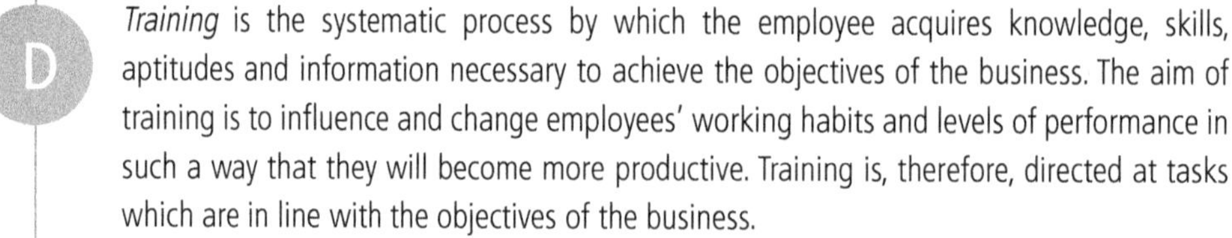

D

Training is the systematic process by which the employee acquires knowledge, skills, aptitudes and information necessary to achieve the objectives of the business. The aim of training is to influence and change employees' working habits and levels of performance in such a way that they will become more productive. Training is, therefore, directed at tasks which are in line with the objectives of the business.

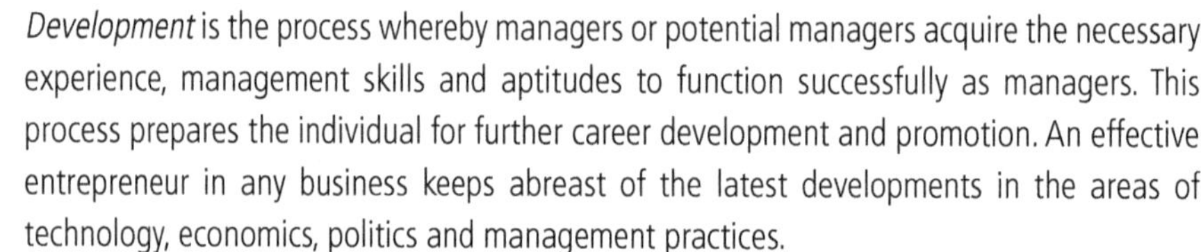

D

Development is the process whereby managers or potential managers acquire the necessary experience, management skills and aptitudes to function successfully as managers. This process prepares the individual for further career development and promotion. An effective entrepreneur in any business keeps abreast of the latest developments in the areas of technology, economics, politics and management practices.

The basic objectives of training and development are:

- to orient new employees with regard to their tasks
- to improve performance and increase productivity
- to maintain a performance level in spite of changes in the work itself or in technology
- to prepare the employee for promotion.

Before any training can be undertaken, you should first determine whether there is really a need for it. An employee may be experiencing personal problems and their work may suffer as a result. A supervisor may not know this and may mistakenly identify the problem as a lack of knowledge or skills. Training costs time and money, and you should therefore ensure that it is not undertaken unnecessarily.

12.4.2 Drawing up a training programme

When you draw up a training programme, the following steps can be used:

Determine training needs

Before training can commence, a needs assessment should be done. These needs are related to the technical, administrative, management or other skills which employees may require in order to perform their duties productively. It is the responsibility of the direct supervisor to identify these needs.

There are different ways to identify training needs, such as:

- The **employee is asked** to say whether they feel unqualified to carry out a task effectively due to a lack of knowledge and/or skills. Although this is not a scientific method to determine training needs and does not provide for long-term needs, it is a practical method which can be used profitably in combination with other methods.
- **Interviews**, where the human resource manager conducts interviews with supervisors, key people and employees in the business to ascertain whether any training needs exist.
- Using a **questionnaire** is a scientific method of ascertaining training needs. Results obtained are usually comprehensive and based on fact.
- The **management by objectives** technique provides ongoing information regarding the work and progress of the employee. You should, therefore, be able to see immediately whether an employee needs training.

The above are active techniques to determine whether there is a need for training. Sometimes, circumstances or problems arising in a business may indicate training needs. Specific problem areas that could point to training needs that should be investigated include low productivity, high costs, poor quality, high wastage, grievances, a high staff turnover, poor discipline, rule-breaking, a high absenteeism rate and standards that are not being achieved.

Establish the objectives and content of training for the training programme

Write down what you wish to achieve with the training. Be specific and use standards so that your objectives are measurable. The difference between what the worker is supposed to do (see job description) and what they can actually do may also be used as a basis for the training programme. Do the employees need basic training, such as training in the use of the telephone, or more specific training, such as training to enable them to use a new computer program?

Determine suitable training methods

Decide whether you will make use of lectures, in-service training, videos, case studies or other methods. Are you going to instruct, facilitate or both? If the training know-how is already in the business, you can do it internally; otherwise make use of external training specialists.

Present the training or send employees for the training

Decide whether it is best to carry out the training on site, or to send your employees to another venue.

Evaluate the training once the employees are back at work

Determine whether the set objectives have been achieved. If not, you will have to reassess the trainer, method, objectives and/or standards (maybe all of these).

Human resource management is not only getting people to work for a business and training them to do the work well, but keeping them motivated and working productively on a continuous basis.

12.5 HUMAN RESOURCE MAINTENANCE

Human resource maintenance involves all those activities that make the work situation acceptable to the employee. It costs the business a lot of money, time and human resources to employ suitable employees. Entrepreneurs should, therefore, do everything in their power to make the best use of employees and motivate them to ensure that they remain on the staff. In order to accomplish this, we need to look at remuneration, performance management, personnel administration, working conditions and labour relations.

12.5.1 Remuneration

Remuneration is what employees receive in exchange for the input they offer the business. Management has certain responsibilities regarding remuneration.

Remuneration should correspond with the remuneration for the same type of work in similar businesses and business sectors. Necessary adjustments should be made from time to time to keep pace with the rising cost of living and inflation.

If the above requirements are not met, it can be expected that staff turnover will be high, employees will lack motivation, unions will be involved in constant wage negotiations and productivity will suffer.

Remuneration can be paid to employees in various ways. We can differentiate between direct and indirect remuneration. Direct remuneration is the salary or wages an employee receives. Salaries are usually paid monthly and wages weekly or daily. To differentiate between productive employees and those who do as little as possible, the latter can be paid per task or piece of work. This is known as the 'piece-wage' system: an employee is paid a sum of money as soon as a specific task or piece of work is completed. For example, an employee is paid R50 for each box of products they unpack, regardless of how long this takes.

Every business has its own particular kinds of indirect remuneration, or fringe benefits. Over and above the salary of the employee, the business may pay the following:

- **Pension:** some employers contribute to an employee's pension.
- **Insurance:** certain types (for example, workmen's compensation and disability insurance) are sometimes borne by the business.
- **Housing:** a subsidy, low interest rates or even free housing can be given.
- **Transport:** various forms of allowances may be given.
- **Leave:** although the Basic Conditions of Employment Act compels employers to allow employees to take leave, this may also be regarded as a fringe benefit.
- **Profit-sharing:** if the profit for a period is higher than a predetermined amount, management could decide to pay the employees a certain percentage of that profit. This makes employees feel that they have a personal stake in the business, which should have a motivating effect.

Indirect remuneration (or fringe benefits) are not necessarily given to all employees. It usually depends on the level of the employee's post. Certain fringe benefits are given only to employees above a specific level in the hierarchy. The combination of direct and indirect remuneration is usually referred to as the employee's package.

The main question is usually how much to pay the employee. When a salary is determined, it is a good idea to look at the salaries of similar posts in other similar businesses. The value of the post must also be compared with the value of other posts in the same business. Remuneration systems may be determined in various ways, but this is usually done by the human resource specialists.

Posts are arranged in order of rank from the employee on the lowest level to top management. A remuneration policy is determined, and a salary scale is assigned to every post in the business. The policy should be made known to the employees, and they should know why they are linked to a particular salary scale or structure. Table 12.2 shows an example of salary scales for a small business.

Table 12.2: Examples of salary scales for a small business

Post level	Job title	Salary scale (per annum)
1	Cleaner/messenger	R42 000 – R60 000
2	Salesperson/administrative official	R50 000 – R140 000
3	Senior clerk	R50 000 – R300 000
4	Supervisor	R100 000 – R400 000
5	Co-director	R170 000 – R525 000

There are other factors that will also determine how much employees are paid. These are:

- the supply and demand of labour in that specific sector or area where the business is located
- the business's ability to pay
- the prevailing minimum wage.

When employees are paid, there are also other aspects that the human resource manager should attend to. Not only the business but also the employees should be registered with the South African Revenue Service (SARS). Each employee must have a tax number. It is the employer's responsibility to deduct tax from the salaries of the employees and to pay this monthly to SARS. The amounts deducted must be according to tables obtained from SARS. At the end of the tax year (February 28), each employee must be issued with an IRP5 form. This is a summary of the employee's income and deductions for the past tax year.

According to the Department of Labour, a payslip must contain the following information:

- employer's name and address
- employee's name and occupation
- period for which payment is made

- total salary or wages
- any deductions
- the actual amount paid
- if relevant to the calculation of pay
  - employee's pay and overtime rates
  - number of ordinary and overtime hours worked
  - number of hours worked on a Sunday or public holiday
  - the total number of ordinary and overtime hours worked in the period of averaging if a collective agreement to average working time has been concluded.

Instead of making use of permanent employees, you might also use 'contractors' to get the job done. These workers do not work for a salary, but are contracted to do a certain job and then get paid for what they have done, similar to the piece-wage system. If they work more, they get paid more; if less, then they get paid less.

Let us assume that there is a need for a job to be done and the human resource manager decides to make use of contractors. Human resources must come to an agreement with the contractor about the job to be done and the amount to be paid for the job. Then a contract is drawn up. Both parties must accept the contract and sign it together with two witnesses.

The contract should include at least the following:

- The particulars of both parties. This would include information such as names, addresses and contact details.
- Details of service or product to be provided. This is the job that is expected of the contractor. Sometimes it is necessary to include a lot of detail so that both parties understand exactly what the contract entails.
- Machines, materials, stock and maintenance. It must be stated who will provide what, and the standards involved.
- Fee structure. The amount you will pay for the completed task, for each section or for specific services rendered.
- Dates of commencement and completion of the job.
- Breakdown or any other hold-up. Discuss the consequences and actions.
- Indemnity, guarantees, liability and insurance, any legalities, safety and security rules and regulations.

Contractors do not have the same rights and advantages as employees. For example, contractors cannot have paid leave, must pay their own medical aid fees and must cater for their own pension and insurance. Contractors work independently for themselves and are in no way part of the business for which the work is being done.

12.5.2 Labour relations

'Labour relations' is concerned with the creation, maintenance, amendment and administration of rules, control processes, ideologies, interactions and relationships in the workplace.

There are three participants to consider: labour, management and government.

Labour is the human effort which is offered with the aim of acquiring an income.

Management (in this case, the entrepreneur), firstly, aims to run the business profitably so that it can continue to exist and grow. The second function of management is to utilise the available production factors optimally. Special attention should be given to labour, which is usually the most important resource. The ability to control and utilise this resource will, to a large extent, determine the success of the business.

The role of *government* differs from country to country, depending on the prevailing socio-economic and political dispensation. The government's role includes providing the legislative framework for labour relations.

NB

The labour relations system is, therefore, a three-way relationship between labour, management and government. It is in the interests of both labour and management to strive for a climate free of conflict and to settle the conflicts that do arise themselves, in an orderly way, with the help of appropriate institutions.

In many cases, employees are members of a union, which is a permanent representation of employees in an industry, business or profession, established to regulate matters of economic interest by way of negotiations with management, so as to improve working conditions and general living standards.

Since a poor relationship with a union can cause much harm to a business, most employers conclude a memorandum of recognition with the unions. The memorandum includes provisions relating to grievance procedures, mediation, safety measures, use of noticeboards and the administration of the agreement. To make this agreement binding, it must comply with the common-law requirements of a valid contract. The proposed provisions should not clash with labour legislation, otherwise the agreement becomes invalid. Recognition of a union implies an agreement, a relationship and a process.

It is essential to keep up to date with the relevant labour legislation, especially the issues contained in the Labour Relations Act. You can find all the details on the website of the Department of Labour: www.labour.gov.za/. Other information that you can find there includes forms, sample documents and guidelines covering many labour relations issues.

12.5.3 Personnel administration

The quality of decisions taken by management with regard to employees is dependent on the availability, completeness and accuracy of information pertaining to each person. The human resource division is responsible for thorough record-keeping of all relevant human resource data including age, qualifications, courses completed and each person's service record in the business, including promotions, merits and transfers. This data should be stored in such a way that it is quickly accessible when management makes decisions regarding promotions, transfers, rationalisation, training, development and other similar changes.

Larger businesses mostly use a computerised database for this function, but a filing system will work adequately in a small business.

Employees must be familiar with the policy of the business. In most businesses, this policy is contained in a personnel manual or online on the website of the business, which is available to employees at all times. Details contained in the manual include conditions of service, leave codes, rights and privileges of employees and disciplinary and grievance procedures. Since we operate in such a dynamic environment, the manual needs to be kept updated.

It goes without saying that management must not deviate from what is contained in the manual. This could lead to conflict and unhappiness. Communication with employees is extremely important. In many cases, it is advantageous for the entrepreneur to discuss or negotiate any policy or other changes to the manual with employees before implementing them.

12.5.4 Working conditions

It is essential that working conditions should be pleasant and safe before one can expect employees to be motivated and productive. Unsafe, unhygienic and unpleasant conditions may result in an employee being injured or becoming ill. The consequences of bad working conditions are usually greater absenteeism, a fall in productivity and a resultant drop in profits.

Accidents in the work situation can be caused by unsafe conditions and unsafe practices. These types of conditions and practices must be eliminated. The elimination of unsafe conditions should come first. Examples of unsafe conditions are unstable constructions, slippery and otherwise dangerous surfaces, overcrowding in workshops, a lack of protective clothing, inadequate ventilation and poor lighting in work areas. Although these conditions cause the smallest number of accidents, they are situations that can be remedied permanently and at relatively low cost. It is the entrepreneur's responsibility to ensure that the workplace is safe and hygienic, and that personnel use the right protective clothing and equipment.

Unsafe practices, on the other hand, are the result of human error and, as such, more difficult to change. It is mostly an attitude or disposition that has to change, and as you might know, this is not so easy. The entrepreneur should, therefore, first do everything possible to ensure that the working environment is safe before expecting personnel to work safely. Accidents caused by human error refer to unsafe acts (practices), while accidents resulting from technical failures refer to unsafe conditions. Examples of unsafe practices are working too fast, working without authorisation, sitting – or working – on moving equipment, taking chances/risks, moving in unsafe places and the refusal to wear protective clothing.

To prevent accidents, you have to know their causes. There are five basic causes, which are divided into the following two categories:

- **Personal factors:** Lack of knowledge and/or skills; physical or psychological distractions; incorrect attitude or motivation.
- **Work factors:** Unsafe conditions and physical environment; inadequate working standards.

Entrepreneurs must exercise constant control over employees to ensure that the above factors do not arise. It is important to be constantly on the lookout for anything that might cause an accident. As far as safety is concerned, it is vital to take preventive action at all times.

There are various ways in which one can help ensure that employees remain healthy and productive, for example:

- a clean workplace, recreation room and cloakroom
- sufficient leave, acceptable working hours and little or no overexertion
- first aid provision in case of an accident or illness
- a suitable and pleasant workplace
- ergonomically designed office equipment, especially desks and chairs
- sufficient lighting that eliminates reflection and, where possible, uses natural daylight regulated by means of blinds

- limiting noise – and noise intensity – by isolating machines and pipes, making use of carpeted and cork floors and/or acoustic tiles
- temperature regulation by air conditioning, especially where large fluctuations occur, as excessive heat results in discomfort and fatigue.

With regard to certain of these factors, entrepreneurs are compelled by law to provide such an environment. You would be well advised to read the Occupational Health and Safety Act 85 of 1993 to ensure that your business does indeed comply. A business cannot afford to neglect the maintenance of its most important resource – the human resource.

There are many other human resource issues related to Basic Conditions of Employment, such as the Unemployment Insurance Fund (UIF). If you wish to know more about these, you should visit the Department of Labour website (www.labour.gov.za/) to get the latest information. There you will find information on everything that you need. The following section outlines some of the issues and subjects discussed and explained on the website.

General issues

- **Basic Conditions of Employment:** This applies to all employers and workers, and regulates employment conditions, such as leave, working hours (ordinary, Sundays and public holidays), employment contracts, employee records, deductions, payslips, overtime and termination.
- **Compensation for Occupational Injuries and Diseases:** This Act provides for, and deals with, injuries, disablement, disease or death caused by work-related activities.
- **Employment Equity:** This Act aims to promote and achieve equality in the workplace by encouraging equal opportunity for all workers.
- **Labour Market Research and Statistics:** The Department of Labour has identified the need to develop an ability to collect, process, analyse and publish labour-market information and statistics in a manner that will report on how effectively the Department is delivering its services.
- **Labour Relations:** Aims to support labour peace, democracy and worker participation in decision-making in the workplace.
- **Occupational Health and Safety:** Provides measures to ensure the health and safety of all workers in the workplace.
- **Skills Development:** Aims to promote the development of skills in the South African workforce.
- **Unemployment Insurance Fund (UIF):** Provides funds to workers who may become unemployed.

Subjects

- **Maternity benefits:** This is a basic guide to maternity issues, such as maternity benefits, leave and application procedures.
- **Registration:** This gives you guidance on, among other things, how to register for the Skills Development Levy, as a trade union and for UIF. The forms for these registrations are also found on the website.
- **Payslips:** Explains everything you need to know about payslips.
- **Annual leave:** All the information that you need to know about annual leave for the different sectors in the economy.
- **Accidents:** All accident issues, such as compensation for injuries and diseases, as well as a guide to claiming for injuries.

The Department of Labour website also provides information on labour legislation and information relevant to a specific industry, sector or interest group, such as domestic workers, employees, employers or bargaining councils, as well as the forms and sample documents that you might need.

12.6 SUMMARY

As an entrepreneur, if you own a small business, numerous staff matters require your attention. The fewer employees you have, the easier it should be to handle these issues. As your business grows and you need to appoint a lot of people, it is advisable to get assistance from a human resource specialist.

The aim of the human resource function in a business is not only to recruit, select and employ suitable staff; it is also to develop, train and, in some cases, educate existing staff, so that employees are utilised to their full potential.

The employment process costs money, requires human resource and takes up a lot of time. It is, therefore, essential that the staff of the business are well looked after. The personnel are indeed the most important production factor in the business and a high staff turnover is very harmful for any business in terms of costs and continuity.

The activities of the human resource division are not always quantifiable, but, as you saw in this chapter, they are in no way inferior to the other functions of the business.

Self-evaluation questions

1. 'The human resource function is one of the eight functions found in most businesses.' Would the human resource functions be managed differently in a small business than in a larger business? Discuss.
2. Write a job description for a human resource manager, or for your own position.
3. You need a person to manage the administration of your small business. You need to fill the post with the most suitable person. Create an advertisement for the position and explain, step by step, what you will do to fill the position.
4. Draw up a list of tasks you need to do regarding the new administrative assistant using the following headings:
   - The week before the newcomer arrives
   - The first day at work
   - The first week in the post.
5. 'Training and development are necessary only for the employees at the lowest levels of a business.' Define training and development and discuss this statement critically.
6. Explain what is meant by 'human resource maintenance' and discuss its effects on the productivity of a business.

REFERENCES AND FURTHER READING

Anon. 2018. Functions of a Human Resource Department. Available from: http://www.dineshbakshi.com/igcse-business-studies/people-at-work/revision-notes/850-functions-of-human-resource-department. Date accessed: 4 April 2018.

Business Dictionary. 2018. http://www.businessdictionary.com/. Date accessed: 1 April 2018.

Business Owner's Toolkit. 2018. Creating job descriptions. Available from: http://www.toolkit.com/small_business_guide/sbg.aspx?nid=P05_0300. Date accessed: 3 April 2018.

Department of Labour. 2018. South African Department of Labour Online. http://www.labour.gov.za/DOL/. Date accessed: 28 March 2018.

Entrepreneur. 2018. Human resources. Available from: http://www.entrepreneur.com/encyclopedia/human-resources. Date accessed: 1 April 2018.

Government Gazette. 1998. http://www.labour.gov.za/DOL/downloads/legislation/acts/employment-equity/eegazette2015.pdf. Date accessed: 28 March 2018.

Grobler, P.A., Wärnich, S., Carrell, M.R., et al. 2011. *Human Resource Management in South Africa.* 4th ed. London: South-Western.

Pavlou, C. 2018. Job advertising on social media with Workable. Available from: https://resources.workable.com/university/social-media-job-advertising. Date accessed: 6 April 2018.

Legislation

Basic Conditions of Employment Act 75 of 1997

Employment Equity Act 55 of 1998

Labour Relations Act 66 of 1995

Occupational Health and Safety Act 85 of 1993

Chapter 13 An introduction to financial management for entrepreneurs

13.1 LEARNING OUTCOMES

After you have studied this chapter, you should be able to:

- explain why financial management is important to a small business owner/manager
- explain how financial management relates to the other functional activities in a small business
- explain and define financial management as a concept and as an organisational function
- explain how the generic functions of management are applied in financial management
- explain the most important concepts (eg different forms of assets and liabilities, fixed and variable capital needed, ROI and ROE) used in financial management
- explain the most important financial activities in a business
- calculate ROI and ROE of a business.

Students should also be able to give everyday examples (preferably from their own experience) for each of the above-mentioned aspects of financial management.

13.2 INTRODUCTION

The following questions are often asked by existing and potential small business entrepreneurs/managers:

- Is this a fair price to ask (or pay) for a specific business?
- How much should my monthly sales be in order for me to survive in my new business?
- How can I know for sure if I am running my business at a profit or at a loss?
- Is the profit I am making satisfactory?
- Is it better (safer, more profitable) to use only my own capital (such as savings), or is it better to borrow additional capital?

- When I use my own and borrowed/outside capital as well, what should the balance be between these two sources?
- When my business needs a sharp increase in stock during a peak season, should it be financed with a long-term loan or short-term credit?
- Should I sell my products and services for cash only or should I also extend credit facilities to my clients?
- What are the advantages and disadvantages of selling on credit?
- How can I be sure that the stock I have purchased for resale purposes will in fact sell?
- How important is cash flow management to me as a small business entrepreneur?
- How important is effective administration to business success?

These are only examples of the many questions a small business entrepreneur/manager should ask (and get answers for) on a regular basis. The success of a small business depends on answering these questions well!

No one can be a successful small business entrepreneur or a successful manager without a thorough understanding of financial management. Small business entrepreneurs do not need to be chartered accountants or specialists in world money markets. However, each and every small business entrepreneur/manager must have a good insight into and understanding of the core concepts and the fundamental elements of financial management. This is an area that is simply too important to ignore. I know about a very, very wealthy entrepreneur who is dyslectic (he cannot read or write properly), but he says the main reason for his business success is that 'I can count very well!' In any business/organisation – even families, individuals, churches, government bodies, not-for-profit enterprises, etc. – one has to watch the figures like a hawk!

The aim of this chapter is to introduce you to the exciting and very important world of business finance. Through an explanation and illustrations of the concepts and elements of basic financial management, you will develop a thorough knowledge and understanding of these concepts and elements. By working through the chapters in this book, you will acquire the expertise to be able to apply these concepts to the management of an existing small business or the launch of a new venture.

Anna Molele is an excellent salesperson with more than 10 years' experience working for a variety of furniture retailers. She is very good at selecting and purchasing the right furniture from manufacturers and communicating with and convincing existing and potential clients to buy. Now she is planning to start her own furniture retail business and has spent much time preparing her business plan. Just last night she said to her husband:

All my plans are in place. I am going to invest as much as possible in purchasing stock and in marketing my business. At the same time, I will spend as little as possible time and effort on administration. I hate paperwork, and will leave that to a bookkeeper, whose only task will be to satisfy the Receiver of Revenue once a year.'

Discuss Anna's view of administration and paperwork. Write down at least five 'common sense' arguments to support and/or to oppose Anna's view.

13.3 THE FINANCIAL FUNCTION IN BUSINESS

For a business (or any other entity) to operate on a profitable, successful and sustainable basis, a number of business functions and activities need to be identified and managed. Typical examples of such activities and functions are marketing, human resources, production, and security and safety. Another one of these functions is the financial function. The financial function is just as important as any other and the owner or manager of any small business must pay close attention to it.

No single business function is more or less important than another. Each and every business and management function is important to business success and all of them are interrelated. Together, they enable the business to achieve its mission and goals.

The financial management function is distinguished from the other managerial and business functions and activities, but should never be seen in isolation from the others. Each of these other business functions and activities has financial implications for the business. For example:

- unproductive employees have a detrimental effect on the financial performance of the small business
- a lack of marketing activities will lead to a lack of income for the small business
- purchasing products for resale that are not in demand in the marketplace leads to high storage and other costs, with less than acceptable financial return for the small business.

A number of functions need to be managed well in any small business:

- human resources management ensures that the business has sufficient capable people who are working productively
- marketing management ensures that there are enough clients supporting the business
- production management (also called operations management) ensures that the business effectively produces high-quality products or services
- financial management ensures that the business has access to needed capital resources and makes the best use of these.

13.4 DEFINING FINANCIAL MANAGEMENT

Financial management is responsible for acquiring the necessary financial resources to ensure the most advantageous financial results for the small business over both the short and long term. The term 'financial management' also covers the responsibility for making sure the business makes the best use of its financial resources.

13.4.1 Examples of financial management

To illustrate the above definition, here are some examples of financial management:

- arranging in time with a bank manager for an overdraft facility on the best conditions possible (acquiring the needed financial resources).
- ensuring that cash received from daily (or evenly hourly) sales is safeguarded and banked as quickly and as efficiently possible (making the best use of financial resources).
- ensuring that money allocated for a specific application, is indeed used for that (and no other) purpose.

13.4.2 Comparison with other business functions

It should be clear to you that the financial management function is mainly concerned with financial matters. Although all activities in a business have a financial implication, we cannot say that financial management is responsible for all these activities or that financial management must have the final say over each and every other business activity.

To understand this principle, let us look at an example:

Emily Ngobeni is the owner/manager of Thanda Stores. She is considering the placement of a marketing advertisement in the local newspaper in order to create more sales. Indicate which issues of this project are financial management issues and which are marketing issues.

Questions:

1. The availability of applicable funds, the method of paying for the advertisement, the timing of the payment and the possibility of negotiating a discount are all issues that relate to which function of the business?
2. The wording of the advertisement, appropriate illustrations, colour, placement (page allocation) and size of the advertisement relate to which function?

Answers:

1. All are financial management issues.
2. These are all marketing issues.

In many small businesses, one person (the owner/manager) handles all the managerial and business functions. This means that there is less of a need to distinguish which issues are financial, marketing or other functional management issues. In larger organisations, where different managers are responsible for different functions, this need becomes more important.

13.4.3 The definition of financial management

Financial management may be defined as the responsibility for timeously acquiring the needed financial resources and ensuring the best use of these resources over the short and long term.

Think about the functions and activities of a small business. From your own experience, give every day examples of financial management in the following areas:

(a) the acquisition of capital (money to buy something)

(b) the utilisation of capital (using the money available wisely).

13.5 THE MANAGERIAL FUNCTIONS OF FINANCIAL MANAGEMENT

Now that we have defined financial management, we need to ask the following important question: 'How do the generic functions of management apply to financial management?' (In general, the generic functions of management are: planning, organising, activating and controlling.)

13.5.1 Financial planning

Financial budgets (annually or even monthly and/or per singular projects) are the most visible and most common outcomes of the financial planning function. The importance of financial planning can be summed up in the following saying: 'If you fail to plan well, you plan to fail well!'

But financial planning is not concerned only with financial budgets. Typically, financial management planning includes planning, developing and finalising an appropriate bookkeeping system and deciding on effective pricing and credit policies, financial procedures and processes to be followed. This planning function and process is a continuous activity and process, and by far not a once-off (or annual) activity.

13.5.2 Financial organising

Another part of financial management is the responsibility to arrange and to organise needed activities, equipment and people in the most effective way to carry out the financial function. This includes the delegation of financial responsibility to others: for example, who will be authorised to make payments on behalf of the small business? Who is going to be responsible for verifying the records and cash receipts of cashiers? Who determines selling prices, how is it done and how often is this re-evaluated? And who will be in charge of credit control? This organising function and process is a continuous activity and process, and by far not a once-off (or annual) activity.

13.5.3 Financial activating

This managerial activating function means inter alia a manager's responsibility to lead and motivate the other people in the business and to ensure effective and efficient communication. An example of this function in financial management is ensuring that employees doing financial work (for example, bookkeeping, cashier work, debt collection, banking, budgeting and pricing) are well trained and motivated to carry out their tasks as diligently as possible. Another example is making sure other functional managers (for example, marketing, human resources, security, production) are always involved with and know the full details of the next annual financial budgeting project in good time. In fact, financial management cannot and should not be isolated from these other operational functions – all should work together on a continuing basis to ensure the best results for the business!

13.5.4 Financial controlling

It is a common mistake of many small business owners and managers to focus only on the controlling aspects of the financial management function. Many people will point out that financial management is only about 'checking' records, bookkeeping and all financial transactions. These are all part – but definitely not all – of the financial management function. It is safe to say that you cannot control something that has not been properly planned, organised and activated, because any control activity must have a set standard against which an outcome can be measured and judged to be in order or not.

The better you plan, organise and activate, the better you will be able to control the activities of your business.

There are four steps in the controlling function:

1. **Determining performance criteria** (planning what should be done, what is expected to happen): drawing up and finalising financial budgets is a typical example.
2. **Measuring the actual performance** (the actual results): setting up an administration and bookkeeping system, with regular reporting outputs, is a typical example.
3. **Comparing the expected with the actual performance** to indicate positive and negative variances: this indicates acceptable and unacceptable deviations from the budget and other set and agreed criteria.
4. **Taking corrective action**, where necessary: for example, retraining cashiers to ensure that clients are billed and pay 100% correctly and on time.

13.5.5 Some financial activities in business

By now, you should have an idea why financial management is so important in business, how it is defined and its relationships with other functions in business.

Think about the activities of a typical small business. Can you identify at least ten financial activities in that business?

There are many financial activities in a small business. Here are some examples:

- **Collecting external information on financial matters:** for example, changes in interest rates; the exchange value of the rand; the availability of capital; trends in debt collection; the profitability of similar businesses in the same industry.
- **Preparing financial budgets:** for example, working together with the marketing function to forecast expected/needed sales volumes in the forthcoming year, even breaking it up into monthly figures; working out a cash flow budget.
- **Recording all financial transactions on a regular basis:** for example, making sure that credit sales to customers are effectively and efficiently recorded and administered.
- **Analysing financial performance:** for example, continuously and timeously assessing whether actual budgeted income and expenses are on course, according to the annual business plan and budgets.
- **Financial reporting:** supplying the other functions of the business with needed financial information (for example, indicating to the production department whether labour and/or material expenses are still within the budget or not).

- **Safeguarding cash resources:** for example, ensuring that cash received daily from cash sales and debtors' payments is safeguarded and banked as soon as possible.
- **Formulating credit policy:** for example, investigating the advantages and disadvantages of selling to customers on credit; ensuring that only creditworthy clients are allowed to buy on credit.
- **Debt collection:** for example, ensuring that debtors honour their commitments regularly and on time.
- **Salary administration:** for example, ensuring that all employees receive their correct remuneration exactly on time.
- **Negotiating with suppliers of capital:** for example, negotiating with banks or other financial institutions the availability of needed bridging capital (say, an overdraft facility) on the best terms possible.

The above-mentioned activities are only some examples. A number of other activities may be added to this list.

13.6 IMPORTANT CONCEPTS IN FINANCIAL MANAGEMENT

As an introduction to financial management, this section of the chapter briefly explains the meaning of a number of financial management concepts. Most of these concepts will reappear in other chapters, where they are more fully explained and illustrated.

The following concepts will be covered:

- assets: fixed assets; current assets; other assets
- capital: own capital (equity); outside or borrowed capital (long-, medium-, short-term); permanent and variable capital; current capital; working capital
- financial structure
- profitability
- liquidity
- solvency.

13.6.1 Assets

The overall objective of a business is to maximise the rate of return on investment to the owner/s over the long term, taking into consideration the interests of all applicable stakeholders.

To achieve this, the business needs assets, which vary greatly in nature. For example, a manufacturing enterprise will definitely need manufacturing equipment, a transport enterprise will need vehicles, a retailer will need shop premises, while a management consulting enterprise will need people trained in business management techniques.

In all cases, the assets of a business enterprise can be divided into two major categories: fixed assets and current assets.

- **Fixed assets** are those assets owned and required by the enterprise for a period of longer than 12 months. (Assets that are required but that do not belong to the business, such as items that are leased or rented, are not part of fixed assets for the purposes of the balance sheet.) Typical fixed assets are: land and buildings; equipment and manufacturing machinery; vehicles; furniture.
- **Current assets** are assets owned by the enterprise that will be turned into sales or cash within a period of 12 months. Typical current assets are: outstanding debtors (people who owe the business money); raw materials in a manufacturing enterprise; stock (inventory); cash (on hand or in the bank).

There is a third category of assets: other assets. These are assets not directly involved in the normal operational activities of the business, for example: shares in another business; investments in a financial institution.

To test your understanding of the differences between fixed, current and other assets, consider the following small businesses and answer the questions.

1. Business A manufactures school uniforms and has machinery and equipment valued at R100 000.
2. Business B buys and sells all sorts of manufacturing machinery and equipment. At present, the available stock is valued at a cost price of R100 000.
3. Business C is an accounting firm. It bought some shares on the stock exchange for R100 000 as an investment.

In each of the three cases, is the R100 000 sum a fixed, current or other asset? Why?

1. Business A? Why?
   (**Answer:** fixed asset; the machinery will be used for more than 12 months)
2. Business B? Why?
   (**Answer:** current asset; the inventory will be sold within 12 months)
3. Business C? Why?
   (**Answer:** other asset; the investment is not required for operational purposes)

13.6.2 Capital

The assets required by a business have to be financed, supplied and paid for. For this, the business requires capital. We can identify a number of sources: for example, banks and manufacturers, that act as the suppliers of the necessary capital or assets to the business. Capital supplied is also sometimes called liabilities.

The major types of capital are:

- **Owners' capital (equity):** This is the capital supplied by the owners/shareholders of the business, in the form of an initial start-up investment (either in the form of assets or as cash) or as accumulative retained net profits, or both. In the case of a close corporation (cc), this type of capital is called members' interest. In the case of a company, this may be called share capital.
- **Outside** (borrowed, loan, foreign) capital: This represents all the capital supplied (either in the form of assets or as cash) or made available to the enterprise by sources other than the owners/shareholders. When such capital is supplied for a period of longer than 12 months, it is called long-term capital. Short-term capital is repayable within 12 months.
- **Trade credit** (when buying stock/raw materials on credit from suppliers) is a form of borrowed short-term capital. The same applies to a bank overdraft, while a 10-year mortgage loan (to help finance a factory building) is regarded as a long-term loan.
- **Permanent and variable capital:** Permanent capital is that amount/value of assets/ funds/ money that is required by an enterprise at all times (say, over a year). Variable capital refers to the additional amount/value of assets/money (over and above the amount of permanent capital needed) that the enterprise needs from time to time: for example, during seasonal peaks such as Easter and Christmas.

Mrs Tshabalala owns a boutique selling ladies' dresses. A minimum stock level of R600 000 is needed all year round in her business. But three times a year, during the December holidays as well as at the start of the winter and summer seasons, she increases her stock levels to R1 000 000. In her case, the R600 000 needed to finance the minimum stock level all through the year will be regarded as permanent capital, while the additional R400 000 required only for the three peak periods can be regarded as variable capital.

- **Current** (liquid, operational) **liabilities/capital:** This is capital utilised on a short-term basis (less than a 12-month period) and should normally only be used to finance part of the current assets of the enterprise. Examples are: trade creditors, bank overdrafts, short-term loans.
- **Working capital:** This normally refers to the current assets, while net working capital refers to current assets less current liabilities.

13.6.3 Some other concepts

Financial structure

This concept relates to the composition of the business's assets in relation to its sources of capital. It also shows the relationships between owners' capital and long- and short-term outside capital, and how these capital resources were utilised in total to finance fixed and current assets.

Profitability

Many people will say, 'This is what business is all about', and in a sense this is correct.

The owners of a small business expect to earn a satisfactory profit (as a just/fair return on their money, effort and time they have invested as well as remuneration for the risks they have taken). This is called return on investment (or ROI) and is expressed as a percentage. Profitability is one of the most frequently used and best measures available to determine the ultimate degree of success or failure of business operations. Profitability is therefore one of the most fundamental and most important concepts in business.

Two major forms of profitability (there are more than 20 variations) are:

- Return on total investment (ROI): This indicates the rate of return on total capital, or the profitability of the business as a whole. A high return on investment is proof of management's ability to make good use of capital and assets. A low (or no) return on investment indicates management's inability to add value to the enterprise.
- Return on equity (ROE): This indicates the rate of return on own capital, or the profitability of own capital. The actual owners/shareholders of a business are often more interested in this measure than in ROI. Fundamentally, the owners are in business to maximise the return on their own investment over the long term. This ratio can thus be regarded as the bottom line for the small business entrepreneur/ manager.

It is important to point out that the two kinds of profitability mentioned above should not be confused. They are two totally different (but related) concepts.

eg

Jabulani Moloketi has a small business called J's Jewellery. He buys and sells all sorts of costume jewellery. At the end of the financial year, his business's financial statements show the following:

Net profit before interest:	R100 000
Net profit after interest:	R70 000
Total capital employed:	R400 000
Owner's equity:	R200 000

In Jabulani's business, the two kinds of profitability will be determined as follows:

$$\text{Return on total investment (ROI)} = \frac{\text{net profit before interest} \times 100}{\text{total capital employed}}$$

$$= \frac{\text{R}100\ 000 \times 100}{\text{R}400\ 000}$$

$$= 25\% \text{ per annum}$$

This means that Jabulani has utilised all the capital (or assets, as they are of the same monetary value) available to his business in such a way as to show 25c net profit for each R1 of total capital (or assets) employed.

$$\text{Return on equity (ROE)} = \frac{\text{net profit after interest} \times 100}{\text{owner's equity}}$$

$$= \frac{\text{R}70\ 000 \times 100}{\text{R}200\ 000}$$

$$= 35\% \text{ per annum}$$

This means that Jabulani Moloketi was able to use outside and own capital in such a way as to show 35c net profit for each R1 of own capital employed per annum.

Liquidity

The liquidity of a business has nothing directly to do with its profitability. Many profitable (even very profitable) small businesses go bankrupt because of insurmountable liquidity problems. Liquidity refers to the ability of the enterprise to pay its short-term financial commitments continuously and on time. For example, a business has a liquidity crisis if it is unable to pay its trade creditors when payment is due because of a lack of cash (liquid) resources. The same applies to an inability to pay for other liabilities and obligations, such as taxes, wages, salaries and/or municipal levies.

Solvency

Solvency is the degree to which the total assets of the business cover its total liabilities. If an enterprise's total commitments or liabilities are larger than the value of its total assets, it is considered to be insolvent. The reliability of the value of the assets in a business is therefore critical in any calculation of solvency.

13.7 SUMMARY

In this chapter the definition and concepts of financial management were introduced. The chapter explained how financial management fits together with the other functions of business, and some major financial concepts (such as assets, capital, profitability and liquidity) were introduced as important background to all the other parts of this book.

Self-evaluation questions

1. Explain why a thorough knowledge and understanding of financial management is a requirement for anyone in any profession in any industry.

2. Explain how financial management relates to and integrates with the other functional areas of a business.

3. Define financial management and illustrate the elements of this definition.

4. Explain and illustrate how the generic managerial functions (planning, organising, activating and controlling) are applied in financial management. Try to think of examples from your own experience.

5. Briefly explain the following financial concepts:
   a. fixed assets
   b. long-term capital
   c. current assets
   d. current liabilities
   e. owner's capital
   f. variable capital
   g. permanent capital
   h. profitability
   i. liquidity
   j. solvency
   k. working capital
   l. financial structure
   m. return on total capital
   n. return on equity.

6. You can review the various concepts covered in this chapter by considering the following example of a small business. Think about all the concepts discussed in this chapter and try to identify them in the example. You should also be able to explain what each of the concepts means.

Ismail Naidoo opened his grocery shop 12 months ago. He inherited the building, furniture and equipment from his late uncle (total value R800 000), but had no money of his own to buy stock or to pay monthly expenses (excluding rent) for six months. All the trade suppliers to his business agreed that he could buy his monthly stock (average R100 000) on a 30-day credit basis, but he had to borrow the R80 000 needed for monthly operational expenses (multiplied by six months = R480 000). His banker only agreed to a R100 000 bank overdraft facility, and he had to borrow the other R380 000 from family and friends (who agreed that he could repay the loans after 10 years have passed, but required him to pay interest monthly).

Ismail seems to be satisfied now that these 12 months have come to an end. The net profit (after paying R72 000 interest) was R200 000, while his own total investment was only the building, furniture and equipment (R800 000) and the outside capital, worth R580 000 (overdraft 100 000, trade creditors R100 000 and long-term loans R380 000).

a. Can you indicate at least four financial functions in this business?
b. Can you indicate some managerial functions (planning, organising, activating and controlling) in this business?
c. Can you indicate different kinds of assets in this business?
d. Can you indicate the different forms of capital in this business?
e. Can you explain the financial structure of this business?
f. Can you calculate the annual ROI and ROE for Ismail's business?
g. Based on your calculations, what conclusions can you draw about the ROI and ROE for Ismail Naidoo's grocery business?

Chapter 14 Financing the capital requirements of a small business

14.1 LEARNING OUTCOMES

After you have studied this chapter, you should be able to:

- define the two primary sources of capital: own capital (equity) and outside capital (foreign, borrowed, external)
- describe the major characteristics of: permanent finance and its sources; long-term finance and its sources; medium-term finance and its sources; short-term finance and its sources
- explain what is involved in choosing the applicable sources of finance
- discuss the typical problems experienced by a small business in obtaining finance.

14.2 INTRODUCTION

The investment decision determines what assets are required to do business successfully. The small business entrepreneur/manager must make investment decisions on what fixed assets (land and buildings, machinery and equipment, vehicles and furniture) and current assets (cash, raw materials, stock or inventory and size of the debtors' book) are required by the business.

In this chapter we will look at the other side of the capital requirement: the financing decision. Once you have decided in detail on all the required fixed and current assets for your business, you need to ask yourself a number of important questions. These are:

- How will I be able to acquire these needed assets?
- How will I be able to afford and pay for these assets?
- If my (the owner's) capital is not enough, who will be willing to help me to finance these assets?
- Is it wise to use only my own capital or should I also allow other parties to be involved?
- Are there certain important principles involved in ensuring that I make the right financing decisions?

- I am sure that some other people may be willing to assist me, but what are their requirements and motives? Will it be to my advantage, or theirs?
- Are there specific problems experienced by the average small business entrepreneur/manager and how can I learn from them?

In this chapter, we will show you how to find the answers to these questions.

14.3 SOURCES OF FINANCE

The two major sources of finance for a small business are own capital (internal sources) and outside capital (external sources). Each of these has its own characteristics, as well as advantages, disadvantages and requirements.

It is important to understand that the words 'capital' and 'finance' do not necessarily refer to physical cash or money. Finance may be cash (in one or another form), but may also take the form of an asset supplied: for example, when I start my own transport business and use my existing paid-up bakkie, the value of this bakkie represents my own capital contribution to the business.

14.3.1 Own capital (equity)

Own capital (also known as owner's capital, shareholders' funds or owner's interest or equity) is one of the most important sources of finance for a small business. The characteristics of own capital are as follows:

- Often, it is the first source of capital available to start a new business.
- It is that part of the total capital used in a business that is legally recognised as the total value (at a certain point in time) of contributions made by all the legal owners of the business.
- It serves as the basis from which other (mostly outside) capital can be attracted.
- Without own capital invested in the small business, it is very unlikely that other potential suppliers of capital will be interested in putting money into your business.
- Own capital is permanent. The investment will last as long as the business itself, provided that the business is not sold or terminated (although exceptions to this rule are possible).
- It is not easy or advisable to withdraw a part of own capital, especially if the business is not very solvent and/or not in a highly liquid position or a single proprietorship – normally such a step changes the nature of the ownership of the business.

- There are a variety of sources for own capital, including owner's savings, pension payouts and existing owned assets put to use in the business. It may even consist of unrelated assets (for example, a house or household furniture) that may be sold or bonded and changed into cash.
- A person starting a small business does not need to depend solely on his or her own contribution to complete the full picture of own capital.

There are two other supplementary sources of own capital:

- If the founder borrows money from someone else in his or her personal capacity (and not on behalf of and in the business's name) and invests it in the business, such monies are also considered to be own capital.
- If the founder wishes to bring co-owners (partners, other shareholders) into the business, these co-owners may also be additional sources of own capital.
- Another, very important, source to add to the value of own capital is the reinvestment of net profit (after tax) as time goes on.

Vusi, the founder of Vusi's Engineering Works, had no cash to invest in his business when he started it, but he was at that time the proud owner of engineering equipment to the value of R80 000 and a delivery vehicle to the value of R60 000. He was also able to convince his previous employer to sell additional engineering equipment to him. They agreed that he needed only to repay the total value of R100 000 in five years' time.

1. How much 'capital' did Vusi initially 'invest' in his new business? Is this own or outside capital?
2. How much did Vusi's previous employer 'invest' in the new business? Is this own or outside capital?

Talk to the owner of any small business that you know, and ask how the business started off. Ask the owner to indicate to you the different sources of assets/capital he or she had available at the beginning. Find out: the name of the small business, the name of the owner, initial assets/capital at start; who supplied these assets?

14.3.2 Outside capital (foreign, borrowed, external capital)

As the name suggests, outside capital is finance that comes from sources outside (not the owner/s) the business.

A more formal definition is that outside capital is the sum total of all claims by other parties (other than the legal owner/s of a business), who have supplied the business with assets and/or cash and/or services, and who have not yet been paid in full.

To understand the nature of outside capital, note the following points:

- Outside capital is normally made available to the small business on either a short-, medium- or long-term basis. This is different from own capital, which remains in the business permanently.
- Outside capital therefore has to be repaid at some time in the future. In contrast, it is rare that own capital must be 'repaid'.
- Suppliers of outside capital are sometimes paid financing fees (for example, interest) as remuneration (reward or payment) for helping to finance the business. The exceptions are trade creditors (businesses that supply the small business with commercial goods and services on a credit basis). In contrast, the suppliers of own capital are normally paid a dividend as remuneration (they also benefit from the growth in the value of their investment in the business).
- If the business is liquidated or sold, the suppliers of outside capital normally have distinct and preferential claims when it comes to being paid. Normally, staff and the Receiver of Revenue and then financiers like hire purchase suppliers and thereafter trade creditors have first priority. The last parties to be paid (if anything is left) are the suppliers of own capital (the owners of the business).

Table 14.1: General characteristics of own and outside capital

Own capital	Outside capital
has a permanent nature	may be of a short-, medium- or long-term nature (no permanence)
seldom withdrawn	withdrawal is common
is remunerated in the form of dividends and growth in value	is remunerated in the form of interest paid and/or goods sold
is in full charge of the management of the business	has very little or no control at all over the business
has the last claim to be remunerated when business is liquidated/terminated	has preferential claim over owners to be remunerated when business is liquidated/ terminated

14.4 FORMS AND SOURCES OF FINANCE

In Chapter 13, we explained that the capital needs of a small business include fixed and current assets. Remember, too, that every small business has a permanent need for capital and a variable need for capital.

We also emphasised how important it is to satisfy the need for permanent capital only from long-term sources of capital. Similarly, the need for variable capital should be satisfied only by using short-term sources of capital. (If you need to review these important principles, turn back to Chapter 13.)

The small business entrepreneur/manager must make use of the appropriate forms and sources of finance to satisfy these needs and requirements. In this section we will look at four forms and sources of finance that are relevant to the small business sector.

14.4.1 Permanent finance and its sources

Normally, the only source of permanent finance for a small business is own capital – the initial or subsequent investment of the owner's capital in the business. The only other source may be the reinvestment of net profit (after tax) in the form of undistributed profits or reserves. There are quite a variety of legal forms of own capital (for example, share capital and loan accounts by shareholders).

Although it is rare to find suppliers of outside capital who are interested in taking up shareholding in a viable small business, sources do exist. The former Small Business Development Corporation, nowadays known as Business Partners, is one such organisation.

14.4.2 Long-term finance and its sources

Long-term finance consists of those monies or goods made available on credit to the business for a period of five years and longer (normally not longer than 20 years).

The major characteristics of long-term finance and its sources are as follows:

- Normally, a **formal written document** signed by all parties and drawn up by an attorney will spell out the detailed agreement and conditions of agreement between the supplier and receiver of such monies or goods.
- In most cases, **interest has to be paid** to the supplier. In the past, it was not uncommon to have a fixed interest rate lasting for the full period. Nowadays, the interest rate will be linked, for instance, to changes in the prime banking rate and will be adjusted accordingly as time goes on.
- In most cases, long-term finance will only be made available to the small business if it can be directly linked to one or another form of fixed asset. Normally, such a fixed asset will also be legally registered as **collateral** for the amount due to the supplier.

Table 14.2: Assets, the type of collateral and contribution to small businesses

Nature of asset	Form of collateral	Contribution
land	mortgage bonds (1st, 2nd or 3rd)	money to buy land from seller
buildings	mortgage bonds (1st, 2nd or 3rd)	money to buy or erect buildings
equipment with a life expectancy of longer than five years	contract of pledge	money to buy it or the sale of the equipment itself

- This form of finance will normally be indicated as a long-term loan on a small business's balance sheet.
- In some cases, long-term loans may also be supplied by the owners of a business, and are not regarded as equity. In these cases, no form of collateral will be required.
- In rare cases, other outside parties (such as a family member or a friend) may supply a long-term loan without expecting or insisting on adequate collateral.

Questions:

1. What are the assets most commonly financed with long-term loans?
2. What are the most likely sources of finance for acquiring these assets?

Answers:

1. a. land;
   b. buildings;
   c. machinery and equipment with a five-years-plus life expectancy.
2. a. Own capital; banks; other (governmental and private) financial institutions; the seller of the asset;
   b. As in 2a., plus the building contractor him- or herself, demanding from the buyer a registered mortgage bond as collateral that the building will be paid;
   c. As in 2a.

Wealthy private individuals (so-called business angels) may also be possible sources of long-term finance for a small business. These are people who are looking for alternative investment opportunities. They prefer to invest their capital in local businesses where they have a more personal relationship and interest. If the small business grows and becomes bigger and more profitable, these investors also expect to be additionally remunerated. They may even sometimes wish to become minority co-owners of the business!

14.4.3 Medium-term finance and its sources

Medium-term finance consists of assets and/or monies supplied to the business for periods lasting between one and five to seven years.

The major characteristics of medium-term finance and its sources are as follows:

- A written and signed document of agreement is usually an integral part of the whole transaction.
- Normally interest will have to be paid by the small business. A variety of forms of interest may apply: in some cases, it will be a single, fixed interest rate, in other cases, the interest rate may change in direct relation to changes in the official banking rate.
- Regular instalments are used to repay the amount of the initial capital (plus interest and other finance charges). Instalments may be staggered in equal monthly payments for the whole period; sometimes only interest and finance charges must be paid monthly, while the capital is repaid only at the end of the period (or every six or 12 months).

It is important to know that the conditions applicable to this type of finance are generally negotiated and packaged to suit the requirements and circumstances of individual businesses. The suppliers of medium-term finance are generally able to offer a wide variety of options and conditions.

Even more important to remember is the fact that the small business entrepreneur should never blindly accept the initial conditions and demands put forward by the willing supplier of goods or capital. The entrepreneur has to make sure that each and every condition is (also) to the advantage of the small business. Before signing anything, the entrepreneur should negotiate and query all conditions of the credit transaction.

Renting (or leasing) an asset is also a form of financing. There are a variety of renting/leasing options, each with its own characteristics and conditions.

A hire-purchase agreement is also a typical form of medium-term finance.

Questions:

1. What are the assets most commonly financed with medium-term finance?
2. What are the most likely sources of medium-term finance for acquiring these assets?

Answers:

1. a. machinery and equipment; b vehicles; c furniture

2. a. own capital; banks; other financial institutions; the seller of the asset; private individuals

   b. same as 2a. above

   c. same as 2a. above.

Another form of medium-term finance, offered by most banks and some specialised financing institutions, is factoring. Factoring takes place when the small business sells (as a once-off transaction or even on a monthly basis) its debtors' book (all or some of its debtors' accounts) to the bank or a specialised financing institution. The latter will pay cash for the debtors' book and will then collect the outstanding monies for itself. Remember that any buyer will want to make sure there are no bad debts to be realised. Thus the buyer (who is known as the factor) will negotiate to buy the debtors' book at, say, only 60–90% of its invoice or book value. This form of finance is not readily made available to most small businesses.

Visit a branch of one of the well-known banks and ask to speak to a loan officer. Ask this person to explain to you the variety of forms of finance that the bank makes available to small business. Write down at least five forms of finance and the major characteristics of each.

14.4.4 Short-term finance and its sources

Short-term finance is made available to the small business for a period of less than 12 months. Normally, the specified period of availability is 30 to 90 days (in the case of suppliers' credit) or even 24 hours (a bank overdraft facility may be withdrawn within 24 hours, although normally it will be available for much longer but may be called up if the bank so decides).

The major characteristics of short-term finance and its sources are as follows:

- When short-term goods or services, stock and materials are made available on credit terms to a small business, we say that such goods or services are being temporarily financed by the suppliers – the suppliers are then considered to be the suppliers of short-term finance to the small business.
- Normally, supplier creditors of short-term goods and services (for example, raw materials needed for manufacturing purposes, stock or inventory) will not charge interest on the outstanding balance owed by the small business. However, they may charge a high interest rate in the case of accounts/payments in arrears. They may also have a higher pricing policy for goods sold on credit than for goods sold for cash, so this may imply an indirect cost to the small business.
- The suppliers of short-term cash loans to the business (banking overdraft facilities or loans forwarded by individuals) will normally charge the small business interest.
- Suppliers of short-term goods and services on credit are normally not very strict or disciplined in assessing the creditworthiness of their credit purchasing customers. This is because they wish to encourage sales, among other reasons. However, they may become very strict and unforgiving if and when their trust in a customer proves to be unjustified.

- Suppliers' short-term credit is not only restricted to those goods the small business owner/manager needs for reselling purposes (which is called stock or inventory). Other goods and services needed to facilitate business activities (for example, marketing or administration) may also be acquired on a credit basis.

The term 'trade creditors' refers to the credit suppliers of goods and/or services needed for reselling purposes (manufacturing works in exactly the same way). The term 'other creditors' refers to the outstanding monies owed to the suppliers of goods/services (other than for manufacturing and/or reselling purposes) that are needed for support operations. An example of this is when I required a shop fitter's services and had to pay within 30 days after the work was done.

In some cases, the short-term capital needs of a small business may even be partially financed by one or more customers (such as when a customer places an order with a manufacturer and pays a deposit at the same time).

Visit a manufacturer (or a wholesaler) and ask to speak with the credit control officer/manager. Ask this person to explain to you the variety of credit forms available to small business clients when they need short-term assets/services.

14.5 CHOOSING SOURCES AND FORMS OF FINANCE

Over the long term, the small business entrepreneur/manager is responsible for ensuring the optimum added value to the business's equity. To do this, he or she needs to make sure that the specific sources and the specific forms of finance used will contribute to the achievement of this goal.

This section will look at the critical considerations that must be analysed before each financing decision is made.

14.5.1 Matching life expectancy of assets and the length of time for which credit is available

As mentioned in Chapter 13, it is extremely important to match the life expectancy of the asset(s) with the length of time for which the source of credit is made available. We saw in Chapter 13 that an understanding of a business's needs for fixed and current assets requires an understanding of the needs for permanent and variable capital. As a general rule the time length of repayment for the outside gained finance should never exceed the life expectancy of the specific asset.

14.5.2 Availability and accessibility issues

In real business situations, it is sometimes not possible for the small business entrepreneur/manager to follow prudent financial management principles. Sometimes the appropriate sources and forms of finance are not available to a small business (see Section 14.6). However, you should take care not to be misled by the easiest source and form of availability and accessibility.

14.5.3 Costs associated with a specific source

Often small business entrepreneurs/managers are so relieved to find willing sources of finance that they completely forget to negotiate the best possible conditions, costs and requirements. Always negotiate and re-negotiate with suppliers of credit.

14.5.4 Independence versus dependence and control

One of the strongest motivations for starting a small business is the desire to be independent – to initiate your own plans and to do things your own way. However, the more outside capital you use in the business, the more your independence is threatened. If you don't have enough own capital resources, a needed piece of equipment will only become available if and when you find an outside supplier of finance and thus on the supplier's conditions. The same goes for bringing in extra partners or extra shareholders. This strengthens the own capital base but also reduces the independence of the small business entrepreneur.

14.5.5 Freedom of application of finance

Most of the various sources and forms of finance available in the marketplace will only be made available to the small business entrepreneur/manager as long as the money is used for a specific and predetermined purpose.

Table 14.3: Freedom in application of finance

Form of finance	Can only be used for
mortgage bonds	the acquisition or renovation of land and fixed buildings
rental/leasing/hire purchase	the acquisition of certain equipment and/or machinery and/or vehicles and/or furniture and fittings
suppliers' credit	the acquisition of specified goods and services bought on credit from the supplier
a bank overdraft	one of the rare cases where the entrepreneur has almost total freedom of use
own capital in the form of cash	the only other source and form of finance where the owner has almost total freedom of use

14.5.6 The positive and negative effects of financial leverage

Financial leverage is related to the cost and use of borrowed capital in the enterprise. If the profitability (ROI) of the enterprise is greater than the interest rate on borrowed capital, an increase in profitability of the own capital (ROE) is caused by the use of borrowed capital. The enterprise therefore uses borrowed capital in the hope that it will cause the profitability of own capital to rise. This is called a positive financial leverage.

However, if the interest rate on borrowed capital is greater than the profitability (ROI) of the enterprise, the profitability (ROE) of own capital is negatively influenced and it drops. This factor may even mean that all (and more) of the profits of a business could be absorbed by interests to be paid over! This is called a negative financial leverage.

It is important to stress certain factors:

- the relationship (weight) between own and outside capital
- the profitability of the whole small business (its return on investment, or ROI)
- the costs of outside capital compared to the ROI
- the final outcome of profitability as expressed in the return on equity (ROE).

In the attempt to attract own or outside capital, the small business entrepreneur must not forget to work out whether the result of the decision will lead to either a positive or negative financial leverage on own capital (ROE).

14.5.7 Considerations of liquidity and profitability

Deciding on the form of finance has a direct impact on the small business's liquidity and profitability. This is closely related to the considerations in sections 14.5.3 and 14.5.6.

Sometimes over the short term it is wise to forget about profitability issues and to make sure that major liquidity threats do not sink the ship – there are many, many examples of profitable small businesses that had to close down because of sudden liquidity crises they could not overcome.

14.5.8 Taxation considerations

There are important taxation issues that are relevant to the well-being of a small business. For now, remember that almost every decision on the required assets, as well as on the sources and forms of finance, has tax implications.

Peter Nkosi buys a vehicle to use in his delivery business. He has three options:

1. If he pays cash for the vehicle (using own capital), he will not be able to deduct any part of the purchase price from his business's income for income tax purposes (although depreciation, insurance premiums and maintenance costs may be deductible).
2. If he purchases the vehicle on a hire-purchase basis, he may pay a deposit (not deductible) and a monthly instalment (where only the interest and insurance part of the instalment and accrued maintenance costs may be deductible, but not the capital down payment part of the instalment).
3. If he rents the vehicle without ever becoming the legal owner, the total costs of renting may be deductible for income tax purposes.

14.5.9 Building long-term relationships

One of the major strengths of small business owners/managers (compared to very big businesses) is their dedication and expertise in building and developing strong and relevant long-term networks. This is something to remember and to build on.

There are many people involved in any small business: the owner(s), relatives and friends, bankers, lawyers, suppliers, existing and potential customers, employees, local authorities, the local communities and even staff of the South African Revenue Service.

The more the small business entrepreneur succeeds in building and developing sound relationships with the vast range of constituencies, the more he or she will be able to combine the wisdom and strengths of all these resources. If these networks are neglected, isolation and ultimate failure may be the result.

Using your own words, and without looking back at section 14.5, write down at least five major things to consider before deciding on the sources and/or forms of finance for your business and give your major consideration and motivation for each one.

14.6 TYPICAL PROBLEMS IN OBTAINING FINANCE

Small businesses have certain advantages when compared to big businesses (for example, building strong personal relationships and networks over the long term). But the size and influence of the small business can also be a disadvantage when it comes to obtaining finance.

This section deals with typical problems experienced by small business entrepreneurs/managers in their quest for the right sources and forms of finance.

14.6.1 When own capital's contribution is too small

To finance all the assets needed in a business, prudent financial management dictates that the contribution of own capital should be at least 50%. In other words, own capital should never be less than half of the business's total capital required.

To start a business, an entrepreneur generally uses all available savings and own capital. As the business grows and expands, it creates an increased need for assets (and sources of finance to acquire these assets). Because all of the entrepreneur's savings have been used initially to start up, he or she depends more and more on outside capital sources.

A related problem is that potential suppliers of outside finance many times also want to know about the financial structure of the small business. The smaller the relative portion of own capital to total capital, the less willing these suppliers will be to supply additional funding because they will deem that a higher risk. If they do provide funding, there will always be an additional cost to the small business.

14.6.2 Lack of experience in financial management

Normally, the small business entrepreneur will have excellent experience and knowledge in a number of disciplines – for example, manufacturing and/or selling and marketing and/or in supplying unique goods/services to customers. But very few entrepreneurs are also experienced and knowledgeable about financial management. This lack of expertise creates difficulties when approaching potential suppliers of needed finance, and the entrepreneur may not be able to convince the potential suppliers of finance to help him or her. Such owners/managers have to admit this fact and should seek assistance in preparing them well in this field.

14.6.3 Lack of financial expertise in managing a small business

This problem is related to the lack of experience in financial management but specifically concerns the running of the business. An entrepreneur who is experienced and knowledgeable about, say, marketing and/or manufacturing will tend to be heavily involved in these activities because they have very positive and added-value contributions to make in these matters. An entrepreneur who does not understand financial management issues will be more inclined to ignore or skirt these issues. This tendency signals great danger for any small business and its owner/s.

Try to relate the two statements above to an everyday small business operation. Do you agree or disagree with these statements? Give two reasons for each answer.

14.6.4 Too much emphasis on collateral by suppliers of finance

Inexperienced small business entrepreneurs/managers may be aware of only some of the sources and forms of finance – perhaps only the large national banks and a few other major financial institutions and trade creditors. If they approach only these sources, the results can be disappointing. Generally, the first question asked by these suppliers is, 'How much collateral can you put up to guarantee your debts?' Banks in particular are often accused of using this quick and easy method of credit assessment. This approach is like saying to someone, 'If you don't already have an umbrella, I can't help you get one!'

Although this is a valid criticism of banks, it is also true that they often have no other choice. If the entrepreneur/manager has not done his or her 'homework' and chosen the right form of finance (see section 14.4), the banker can only accurately assess one of the aspects of credit, such as collateral.

14.6.5 Lack of planning

The planning function is a big part of business management. The saying, 'If you fail to plan, you plan to fail' contains a great deal of truth. On the other hand, if you prepare an elaborate business plan and then do not implement your plans, you will have wasted of lot of energy and other scarce resources.

Many business textbooks discuss the steps, contents and issues that should be addressed in the business plan. Most of these textbooks point out that one of the major purposes of a business plan is to convince potential suppliers of finance to invest in the business or supply capital. (Refer to Chapter 5 for the details of a concise business plan.) This is true, but remember that the well-prepared business plan is in the very first and foremost instance also there to help the entrepreneur/manager to make a success of the business.

14.6.6 Creditworthiness

Just as a small business entrepreneur/manager needs to make a careful analysis to determine the creditworthiness of a client, so the suppliers of finance need to analyse the strengths and weaknesses of the small business.

The challenge for the small business entrepreneur/manager is therefore to be very well prepared, to have substantiated facts and motivations ready to convince the selected source of finance to provide needed capital, and to maintain this trust into the future.

14.7 SUMMARY

In this chapter, we discussed the major issues relating to how a small business's needs for assets should be financed. We emphasised the differences between own and outside sources and forms of finance. In direct relation to these issues, we examined the various sources and forms of permanent and variable finance available in the marketplace. These include permanent, long-term, medium-term and short-term finance.

There are a number of critical considerations involved in choosing the best form and source of finance. However, the availability and accessibility of finance often forces the entrepreneur/manager to adapt or to bypass these considerations.

The chapter concluded by discussing some typical problems encountered by entrepreneurs/managers in their attempts to obtain finance.

Self-evaluation questions

1. Name and explain at least four characteristics of 'own capital' in a small business.
2. Name and illustrate at least five characteristics of 'outside capital'.
3. What are the nature and sources of permanent finance?
4. Briefly discuss at least five characteristics of long-term finance and its sources.
5. Explain in your own words who 'business angels' are.
6. Briefly discuss at least five characteristics of medium-term finance and its sources.
7. Briefly discuss at least five characteristics of short-term finance and its sources.
8. Briefly discuss at least five characteristics of long-term finance and its sources.
9. There are at least nine important considerations in choosing the right sources and forms of finance. Can you think of five of these? Give a short explanation for each of your answers.
10. Small business entrepreneurs/managers face unique problems in obtaining finance. What are five of the problems they face? Give a short explanation for each of your answers.

Chapter 15

The break-even analysis

15.1 LEARNING OUTCOMES

After you have studied this chapter, you should be able to:

- indicate some of the important things to consider in starting a new business and/or new initiative or project
- indicate, explain and illustrate the three pieces of information required to calculate the financial break-even point
- calculate the break-even point using the correct break-even formulae
- explain the financial break-even concept using a graph
- assess the impact on the break-even point when any one of the three critical elements changes
- explain the advantages and disadvantages of the break-even analysis.

15.2 INTRODUCTION

The small business entrepreneur/manager must answer many important questions when considering starting a new venture or a new project. Some of these questions are:

- At what cost prices will I be able to acquire the products and services I now intend to sell to the market?
- At what selling prices will I be able to convince potential customers to buy from me instead of from my competition?
- Apart from the actual cost prices of these products and services, what other basic costs will I have to incur in order to be able to buy and sell these products and services?
- How can I know, in advance, how many products/services I need to buy/acquire and utilise and sell in order to realise a satisfactory profit figure?

- After I have started the business, if there is a change in one or more of my cost prices/expenses, how will that influence the quantity of products and services and their monetary value that I need to sell in order to realise the same profit as before? (This question is also relevant whenever a change may occur in the selling prices and/or the other basic costs/expenses of business operations, like an increase in rental to be paid or higher wages and salaries agreed on.)

In this chapter, we will answer these questions by looking at very basic and realistic everyday business examples, in order to learn about and understand the issues relating to the break-even analysis.

15.3 CRITICAL ASPECTS OF STARTING A BUSINESS

In this section we will review some of the factors that must be considered before starting a small business. To do this, let us look at a practical example.

Mary Khoza is a second-year university student and needs to supplement her income. Because she is good at making hamburgers for herself and her friends, she is considering opening up a hamburger stall on weekends at one of the popular flea markets near the campus.

What do you think are the most important things to consider when starting a new business? What does Mary need to look at to decide whether her weekend hamburger stall will be viable or not? List at least ten things she will need to investigate.

Here are a few of the factors Mary will have to consider:

- **Location:** Where will the very, very best locality be to establish this initiative? Is there a site available at the nearest flea market? How much will the rent per day be? What about alternative flea markets or other localities?
- **Competition:** Are there other suppliers of hamburgers at (or near) the flea market? At what price do they sell their hamburgers? How many hamburgers do they approximately sell on an average weekend day?
- **Equipment:** What kind of equipment will be needed at the flea market site to make and sell hamburgers? Is this equipment available on a rental basis or will Mary have to buy it all herself?
- **Ingredients:** Mary needs to make a list of all the ingredients required to make her Super-Duper special hamburger (for example, meat patties, spices, bread rolls, sauces, etc.). It is also very important that she calculates exactly what the ingredient costs will be per hamburger.

- **Salary and wages:** A basic principle of small business management is that the profit to the business and the salary/remuneration of the entrepreneur are two different things. An entrepreneur who operates and manages his or her own business should pay him- or herself a competitive, market-related salary. This is part of the overall expenses of the business. Profit is always calculated after all business expenses are deducted from income. Mary should therefore make provision for her own market-related remuneration. And if business is good, she may need to employ an assistant. She will then also have to work out how much to pay her assistant.
- **Marketing:** It is not enough to have an excellent product or service – you have to be able to inform, invite and convince the target market about your product or service and make it easy for customers to actually buy it. These activities are part of marketing. Mary will need to market her hamburgers in an efficient and effective way, otherwise her business will not be a success.

Mary's investigations, inquiries and negotiations had the following results:

- **Site:** Mary can rent an exclusive site, situated close to where visitors enter the flea market, at a daily rate for Saturdays and Sundays of R1 600 (payable in cash on the preceding Monday).
- **Selling price:** There is one existing regular competitor in the flea market, selling hamburgers at R25 each. Mary reckons that she will do well in selling her Super-Duper special hamburgers at the same price. She could not find out how many hamburgers this competitor sells, but the landlord reckons that an average of 5 000 people visit the flea market per weekend day.
- **Equipment:** After investigating many alternatives, Mary determined that the best option was to rent a fully equipped trailer, custom-made for a hamburger stall, with all the gas bottles, utensils, signboards, etc. The daily rent is R400 and is payable one week in advance.
- **Wages:** Mary reckons that a market-related daily wage for herself could be R900 (R90 per hour for 10 hours). Her younger sister is willing to assist her for R300 per day (R30 per hour for ten hours). Her sister expects to be paid this figure whatever the quantity of hamburgers (zero or 1 000) they sell per day.
- **Ingredients:** After many hours of experimenting, measuring and calculating, Mary worked out that the total cost price of all the ingredients needed in one hamburger is exactly R10. This includes bread rolls, meat patties, butter, mustard, onions, salt and pepper, lettuce, as well as her 'mystery' Super-Duper sauce mixture. Packaging is also included.
- **Marketing:** The owner of the trailer rental business introduced Mary to a marketing consultant. After weighing many possibilities, Mary accepted the consultant's advice to put a large sign on top of the trailer to make the stall visible from far away. The total cost of this permanent sign is R2 000.

- **Transport and Communications:** After considering all relevant aspects, Mary worked out that her transport and communication costs will be R80 per day.

A very important question (relevant to any business venture) needs to be asked and needs to be answered well: How many hamburgers must Mary sell per day to just cover all her costs (not making any loss or profit)?

15.4 THE BREAK-EVEN POINT

Now that Mary has worked out what she needs to start her hamburger stall, she needs to calculate how many hamburgers she must sell each day to cover all her costs. The answer to this question is called the break-even point.

The break-even point of a business can be defined as the level of business where neither a profit nor a loss is realised, the level where the income from sales is equal to the total operational costs (including the owner's remuneration) of the enterprise.

At this point the business is neither making any profit nor realising any loss. It is breaking even – no profit, no loss.

How many units must Mary sell per day to break even? To answer this question, we need three pieces of information or critical factors:

a) **The selling price of a single product/service:** Mary will sell her hamburgers for R25 each.

b) **The direct cost price of a single product/service:** This relates to all the costs directly incurred in acquiring/manufacturing/buying a single product. In Mary's case this will be R10, representing the accumulated cost prices of all the ingredients needed to make one Super-Duper special hamburger.

c) **The total indirect costs of the business:** This covers all other costs necessary to operate a business. In Mary's case, these daily costs are: the rental of a site (R1 600), the rental of the custom-made trailer (R400), and wages paid (R900 + R300 = R1 200) as well as transport and communications R80 per day. Added together this amounts to R3 280 per day. The marketing sign of R2 000 needs a little more explanation. All the other costs (wages, rental of site and trailer) are daily costs, but the marketing sign will last say at least one year – its life expectancy is deemed to be one year. Its daily cost can therefore be calculated as follows: R2 000 divided by 100 weekend days per year and this gives a daily cost of R20 for marketing/advertising costs. Thus the total indirect costs to Mary's business are R3 300 per day.

15.4.1 Using the break-even formula

The following formula can be used to answer the question of how many hamburgers Mary must sell per day in order to break even:

$$\frac{\text{total indirect costs}}{\text{selling price per unit less direct costs per unit}}$$

This gives: Number of hamburgers to be sold per day to break even

Thus: $\frac{\text{R3 300}}{\text{R25 } - \text{R10}}$

= 220 hamburgers must be made and sold per day to break even

Mary needs to sell 220 hamburgers per day in order to break even (making neither a profit nor loss). If she sells more, she will make a profit. If she is unable to sell 220 on a specific day, she will make a loss.

Verifying your answer

How can you be sure that you have correctly calculated the break-even point?

You can verify the answer by answering the following questions:

- How much will Mary's total income be if she sells 220 hamburgers at a selling price of R25 each? (**Answer:** 220 × R25 = R5 500)
- How much will her total direct costs be when making and selling 220 hamburgers at R10 direct cost price per hamburger? (**Answer:** 220 × R10 = R2 200)
- How much are her total indirect costs (excluding total direct costs) to operate the business? (**Answer:** R400 for trailer rental plus R1 600 for site rental plus R20 for advertising plus R1 200 for wages, plus R80 for transport and communications = R3 300)

So:	Total income	=	R5 500
Less:	Direct costs	=	R2 200
Less:	Indirect costs	=	R3 300
Gives:	Profit (loss)	=	R0 000

Remember that you cannot calculate the break-even point without any of the following three pieces of information:

i. selling price per unit

ii. direct cost price per unit

iii. total indirect costs of business operation.

15.5 OTHER FINANCIAL MANAGEMENT CONCEPTS

Now that you understand what is meant by the break-even point, let us look at some other important concepts in financial management. First we will examine terms we have used already in our calculation of the break-even point, namely indirect costs (or overheads) and direct costs. We will then discuss marginal income.

15.5.1 Overheads

Overheads (also called indirect costs, operational costs or fixed costs) are those costs, other than the direct costs (see section 15.5.2), that are unavoidable in business. Normally, overheads consist of the costs of facilities and resources that enable the entrepreneur/ manager to do business.

Typical examples of overheads are:

- rent paid for business premises and equipment
- wages and salaries paid to yourself and other employees
- monies paid for marketing campaigns, insurance instalments and fees for local authority services.

Overheads are mostly relatively fixed (site rental will be fixed but Water and Electricity may vary a bit between two extremes) and whether you sell many products and services per month or nothing at all, these expenses still have to be incurred. Overheads are an essential part of doing business, but cannot be related directly to the individual cost price of a product unit. These costs are, however, indirectly related to all products.

If we look at Mary's hamburger stall, a useful way of determining whether a cost is direct or indirect is to ask (and answer) the following question: If she sells no hamburgers, will this cost be more or less? For example, if she sells 1 000 hamburgers, will that cost be more or less?

Mary will pay R2 000 for the advertising sign. She has to pay this money to the sign-writer whether she sells one hamburger or 1 000. The same applies to the R400 rental for the trailer, the R1 600 rental for her site as well as the R900 needed for wages or the R80 for transport and communications. All these costs are therefore regarded as indirect costs (overheads).

Indirect costs are the costs (expenses) incurred in order to do business regardless of whether one or 1 000 items are sold.

In our example of Mary's hamburger stall, the costs of renting the site, renting the trailer, and paying for the sign and the obligation to pay wages to her sister are fixed. Whether she sells one or 1 000 hamburgers per day, she will still have to pay these costs in full.

In business, fixed costs are fixed only for particular periods of time. For example, after a period of time (for example, 12 months), the rent on the premises may be raised or employees may demand higher salaries. If sales increases require more employees, the fixed cost of wages will change as well.

Overheads (fixed costs, indirect costs, operational costs) are committed, unavoidable costs that have no direct relation to the volume of sales. If sales are low, the fixed costs will still be incurred. If sales rise, fixed costs will still be the same (up to a certain point, of course).

15.5.2 Direct costs

Direct costs (also called variable costs or cost of sales or manufacturing costs) are the direct, exclusive costs (expenses) incurred to acquire (or to manufacture) specific units of products/services. For a retailer, direct costs normally consist of the cost price of a product the retailer pays to the supplier/wholesaler of the product/service. For a manufacturer, direct costs normally consist of the accumulated cost prices of all the raw materials (ingredients) and the direct labour cost used in manufacturing a specific product or unit.

Mary calculated the combined cost of all the ingredients needed to make one Super-Duper special hamburger at R10 per hamburger. If customers do not order a single hamburger, Mary will accrue no direct costs in making the hamburgers. If she sells 200 hamburgers, the variable cost to the business that day will be 200 × R10 = R2 000.

Thus we can see that direct costs are directly related to the volume of sales. If sales volume is low, direct costs will be low; if sales volume increases, the direct cost will directly increase proportionally as well.

In real life, Mary might consider making hamburgers beforehand, so building up an inventory in advance of the flea market (but this then will bring many other aspects to the front: for example keeping them 'fresh', transport, not to over- or under-produce, etc.). For now, we will not discuss all the intrinsic aspects of building up stocks and related stock planning and control.

Direct costs are those costs directly incurred and directly related to acquiring a single product/service. The accumulated direct costs are called the cost of sales (or cost of manufacturing).

15.5.3 Marginal income

Marginal income (also more commonly called gross profit) represents the positive difference between the selling price per unit and the direct cost price per unit.

In Mary's case, R25 less R10 gives R15 per unit marginal income. This means that for each hamburger sold at R25, R10 is needed to pay for ingredients (direct costs) while the R15 marginal income contributes to the payment of the indirect costs (overheads, fixed or operational costs). Once the total indirect costs have been defrayed (covered) by this marginal income, the business starts to make a profit only then. If the accumulated marginal income is not enough to cover the total overheads, the result will be a net loss.

Marginal income percentage (gross profit percentage)

Whenever marginal income (gross profit) of a product is expressed as a percentage, it is calculated either as a percentage in relation to the selling price or to the cost price of that product.

In Mary's case:

$$\text{Gross profit percentage} = \frac{\text{gross profit} \times 100}{\text{selling price}}$$

$$= \frac{\text{R15} \times 100}{\text{R25}}$$

$$= 60\% \text{ gross profit percentage}$$

This means that for every R1 sales, 60 cents are realised as gross profit/marginal income.

Gross profit percentage is different from the mark-up percentage, which is the percentage a small business entrepreneur will add to the cost price of a product in order to arrive at that product's selling price. The mark-up percentage is therefore calculated where the marginal income (gross profit) of a product is expressed in relation to the cost price of that product.

In Mary's case:

$$\text{Markup percentage} = \frac{\text{gross profit} \times 100}{\text{cost price of the product/service}}$$

$$= \frac{\text{R15} \times 100}{\text{R10}}$$

$$= 150\% \text{ markup percentage}$$

This means that for every R1 invested in direct costs (acquiring or manufacturing a product), R1,50 is added to arrive at the selling price.

Question:

We can now ask the second big question: How many hamburgers must Mary sell if she wishes to make a net profit of, say, R1 000 per day? After all, she is not in business to break even, but to make a profit!

Answer:

The same three pieces of information are required. We need to know Mary's selling price per unit, her direct cost price per unit and her total indirect costs per day. Now add Mary's required net profit to her indirect costs and then recalculate the 'new' break-even point, which now includes profit desired.

The formula now is: $\dfrac{\text{total indirect costs + required profit}}{\text{selling price per unit – direct cost per price}}$

In Mary's case: $\dfrac{\text{R3 300 + R1 000}}{\text{R25 – R10}}$

$= \dfrac{4\ 300}{15}$

$=$ 286.67 hamburgers to be made and sold

So she must sell 287 hamburgers in order to make R1 000 net profit per day.

Verifying your answer

Once again it is quite easy (and also a good idea) for you to check whether the answer of 286.67 hamburgers is correct.

All you have to do is to answer the following questions:

- How much will Mary's total income be if she sells 286.67 hamburgers at R25 each? (**Answer:** 286.67 × R25 = R7 166.67)
- How much will her total direct costs be when making and selling 286.67 hamburgers at a direct cost price of R10 per hamburger? (**Answer:** 286.67 × R10 = R2 866.67)
- How much are the total indirect costs (excluding total direct costs) involved in operating Mary's business? (**Answer:** R3 300. This is unchanged because these costs are still the same: R400 for trailer rental, R1 600 for site rental plus R20 per day for the marketing sign plus R1 200 for wages and R80 for transport and communications per day.)

  So: Total income R7 166.67

  Less: Direct costs R2 866.67

  Less: Indirect costs R3 300

  Gives: Net profit R1 000

15.6 CALCULATING THE BREAK-EVEN POINT IN TERMS OF MONETARY SALES VOLUME

When we know the marginal income percentage (or, in other words, the gross profit percentage) of a business, we can use the following formula to indicate its break-even point in monetary sales volume:

$$\frac{\text{total indirect cost} \times 100}{\text{gross profit percentage}}$$

Thus in Mary's case:

$$\frac{\text{R3 300} \times 100}{60}$$

= R5 500 monetary sales required daily to break even (220 hamburgers at R25 selling price each)

This formula may also be used to calculate the needed monetary volume of sales in order to realise a given net profit. The required profit must first be added to the total indirect costs.

In Mary's case, if she wants a profit of R1 000, this will be:

$$\frac{\text{total indirect cost} + \text{required profit}}{\text{gross profit percentage}}$$

$$= \frac{(\text{R3 300} + \text{R1 000}) \times 100}{60}$$

= R7 166,67 sales required per day to arrive at R1 000 net profit (286.67 hamburgers at R25 selling price each).

R5 500 in monetary sales is required to break even (220 hamburgers at R25 selling price each).

And R7 166,67 income is required for Mary to realise R1 000 net profit (286.67 hamburgers at R25 each).

15.7 USING A GRAPH TO EXPLAIN THE BREAK-EVEN POINT

15.7.1 Indirect costs

The total indirect (fixed, operational) costs of a business remain the same regardless of the sales volume of the enterprise. It does not make a difference whether one or 1 000 items are sold. For Mary's hamburger stall, we can see this clearly on the graph in Figure 15.1 below.

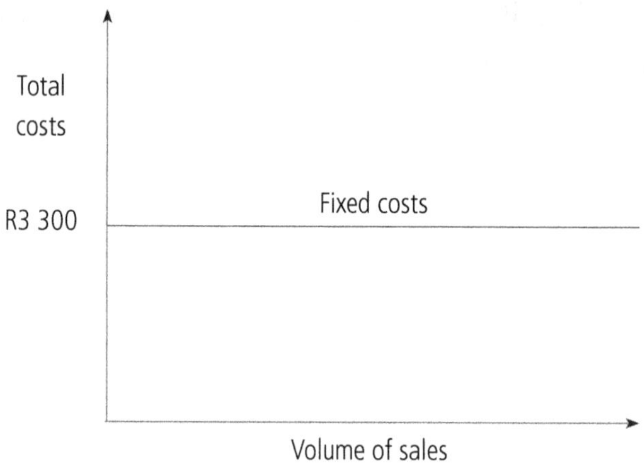

Figure 15.1: Graph to explain the relationship between fixed costs and volume of sales

15.7.2 Direct costs

The direct (variable) costs needed to purchase (or to manufacture) a single product vary according to the volume of sales. If Mary makes and sells only one hamburger, her direct costs will be only R10; if she makes and sells 1 000 hamburgers, her direct costs will increase in direct relation to the increase in sales volume, thus 1 000 × R10 = R10 000.

In Mary's case, we can show this on a graph as depicted in Figure 15.2.

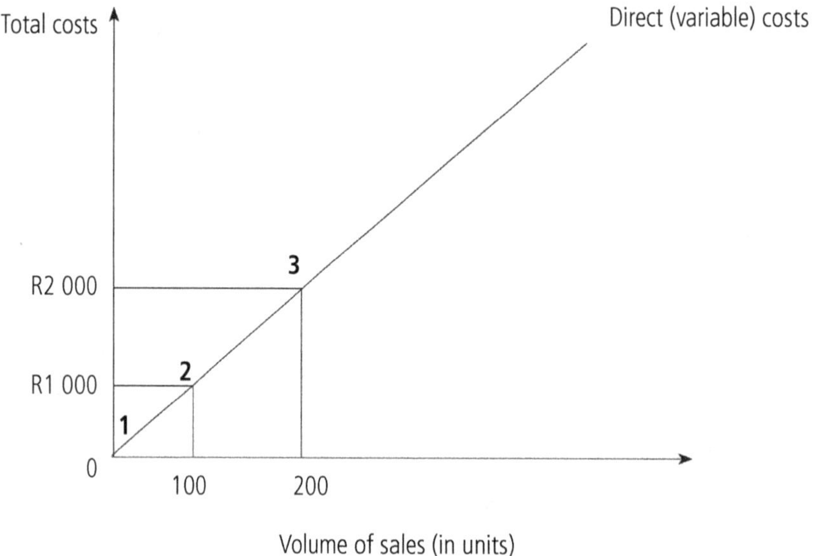

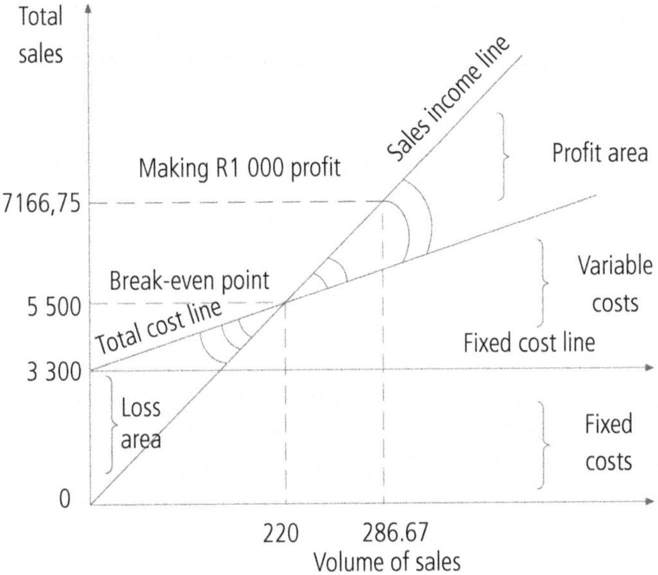

Figure 15.2: Direct costs for Mary's hamburger stall

Above are two different graphs. The first one explains the relationship between direct/variable costs and volume of sales. The second one explains all the break-even components.

15.8 ADVANTAGES AND DISADVANTAGES OF THE BREAK-EVEN ANALYSIS

The break-even analysis is an essential and useful tool for the small business entrepreneur/manager. There are no real disadvantages to it, although it can be misunderstood, for example:

- Sometimes it is not easy to draw the exact line between direct and indirect costs. For example, if you make a phone call to order a product, should this cost be calculated as a direct cost in acquiring the product? And how?
- The elements affecting the direct cost price per unit, as well as those making up the total indirect costs of a business are not constant but may change continuously.
- Most new businesses will not be in a position to initially realise a profit – in normal conditions, a retail business will take up to nine months to get to their break-even point and then to go beyond that to earn net profits thereafter.

In spite of these problems, doing the break-even analysis regularly is necessary for successful financial management and eventual business success. Profit is realised by calculating income less direct costs, less indirect costs. Unless all three of these critical elements are continually measured, calculated and managed, the achievement of the business's objectives will be endangered. The aim of business is to make a profit and the small business entrepreneur needs to make sure this is achieved.

When something is not measured, it cannot be managed. And the better something is measured, the better it can be managed!

15.9 CHANGES TO THE THREE CRITICAL FACTORS

Any change to one (or more) of the three critical factors in the profit analysis will have a very important impact on the profitability of the business. Price changes (in selling prices, direct cost prices and changes in direct cost) are common in business, and the entrepreneur/manager must have a sound knowledge and understanding of these changes at all times. In Mary's case, the following three scenarios illustrate the impact of such changes.

15.9.1 If the selling price per unit changes

As an example of this, if the selling price is raised to R30 per unit, what will be the new break-even point?

$$\frac{\text{total indirect costs}}{\text{selling price per unit less direct costs per unit}}$$

$$= \frac{\text{R3 300}}{\text{R30} - \text{R10}}$$

$$= \frac{\text{R3 300}}{\text{R20}}$$

= 165 hamburgers needed to be sold in order to break even

So Mary now needs to sell only 165 hamburgers in order to break even (instead of 220 when the selling price was R25 each).

15.9.2 If indirect costs change

If any or more indirect costs increase, for example, the landlord raises the site rental to R2 000 (previously R1 600) and the trailer company raises the trailer rental to R600 a day (previously R400), the break-even point will be:

$$\frac{\text{R3 300} + \text{R400} + \text{R200}}{\text{R25} - \text{R10}}$$

$$= \frac{\text{R3 900}}{\text{R15}}$$

= 260 hamburgers

So Mary will now have to sell 260 hamburgers (previously 220) in order to break even.

15.9.3 If the direct costs per unit change

Say, for instance, that the cost price of the ingredients of the hamburger increases from R10 to R12. The new break-even point will be:

$$\frac{\text{total indirect costs}}{\text{selling price per unit less new direct costs per unit}}$$

$$= \frac{\text{R3 300}}{\text{R25} - \text{R12}}$$

$$= \frac{\text{R3 300}}{\text{R13}}$$

= 253.85 hamburgers

So Mary now has to sell 254 hamburgers (previously 220) for her hamburger stall to break even.

You can see that any change in any one or more of the three factors influencing the break-even point has a direct impact on the profit, loss or break-even results of the business. Each of these factors must be monitored continually.

15.10 BUT THE BUSINESS INTENT IS TO MAKE A PROFIT!

One must remember that actually the intent of business is to make a satisfactory profit over the longer term (and not to break even). But it is only after the break-even point is reached that the business will start showing profits. It is therefore very important to continually calculate the break-even point and to ensure the business volumes will continually be beyond that point! The further a business's sales are beyond its break-even point, the bigger net profit is earned for each rand's sales beyond that point, as gross profit then becomes net profit.

15.11 CALCULATING THE BREAK-EVEN POINT WHEN SELLING A VARIETY OF PRODUCTS/SERVICES

Most businesses sell more than one unique product. How then must the small business entrepreneur/manager also determine and manage break-even, not only of a specific unit, but of the business/project/enterprise as a whole selling a wide variety of products and/or services?

Two points applicable here are important:

i) Firstly, it remains very important also to the extended and well-established business to continually monitor its direct costs, indirect costs and its required overall break-even volumes;

ii) Secondly, the contribution of each product/service (or at least each of the sub-departments with the same kind of products, costs, pricing practices and income structures) to overall break-even and profitability must be known in order to make sure only the most profitable and greatest contributors to the success of the small business are maintained and built up.

The 80/20 Pareto-Principle must always be borne in mind as it is applicable to every business or organisation: Twenty percent (20%) of products/services/team members will always contribute eighty percent (80%) to the outcomes. The opposite is also true: Eighty percent (80%) of products/services/team members will always contribute to only twenty percent (20%) of the outcomes.

The gross profit percentage planned/achieved by the business, is more than a handy tool to answer this question. This may even applied to a range of products/services that has similar gross profit percentages: eg in a retailer one may find a grocery department, a hardware department, a fresh produce department, etc, where different pricing policies (mark-ups and gross profit percentages) are required and implemented.

Lerato's Store is selling a wide variety of goods. Her pricing policy is to implement a 200% profit margin to whatever she pays her suppliers for any product bought. Her average gross profit margin will therefore be 66.67% (cost price eg R100, adding 200% mark-up gives R200 added to sell it at R300 and R200 gross profit gives a gross profit percentage of 66.67%). Her total overheads (fixed or indirect costs) per month are at present R900 000.

Calculating Lerato's Store break-even in monetary terms:

$$\frac{\text{Total indirect costs/overheads} \times 100}{\text{Gross profit percentage}}$$

Thus: $\frac{900\ 000 \times 100}{66.67\%} = 1\ 349\ 932.50$

Gives: Monthly sales of R1 349 932.50 are required to break even.

Test: Sales	R 1 349 932.50	
Minus gross profit	R 449 932.50	(66.67% of R1 349 932.50)
Balance to pay overheads:	R 900 000	
Result:	No net profit or net loss.	

15.12 SUMMARY

In this chapter, we looked at the importance and the critical elements of the break-even analysis. You learnt that the entrepreneur/manager has to identify three critical things in order to do the break-even analysis: the selling price per unit, the direct costs to acquire or to manufacture the unit and the total costs of indirect but necessary operational activities.

By using the example of Mary's hamburger stall, we identified many issues that an entrepreneur/manager must consider. You learnt the important difference between direct and indirect costs, and this was applied to Mary's business. By using this data, two different formulae were used to calculate Mary's break-even point, both in terms of number of units that had to be sold and also in terms of the monetary sales income Mary requires. We stressed that you should always verify the calculation of the break-even point.

All these principles and methods to calculate the financial break-even point, are even more applicable to businesses and enterprises selling a multitude of different products and services and also those having different sub-departments and/or branches: what is important in the singular, is also important in the plural (profitable and contributing products/services/departments/branches should not subsidise unprofitable and non-contributing ones, unless there is a very good reason for that).

Lastly, we looked at how the break-even point changes when one (or more) of the three critical elements changes. The important thing to keep in mind is the need to recalculate the break-even point continually.

Remember: When something is not measured, it cannot be managed. And the better something is measured, the better it can be managed!

Self-evaluation questions

1. Explain the following concepts in your own words and give an everyday example for each:
   a) fixed costs
   b) variable costs
   c) marginal income
   d) gross profit percentage
   e) the break-even point
   f) mark-up percentage.

2. Give the formula for each of the following:
   a) break-even point (number of units)
   b) break-even point (monetary volume of sales)
   c) marginal income percentage
   d) Mark-up percentage.
3. Suppose Ali is considering starting his own business, manufacturing and selling fishing rods. The costs of the components needed to manufacture one rod amount to R60 and direct labour costs are R15 for one rod. The rental of premises amounts to R200 per month (his father's garage at home) and other indirect costs will be R2 800 per month (including his own part-time salary). Ali is confident that he will be able to manufacture and sell 100 fishing rods per month. The budgeted selling price is R250 per rod.
   a) How many fishing rods should be manufactured and sold per month to break even?
   b) Verify whether your answer above is correct.
   c) How many rods must be manufactured and sold to make a net profit of R5 000 each month?
   d) Verify the correctness of the above answer.
   e) If the price of rod components changes to R70, what happens to the break-even point in a. above?
   f) Draw a graph to illustrate the break-even point in question c. above.

Chapter 16

Budgets

16.1 LEARNING OUTCOMES

After you have studied this chapter, you should be able to:

- give reasons for items included in your budget
- distinguish between the various components used to compile a master budget
- draw up the budgeted income statement and balance sheet
- draw up the cashflow budget
- draw conclusions and make decisions on the basis of the completed budgets
- compare actual costs with budgeted costs and use it as a tool for management decisions.

16.2 INTRODUCTION

Whether you are budgeting your time or your available funds, everyone uses a budget in one way or another.

A business needs to take time to put goals in place to determine what they want to achieve in the next year or other specific time period. This usually goes well with reviewing what the business has done in the previous period and how they can improve on it.

The financial budget will put in writing the formal approved plan and how the profit line in the budget can be achieved. The actual results need to then be compared to the budget, preferably monthly, to see whether the business is on track or if it needs to make certain changes. As a budget is usually done three months before the start of the financial year it is quite possible to have changes to the budget for the last six months of the financial year due to unexpected changes. For example:

- a strike in the labour force sector of the business
- changing of law pertaining to their products, eg sugar tax enforced on your products or
- a new competitor that opened in their area.

Budget formats may vary from one organisation to the next, but the principles remain the same. For an entity to be successful, strategic planning for the following year needs to be done and these plans need to be put on paper by doing budgets. The enterprise needs to identify what actions will be necessary to achieve the budgeted sales. The budget process can either be done from the setting of a required margin and how you would achieve it (known as top-down approach) or starting with a zero base and estimating the sales and expenses from there.

A budget is a written document that expresses management's goals and forecasts in financial terms for a specific future period. It constitutes a financial plan and estimation for a future period.

16.3 WHY DO WE DRAW UP BUDGETS?

A budget provides a formal framework for an enterprise to make forecasts and set goals.

- A budget is an instrument that allows management and staff to evaluate whether goals have been achieved. By allowing comparisons between actual results and budgeted results, it aids in financial control.
- Budgets also serve as an aid to financial planning. For example, the budgeting process gives the entrepreneur a chance to determine the capital requirements of the business. The business can then make provision for its financing needs at an early stage.
- Budgets create cost awareness among staff. They are used to control costs in the business. They can also show where possible problems could arise in the future.
- Budgets coordinate the goals of the business and contribute to the effective use of the resources at the business's disposal.
- Budgets give the business the opportunity to take external factors into account – for example, competition and economic cycles – that can influence it during financial planning.

16.3.1 When and for what period is a budget drawn up?

Budgets are drawn up a month or two before the period or year you need the budget for, to be ready for the following year, when they will come into effect. The budgeting process involves collecting necessary information from all the various components of the business and processing it. A medium to large enterprise will have its budget ready in September for the following 12-month period from January to December.

To put it simply, a budget is merely a set of goals that is converted into figures. In this chapter we will look at the process involved in translating goals into figures. The budgeting circle (Figure 16.1) is a diagram of how budgeting works.

Figure 16.1: A budgeting circle

16.4 MASTER BUDGET

A master budget is compiled from a number of different budgets – each drawing on different components of the business.

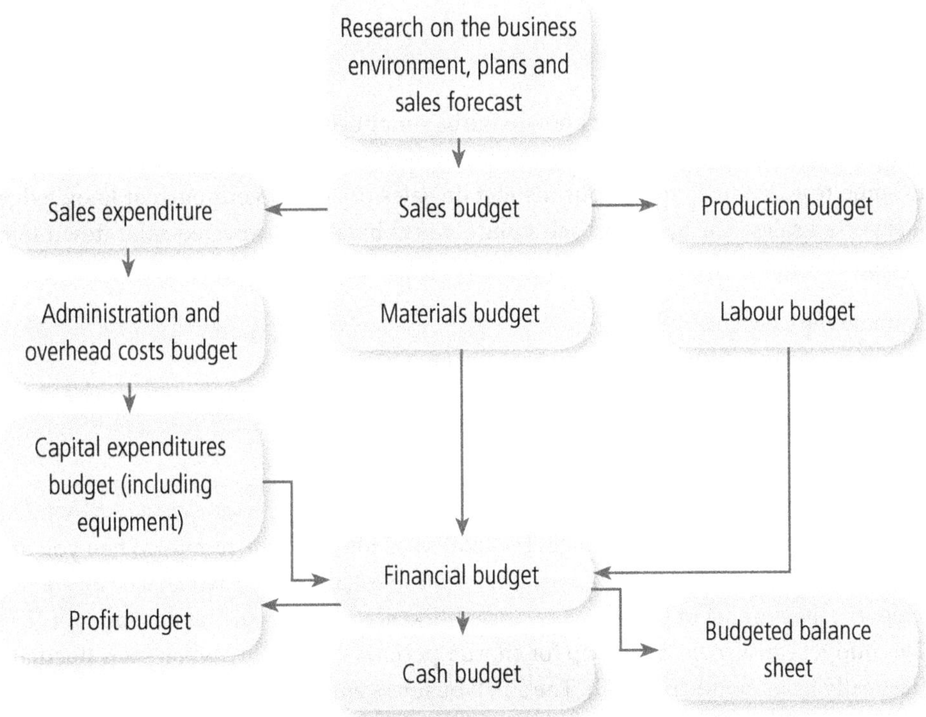

Figure 16.2: Components of a master budget

All information contained in the budgets must be based on challenging but realistic goals. Thorough research must be done on existing situations – for example, current sales and growth in the market – before a budget can be drawn up.

A budget will only work and be applied effectively if all interested parties in the business (such as salespeople) are consulted in the process. It is important that the budget also contain their inputs. In a small business, the owner usually has knowledge of all levels of activity in the business.

When a budget is reasonable and realistic, it motivates staff to attempt to reach the goals set. Conversely, an unreasonable and unrealistic budget will have a negative influence on the staff.

The first budget that must be completed is the sales budget.

16.5 SALES BUDGET

The important thing to remember is that you can draw up the sales budget only if you have already determined your sales forecast.

The sales forecast is an estimate or prediction of the expected sales of the enterprise for a future period.

Forecasting takes good working knowledge of your business. You, as the small business entrepreneur, can forecast or estimate better than any device or statistical analysis. First do some research to confirm your instinct on sales or add to your current knowledge of expected sales. The basis of a sales budget is to break the expected sales down into manageable parts.

Estimate the sales by:

- individual project/product or item
- month per month for a period of one year.

Add up the sales lines to get total sales per product or project for the year.

Months can be added together to get the total sales for a specific month. When you are doing a sales forecast in components, it is easier to establish later which sales were not achieved, the number of units sold or price difference per unit sold against budget. The sales budget can also be drawn up for shorter periods – especially when sales fluctuate drastically from month to month. The small business enterprise should review the sales forecast monthly so that it can make swift adjustments if necessary. The sales forecast is the point of departure for the sales and other budgets.

The sales budget is regarded as one of the most important budgets because it has an influence on so many other budgets. Here is an example of a sales budget:

Table 16.1: Sales budget

Estimated sales:	Total	Jan	Feb	Mar	Apr	May	Jun	Jul	Aug	Sep	Oct	Nov	Dec
Product A													
Number units South Area	7 549	1 700	2 040	1 100	440	105	64	900	120	190	270	220	400
Number units North Area	8 230	1 200	1 350	950	1 400	360	100	1 200	450	250	350	120	500
Total number of units	**15 779**	**2 900**	**3 390**	**2 050**	**1 840**	**465**	**164**	**2 100**	**570**	**440**	**620**	**340**	**900**
Estimated price per unit (Average)	296	315	315	315	280	280	280	295	295	295	295	295	295
Total value of course fees	**4 784 570**	**913 500**	**1 067 850**	**645 750**	**515 200**	**130 200**	**45 920**	**619 500**	**168 150**	**129 800**	**182 900**	**100 300**	**265 500**

The basic calculations are as follows:

Step 1: Determine the expected sales

Expected sales = expected number of units sold × unit price

If you have determined that you are going to sell 20 000 units with a value of R40 per unit for the following month, your sales are 20 000 × R40 = R800 000. This amount will be used for the profit and loss budget.

Step 2: Determine the expected cash collection

For the cashflow forecast, we need to determine the cash collection during the period. If the company sells on credit, cash is received over a specific period usually established by past trends and the effectiveness of the debt collection process. These amounts can be determined as follows:

- For sales of R800 000, 20% will be cash and 80% will be on credit. The credit sales will be collected as follows: 60% in the month following the purchase (30 days) and 40% in the next month (60 days).

	Month		
	1	2	3
Cash sale: R800 000 × 20%	R160 000		
Credit sales: R800 000 x 80% x 60%		R384 000	
R800 000 × 80% × 40%			R256 000

Check your answer: R160 000 + R384 000 + R256 000 = R800 000.

Table 16. 2: Shop-a-Trade sales budget per quarter

	1	2	3	4	Year
Expected sales	3 000	3 500	4 000	4 500	15 000
Unit price	× R60	× R60	× R60	× R60	× R60
Total sales	180 000	210 000	240 000	270 000	900 000
Cash collection: Debtors balance brought forward	65 000				
Cash sales	108 000	126 000	144 000	162 000	540 000
Credit sales		72 000	84 000	96 000	252 000
Total cash	173 000	198 000	228 000	258 000	792 000
Debtors	(R900 000 – R540 000 – R252 000) = R108 000				

We have drawn up the annual budget for Shop-a-Trade, a company selling umbrellas printed with the names of companies (see Table 16.2 above). The following information was collected:

- After thorough research, the owners determined that expected sales would be 3 000 units for the first quarter, later increasing by 500 units per quarter.
- The selling price would remain constant for the year at R60.
- 60% of sales were for cash and 40% were on credit.
- Debtors would pay 30 days after purchase.
- The outstanding debts of R65 000 at the beginning of the year should all be collected in the first period.

The annual sales budget for Shop-a-Trade appears in Table 16.2.

The sales budget can be divided up by shop or region or salesperson.

You are asked to draw up the sales budget of Manufacturer (Pty) Ltd. The company sells sewing machines that are in reasonable demand. The following information must be taken into account:

- Sales for the next year will increase from the second quarter by 15% and 10% for every quarter thereafter. The sales for the current year are 3 100 units per quarter. Selling price per unit is R500, and this will increase by 10% in the third quarter.

- Cash sales amount to 50%.
- Manufacturer's outstanding debts amount to R85 000, of which 50% is collected in period 1 and 50% in period 2. Debtors usually pay 60% in the first period after sales and 40% in the second period after sales.

Draw up the sales budget by filling in Table 16.3.

Table 16.3: Manufacturer sales budget per quarter

	1	2	3	4	Year
Expected sales	3 100	3 565	……..	……..	……..
Unit price	× R500	x	x	x	x
Total sales	R ……..	R ……..	R ……..	R ……..	R ……..
Cash collection: Debtors balance brought forward	R42 500	R ……..	R ……..	R ……..	R ……..
Cash sales	R775 000				
Credit collect 60%		R465 000			
Credit collect 40%			R310 000		
Total cash collect per quarter					

16.6 PRODUCTION BUDGET

Now that you know how much you can sell, you must calculate how many units you must manufacture. Here you must consider the stock you already possess, as well as what you want to retain. The calculation will therefore be as follows:

expected number of sales	– opening stock	+ final stock	= expected number of units to manufacture

If the expected sales are 200 000, opening stock is 50 000 and final stock is estimated at 70 000 (to have enough stock on the shelves to sell), what is the expected number of units that you must manufacture?

200 000	– 50 000	+ 70 000	= 220 000 units

It is important that the business carry the right amount of stock. If too much stock is carried, it can lead to liquidity problems and the dismissal of staff. If too little stock is carried, it can lead to loss of sales.

Suppose the owners of Shop-a-Trade have decided that they want to manufacture 15% of a future quarter's stock in the preceding quarter and have it on the shelves in advance. (This is their stock of finished products.) We can now calculate what the opening and final stock must be for each quarter.

Opening stock (15% × 3 000) = 450 units

Closing stock (15% × 3 500) = 525 units

- Direct material costs are R4.90 per unit.
- Direct material purchases are paid 50% cash in the quarter of purchase and 50% in the following quarter (30 days). Accounts payable of R11 500 at the beginning of the year will be paid in full in the first quarter.

Table 16.4: Shop-a-Trade production budget per quarter

	1	2	3	4	Year
Expected sales	3 000	3 500	4 000	4 500	15 000
Less: Opening stock	(450)	(525)	(600)	(675)	(450)
Plus: Closing stock	525	600	675	750	750
Number of units to produce	3 075	3 575	4 075	4 575	15 300
Material purchases: Units x R4,90	R15 068	R17 518	R19 968	R22 418	R74 970
Payment of materials:					
Balance b/f	R11 500				R11 500
Cash	R7 534	R8 758	R9 984	R11 209	R37 485
Credit		R7 533	R8 759	R9 984	R26 276
Total payments	R19 034	R16 291	R18 743	R21 193	R75 261
Creditors	(R74 970 – R37 485 – R26 276) = R11 209				

The production budget shows a close relationship to the sales budget since enough stock must be produced to meet the demand for goods.

Complete the production budget for Manufacturer. Opening stock amounts to 25% of expected sales. Closing stock must be 25% of the following period's sales:

- Manufacturer pays for its materials 50% in cash in the quarter of sales, 60% of the creditors in the following quarter and the outstanding 40% in the second quarter following the sales.
- Manufacturer's outstanding accounts at the beginning of the period were R42 000 and this is paid equally over the following two periods.
- Material costs are R5 per unit.

Table 16.5: Manufacturer production budget per quarter

	1	2	3	4	Year
Expected sales	3 100	3 680			
Less: Opening stock	(775)				
Plus: Closing stock	920				
Number of units to produce	3 245				
Material purchases: Units x R....					
Payment of materials:					
Balance b/f	R21 000				
Cash (50%)					
Credit (60%)					
Credit (40%)					
Credit					
Total payments					
Creditors					

If a small business does not produce goods but buys and sells goods, it must draw up a purchases budget. The number of products that must be purchased is determined in the same way as the number of products that need to be manufactured. You must therefore determine the quantity that must be purchased for each quarter. After the purchases budget, you immediately complete your cashflow budget (see section 16.10 in this chapter).

16.7 LABOUR BUDGET

It is necessary to draw up a labour budget to determine the need for human resources, and how much they will cost. Without a labour budget, you might find that you do not have enough staff to complete the required production within the given time frame. A labour budget will also assist you in managing your cashflow with regards to salaries and wages.

Your step-by-step process will be as follows:

1. determine how many units you want to make (refer back to production budget)
2. determine how long each unit will take to manufacture (per hour/per day?)
3. multiply calculated time by the labour cost per hour/per day.

Shop-a-Trade manufactures umbrellas, and it takes two hours of labour per umbrella (unit) at an average wage of R10 an hour.

Table 16.6: Shop-a-Trade labour budget per quarter

	1	2	3	4	Year
Expected production	3 075	3 575	4 075	4 575	15 300
× hours of labour per unit	× 2	× 2	× 2	× 2	× 2
Labour hours per quarter	6 150	7 150	8 150	9 150	30 600
× cost per hours	× R10	× R10	× R10	× R10	× R10
Total labour costs	R61 500	R71 500	R81 500	R91 500	R306 000

Manufacturer takes three hours to manufacture one sewing machine, and the average labour cost is R50 an hour. The cost per hour will increase by 10% in the beginning of the fourth quarter. Complete the labour budget for Manufacturer.

Table 16.7: Manufacturer labour budget per quarter

	1	2	3	4	Year
Expected production	3 245				
× hours of labour per unit	× 3	×3			
Labour hours per quarter	9 735				
× cost per hours	× R50				
Total labour costs	R486 750				

16.8 BUDGETED INCOME STATEMENT

Expense budgets for larger entities can be drawn up for every department. Such an expense budget is then assigned to the person responsible for that department or specific expense line, who must control and authorise all expenses against that specific department. There are different methods to budget for expense items, similar to the functional budgets:

- start from a zero base and recalculate all expenses due in the next year
- review the previous year's expenses and, using them as a base, increase or decrease the new expenses depending on the business plan
- use the previous year's expenses and do an inflationary increase to all expense items
- the budgeted income statement is an important summary of all the previous budgets that have been completed. It therefore also indicates the expected profit for the following period. Since the income statement is a summary of all the previous budgets, it also serves as an excellent way to evaluate actual results against budgeted results.

Shop-a-Trade had the following expenses in the preceding year and wants to make provision for an adjustment for inflation of 12% for the coming year:

Table 16.8: Annual expenses

Rent paid	R50 000
Telephone	R5 000
Salaries (admin)	R40 000
Repairs and maintenance	R4 000
Marketing	R50 000
Travel expenses	R1 000

Additional expenses are an interest obligation of R35 000, taxation of R5 000 and operating expenses of R306 000 per year.

Table 16.9: Budgeted income statement for Shop-a-Trade

	R
Sales	900 000
Less: cost of sales	373 500
Opening inventory (450 × R24.90)	11 205
Materials	74 970
Labour	306 000
Less: closing inventory (750 × R24.90)	18 675
Gross profit	**526 500**
Current expenses	(508 880)
Rent paid (R50 000 × 12%)	(56 000)
Telephone	(5 600)
Salaries (admin)	(44 800)
Repair and maintenance	(4 480)
Marketing	(56 000)
Interest paid	(35 000)
Travel expenses	(1000)
Operating expenses	(306 000)
Net income before tax	17 620
Tax	5 000
Net income	12 620

Using the budgets that you already completed, draw up a budgeted income statement for Manufacturer. The company has already incurred the expenses listed below. You should allow for inflation of 10% in your calculations.

Marketing	R2 000
Rent paid	R10 000
Stationery	R1 500
Telephone	R3 000
Travel costs	R18 000

Interest paid is R6 000 for the year and taxation will be 25% of the net income before taxation.

	R
Sales	____
Less: cost of sales	
Opening inventory	____
Materials	____
Labour	____
Less: closing inventory	____
Gross profit	____
Current expenses	
Marketing	(____)
Rent paid	(____)
Stationery	(____)
Telephone	(____)
Travel costs	(____)
Interest paid	(____)
Net income before tax	____
Tax	____
Net income	____

16.9 BUDGETED BALANCE SHEET

Shop-a-Trade had the following balance sheet at the end of the year:

Table 16.10: Budgeted balance sheet as at 31 December

	R
Fixed assets	133 000
Current assets	141 829
Inventory (750 × R24.90)	18 675
Debtors	108 000
Cash	15 154
Total assets	**274 829**

Share capital	100 000
Accumulated profits	13 620
Loan (R150 000 – R5 000)	145 000
Current liabilities	16 209
Receiver of Revenue (tax)	5 000
Creditors	11 209
Total equity and liabilities	**274 829**

16.10 CASHFLOW BUDGET

Let us say you have completed the forecast profit and loss calculation. The difference between the forecast profit and loss and the cashflow is that in the latter you focus on when you will receive cash and when cash payments are made. The cashflow budget is the main lifeline of the business and is the most important result of drawing up the other budgets. The cashflow budget indicates the expected flow of cash and can help management plan to make early provision for cash shortages and to consider the necessary financing possibilities. This allows cash planning to take place; any excess cash can be invested.

You have bought a vehicle for R100 000. This amount will appear in the cashflow budget as an outflow (expense). But in the balance sheet it will be capitalised and depreciation will be written off in the income statement.

The cashflow statement does not take into account non-cash items, such as depreciation and bad debts.

Shop-a-Trade has collected the following information to do their cashflow budget:

- The enterprise's bank account should show a positive balance of R40 000 at the beginning of the year.
- An investment of R4 000 will be sold for cash in the second period.
- Purchases of all current costs are spread evenly over the quarters.
- Direct labour costs are settled in the period in which they are incurred.
- Management wants to purchase a new truck for R133 000 in the second quarter.

- The enterprise pays the tax monthly in equal instalments.
- Loans are paid in the third quarter when there is sufficient cash (rounded off to the nearest R5 000).
- A loan of R150 000 will be granted in the second quarter.

Table 16.11: Shop-A-Trade cashflow budget per quarter (all figures are in rands)

	1	2	3	4
Receipts:				
Debtors & cash	173 000	198 000	228 000	258 000
Sale of investment		4 000		
Total receipts	**173 000**	**202 000**	**228 000**	**258 000**
Less: payments				
Direct material	19 034	16 291	18 743	21 192
Direct labour	61 500	71 500	81 500	91 500
Rent paid	14 000	14 000	14 000	14 000
Telephone	1 400	1 400	1 400	1 400
Salaries	11 200	11 200	11 200	11 200
Repairs & maintenance	1 120	1 120	1 120	1 120
Marketing	14 000	14 000	14 000	14 000
Purchase of vehicle		133 000		
Interest paid	8 750	8 750	8 750	8 750
Operating costs	76 500	76 500	76 500	76 500
Tax	1 250	1 250	1 250	1 250
Total payments	**208 754**	**349 011**	**228 463**	**240 912**
	1	2	3	4
Surplus/deficit	**(35 754)**	**(147 011)**	**(463)**	**17 088**
Cash balance	40 000	4 246	7 235	1 772
Financing				
Loans		150 000		
Repayments			(5 000)	
Closing cash balance	**4 246**	**7 235**	**1 772**	**18 860**

Manufacturer's cash balance is R225 000 at the beginning of the year. A vehicle is bought for R120 000 in the second quarter, and in the third quarter a loan of R30 000 is paid back. Tax is divided in the period and paid in equal payments. Complete the cashflow budget for Manufacturer.

Table 16.12: Manufacturer cashflow budget per quarter

(All figures are in rands.)

	1	2	3	4
Receipts				
Debtors	_____	_____	_____	_____
Sale of investment	_____	_____	_____	_____
Total receipts	_____	_____	_____	_____
Less: payments				
Direct material	_____	_____	_____	_____
Direct labour	_____	_____	_____	_____
Manufacturing overheads	_____	_____	_____	_____
Sales and admin	_____	_____	_____	_____
Purchase of vehicle	_____	_____	_____	_____
Tax	_____	_____	_____	_____
Total payments	_____	_____	_____	_____
Surplus/deficit	_____	_____	_____	_____
Cash balance	225 000			
Financing				
Loans				
Repayments				
Closing cash balance	_____	_____	_____	_____

16.11 COMPILING MORE DETAILED BUDGETS

We have discussed the basic concepts of the budgeting process. However, it might be necessary to do detailed analysis of an expense line in order to justify the increase in spending and be able to track the spending later in the year. Here is an example of a detailed marketing budget.

Here is a an annual budget with supporting reasons for the marketing expenses with the objective for 2026: Increase opportunities through marketing efforts. Direct marketing opportunities include phone calls, emails, website registrations and referrals.

Strategies	Goal	Tactics	Budget
Internet marketing	Drive more activity to website	Increase advertising links to www.xyz.com to get listed higher in search engines.	80 000
		Directory A – R10 000	
		Directory B – R10 000	
		Google AdWords Budget – R20 000	
		Website hosting – R40 000	
Direct marketing	Build awareness in target market	Marketing initiatives: Big event	600 000
Total expense			680 000

Budgets can also be compiled by sections or departments in a company instead of processes. The following is an example of a marketing budget monthly expenses broken down in the different type of expenses. The more detailed the budget is that you submit together with the purpose of the expenses included in the budget, the easier the budget will be for non-financial people to understand. You will note the following budget is for R13.3 million (numbers rounded to R'000) for the whole department including salaries.

Marketing budget													
	Jan	Feb	Mar	Apr	May	Jun	Jul	Aug	Sep	Oct	Nov	Dec	Total
	R'000	R'000	R'000	R'000	R'000	R'000	R'000	R'000	R'000	R'000	R'000	R'000	R'000
Personnel													
Salaries, wages	150	150	150	150	150	150	170	170	170	170	170	170	1 920
Benefits	5	5	5	5	5	5	7	7	7	7	7	7	72
Commissions and bonuses						60						70	130
Personnel: Total	R155	R155	R155	R155	R155	R215	R177	R177	R177	R177	R177	R247	R2 122
Market research													
Primary research	5	5	5	5	5	5	5	5	5	5	5	5	60
Secondary research		3				5			8			4	20
Library management						6							6
Market research: Total	R5	R8	R5	R5	R5	R16	R5	R5	R13	R5	R5	R9	R86

Marketing communications													
Branding	0	14			20				15			3	52
Advertising	5	12		10		5		40	20	32			124
Websites	5	5	5	15	5	5	5	5	5	25	5	5	90
Direct marketing	3	20	5	40	5	20	8	4	12	30	16	1	164
Internet marketing			16					24					40
Press relations	7	7	7	7	7	7	7	7	7	7	7	7	84
Public relations	10	35	10	10	10	10	10	10	15	5	5 000	5 000	10 125
Events			120							150			270
Marketing communications: Total	R30	R93	R163	R82	R47	R47	R30	R90	R74	R249	R5 028	R5 016	R10 949
Other													
Postage	3	4	6	3	4	6	10	3	4	6	2	1	52
Telephone	3	3	3	3	3	3	3	3	3	3	3	3	36
Travel	2	5	10	2	5	10	12	4	2	10	2	2	66
Computers and office equipment					10						20		30
Other: Total	R8	R12	R19	R8	R22	R19	R25	R10	R9	R19	R27	R6	R184
Total: Marketing budget	R198	R268	R342	R250	R229	R297	R237	R282	R273	R450	R5 237	R5 278	R13 341

16.12 FINANCIAL FORECAST

Budgets can also be drawn up on the basis of financial forecasts. This method relies on relationships and forecasts that are based on past data and trends.

Advertising costs have increased by 12% per year in the last five years. They amounted to R20 000 last year. What will next year's current expenditure be if you do a trend forecast?

R20 000 × 112% = R22 400

The following income statement for the past two years is available to you.

Sales for the coming year are estimated to be 20% more than the current year.

Current expenses are expected to follow the latest trend. Other income will remain constant. Interest paid will increase to R20 000 because of the new long-term loan that has been negotiated. All the other costs will remain in the same proportion to sales. Tax rate for the next year will amount to 30%. Now complete the budgeted income statement.

	Last year (R)	This year (R)	Next year (R)
Sales	700 000	750 000	______
Cost of sales	373 000	400 000	______
Gross profit	327 000	350 000	______
Current expenses	(112 500)	(125 000)	______
Current income	214 500	225 000	______
Interest paid	(9 500)	(12 500)	(______)
Other income	5 000	5 000	______
Income before tax	210 000	217 500	______
Tax	(80 000)	(87 000)	______
Net income	130 000	130 500	______
Completed income statement			______
	Next year (R)	Explanation	
Sales	900 000	20% increase	

Cost of sales	480 000	53.33% of sales	
Gross profit	420 000	11.1% trend	
Current expenses	(138 750)		
Current income	281 250		
Interest paid	(20 000)	Given	
Other income	5 000	Constant	
Income before tax	266 250		
Tax	(79 875)	30%	
Net income		186 375	

16.13 ACTUAL AGAINST BUDGET

An important control measure when budgeting is to measure the actual costs against the budgeted costs. This allows you to exercise control over the budget and cashflow.

When actual costs are set against budgeted costs, as is done at a given time, reasons must be given for any deviation from budget. This allows the business to establish possible lack of control in certain areas. Feedback and accountability from these departments are most important. Below is an example of a detailed marketing budget with supporting reasons for the expense.

eg

Strategies	How are we going to achieve this	Budget	Actual	Reason
Internet marketing	Increase advertising links to www.xyz.com to get listed higher in search engines	80 000	90 000	Additional 10 000 was spent on the Google Ads as it seemed to be highly profitable
	Examples:			
	Directory A – R10 000,00			
	Directory B – R10 000,00			
	Google AdWords budget – R20 000			

	Website hosting – R40 000,00			
Direct marketing	Build awareness in target market	600 000	620 000	Increase in marketing material costs
		680 000	710 000	

Mr Wise of Cycle Wheels Supplies, which specialises in the sale of bicycles, has drawn up the monthly sales budget. Mr Wise has cashflow problems and will look for the root of the problem in sales that do not agree with the budget. The budgeted and actual sales figures for the bicycles are as follows (actual figures are only available up to June):

	Budgeted sales	Actual sales	Difference
	(R)	(R)	(R)
January	20 000	10 000	(10 000)
February	20 000	15 000	(5 000)
March	20 000	20 000	NONE
April	30 000	25 000	(5 000)
May	40 000	30 000	(10 000)
June	45 000	40 000	(5 000)
July	40 000		
August	30 000		
September	30 000		
October	20 000		
November	20 000		
December	30 000		

After considerable investigation, Mr Wise came to the following conclusions:

- When he drew up the budget, he thought he would sell more bicycles because of a big race that was due to take place locally in July.
- January's sales are lower than budgeted (due to over-expectation), but still show a 2% growth over the previous year's figures.

- February's budgeted figures were still based on over-expectation and also show a 2% growth over last year's figures.
- March showed no deviation, as Mr Wise launched a major advertising campaign.
- April's sales still show 2% growth over last year's sales but did not come up to expectations.
- Sales for May are weaker, as all potential race participants have already bought their bicycles from a competitor, Wheelly Warehouse, located 2 km down the road from Mr Wise.
- Sales for June are not as budgeted, but it was definitely a good month, as the shop was crowded with cyclist who arrived for the Argus tour. June showed a 20% growth over the previous year's figures.

Mr Wise concludes that he should examine not only the sales budget, but also his expenses to determine where he overspent, resulting in the cashflow problems he is experiencing.

16.14 USING A COMPUTER TO DRAW UP BUDGETS

There are a number of computer programs available to help businesses to draw up budgets. The advantage of using one of these programs is that you can change a single figure and the program will automatically revise your budget. If you don't have a computer package, you can also draw up your budgets using Microsoft Excel or any other spreadsheet program.

> **NB** If you use Excel, remember to work with formulas in your tables, otherwise the program will not automatically recalculate your budgets when you change individual figures.

When using a computer program you can create sales charts of expected sales and use them to review actual sales achieved. Use the charts to understand your sales forecast: Does it look real? Does it make sense? Figure 16.3 is an example of putting your data into a graph to show the previous year's sales in rands, budgeted sales and actual sales for the current year. It is a visual interpretation on growth of sales as well as whether the budget has been met.

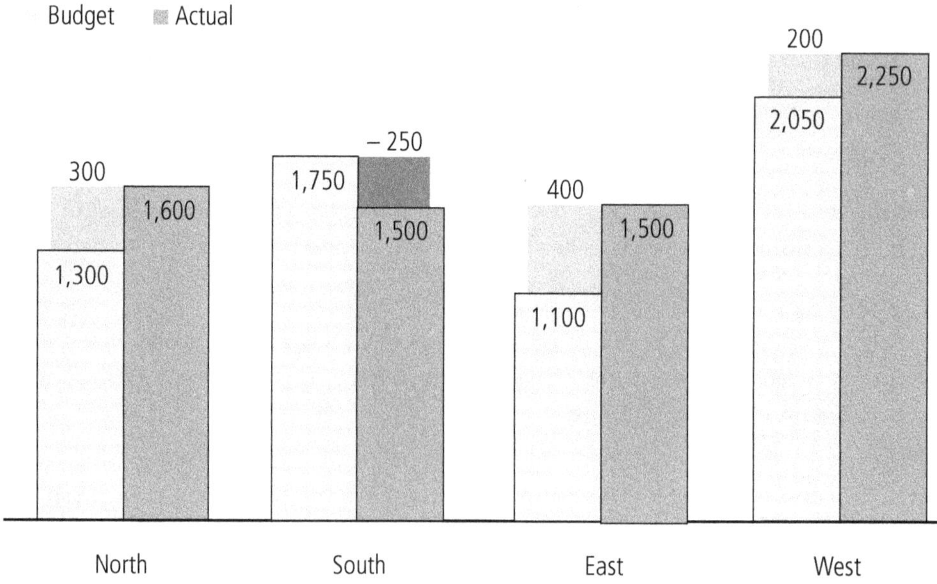

Figure 16.3: Graph reflecting actual sales against budget per month

16.15 SUMMARY

In this chapter we looked at how to draw up budgets. A business uses many budgets, and together these make up the master budget. We learnt that the sales budget is the first budget that must be drawn up, and that the sales budget depends on the sales forecasts. We then discussed the production budget, the labour budget and the cashflow budget, and drawing up the income statement and the balance sheet. Finally, we learnt about assessing the difference between actual and budgeted figures, and the advantages of using computer programs in budgeting.

Self-evaluation questions

1. What is the definition of a budget?
2. List the reasons why it is necessary to draw up a budget.
3. Which factors must be taken into account when drawing up a sales budget?
4. What is the formula that you use to determine expected sales?
5. List the steps you would follow when drawing up the cashflow budget.

6. Current expenses have risen by 8% a year for the last four years. Last year the current expenses amounted to R150 000. What will next year's current expenses be if you do a trend sales forecast? (Answer: R162 000)

7. The cost of sales was 70% of total sales last year. Next year's sales are budgeted at R1 050 000.What will the cost of sales be? (Answer: R735 000)

8. The sales of the business were as follows over the past few years:

Year	2014	2015	2016	2017	2018
Sales (R)	100 000	110 000	121 000	133 000	147 000

Calculate the sales for 2019 on the trend basis.

9. Mike's intention is to start trading on 1 January 20xx. Mike is going to market and distribute a revolutionary anti-static computer device called ANT in KwaZulu-Natal. This device is manufactured in South Korea. He is confident that he can sell an average of 5 000 units of ANT per month, but he recognises that there will be a start-up phase – it will take time to become known and established in the marketplace. He would like to formulate a profit and loss projection and cashflow forecast before starting the business.

The following details are pertinent to the proposed business:

- The Korean company wants a committed monthly order, confirmed for a six-month period at a time.
- The cost price per ANT is R80 and payment terms are cash on delivery. Orders for the six-month period must be placed two months before first delivery. Mike has decided that his first order will be 2 000 units per month for the first three-month period. The order for the next three months will be 2 200 units per month. The first shipment will be received on 5 January 20xx.
- His sales projections, expressed as a percentage of the monthly purchases, are as follows:

Jan 20xx	Feb 20xx	Mar 20xx	Apr 20xx	May 20xx	June 20xx
80%	80%	90%	100%	110%	120%

- The selling price of ANT in KwaZulu-Natal will be R1 200 per unit. The majority of customers are likely to be other businesses. Mike believes that, while his customers will be given 15 days' credit after invoice, in reality an average of 30 days will be taken for payment, even after implementing strict credit control procedures.

- Mike intends to employ a sales representative and pay him or her a fixed salary of R5 000 per month, as well as a sales commission of 2% on sales achieved. The sales commission will be paid in the month following sales achieved. Mike believes that the sales representative will account for 30% of sales, and he himself for 70%.
- Rental expense would amount to R2 000 per month and is payable at the end of each month. A refundable deposit, equivalent to one month's rent, is to be paid when Mike takes occupancy of his premises on 1 January 20xx.
- Mike needs to acquire the following for his business:

Item	Cost	Will acquire	Depreciate over
computer			
equipment	R14 400	1/1/20xx	3 years (straight line)
motor vehicle	R96 000	1/1/20xx	5 years (straight line)

- Other monthly overheads are expected to be:

	R	
Accounting fees	3 000	(one month's credit)
Electricity and water	1 200	(paid in the following month)
Petrol	2 000	(paid in month incurred)
Mike's salary	30 000	
Telephone	1 500	(paid in the following month)
Advertising	10 000	

- Mike has R60 000 of his own money to invest in the venture. He feels that he could qualify for a R70 000 overdraft and could offer his house as security to the bank.

You have to:

9.1. Calculate Mike's closing stock per month for the period 1 January 20xx to 30 June 20xx.

Use the following layout:

	Jan 20xx	Feb 20xx	Mar. 20xx	Apr. 20xx	May 20xx	June 20xx
Opening stock						
Purchases						
Less sales						
Closing stock						

9.2 Prepare a monthly profit and loss budget for the period 1 January to 30 June

9.3 Prepare a monthly cashflow forecast for the period 1 January to 30 June.

Answer 9:

Profit and loss for six months

	Jan	Feb	Mar	Apr	May	Jun
	R	R	R	R	R	R
Sales	448 000	448 000	504 000	616 000	677 600	739 200
Less: cost of sales	192 000	192 000	216 000	264 000	290 400	316 800
Opening inventory	–	48 000	96 000	120 000	120 000	93 600
Purchases	240 000	240 000	240 000	264 000	264 000	264 000
Less: closing inventory	–48 000	–96 000	–120 000	–120 000	–93 600	–40 800
Gross profit (Loss)	256 000	256 000	288 000	352 000	387 200	422 400
Current expenses	62 852	62 852	62 996	63 284	63 442	63 601
Rent paid	2 000	2 000	2 000	2 000	2 000	2 000
Depreciation	2 000	2 000	2 000	2 000	2 000	2 000
Accounting fees	3 000	3 000	3 000	3 000	3 000	3 000
Electricity and water	1 200	1 200	1 200	1 200	1 200	1 200
Petrol	2 000	2 000	2 000	2 000	2 000	2 000
Mike's salary	30 000	30 000	30 000	30 000	30 000	30 000
Sales person salary	10 000	10 000	10 000	10 000	10 000	10 000
Commission	1 152	1 152	1 296	1 584	1 742	1 901
Telephone	1 500	1 500	1 500	1500	1500	1 500
Advertising	10 000	10 000	10 000	10 000	10 000	10 000
Net income before tax	193 148	193 148	225 004	288 716	323 758	358 799
Tax @28%	–54 081	–54 081	–63 001	–80 840	–90 652	–100 464
Net income	139 067	139 067	162 003	207 876	233 105	258 335

Index

Page numbers that refer to figures and tables are in *italics*.

C

D

F

G

H

N

O

P

www.ingramcontent.com/pod-product-compliance
Lightning Source LLC
Chambersburg PA
CBHW061757210326
41599CB00034B/6805

* 9 7 8 1 4 8 5 1 3 0 5 1 2 *